THE M. & E. HANDBOOK SERIES

APPLIED ECONOMICS

THE M. & E. HANDBOOK SERIES

APPLIED ECONOMICS

E. SEDDON, M.A.

Senior Lecturer in Economics,
Faculty of Business and Management Studies,
Liverpool Polytechnic

J. D. S. APPLETON, B.Sc.(Econ.), Dip.Ed.

Lecturer in Economics,
Faculty of Business and Management Studies,
Liverpool Polytechnic

MACDONALD & EVANS LTD
8 John Street, London WC1N 2HY
1972

First published July 1972
Reprinted (with amendments) August 1973
Reprinted April 1975

©

MACDONALD AND EVANS LIMITED

1972

ISBN: 0 7121 0122 5

HANDBOOK *Conditions of Sale*

Reproduced photolitho in Great Britain by
J. W. Arrowsmith Ltd., Bristol

PREFACE

THIS HANDBOOK sets out to analyse the main problems which confront the U.K. economy today and to test the validity of theoretical solutions to these problems against the results which have been achieved. It is intended for a very wide range of students, from those taking G.C.E. "A" Level to those preparing for papers in Applied Economics in the examinations of both academic and professional bodies.

Part One establishes the theoretical framework of macro-economic analysis and appraises the techniques and effective-ness of fiscal policies designed to manage the level of demand.

Part Two continues this approach in the realm of monetary policy by way of examining the structure and operation of the whole monetary system.

Part Three considers the implications for domestic economic policy of external trade and payments transactions.

Part Four is concerned with *direct* Government intervention in specific segments of the economy in an attempt to improve the efficiency of their operation.

The authors are conscious that this is a field of study in which there is continuous change. Old problems assume new forms and require fresh solutions. Moreover, the institutional apparatus of the economy is evolving at a rate which quickly dates written material. Nevertheless it is hoped that this book will provide the reader with a systematic and critical approach to the solutions put forward to current economic problems. Judicious reading of newspapers, periodicals, journals, and Government and banking publications will enable the student to keep abreast of events.

Grateful acknowledgment is due to the following bodies for permission to reprint the examination questions which appear in Appendix III.

The Joint Matriculation Board of the Universities of Manchester, Liverpool, Leeds, Sheffield and Birmingham
(J.M.B.).

University of London.
Liverpool Polytechnic.
Institute of Bankers (I.O.B.).
Savings Bank Institute (S.B.I.).
Institute of Municipal Treasurers and Accountants (I.M.T.A.).
Institute of Cost and Management Accountants—formerly Institute of Cost and Works Accountants (I.C.W.A.).
Institute of Transport (I.O.T.).
Chartered Institute of Secretaries (C.I.S.).

January 1972

E. S.
J. D. S. A.

NOTICE TO LECTURERS

Many lecturers are now using **HANDBOOKS** as working texts to save time otherwise wasted by students in protracted note-taking. The purpose of the series is to meet practical teaching requirements as far as possible, and lecturers are cordially invited to forward comments or criticisms to the publishers for consideration.

P. W. D. REDMOND
General Editor

CONTENTS

Part Three: INTERNATIONAL TRADE AND PAYMENTS

Part Four: GOVERNMENT AND INDUSTRY

LIST OF TABLES

xi

PART ONE

THE MACROECONOMIC APPROACH

CHAPTER I

THE KEYNESIAN SYSTEM

MICROECONOMICS AND MACROECONOMICS

1. Microeconomics. Economics is a study of the allocation of resources between competing alternatives in a way which best alleviates the problem of scarcity. In the past economists concentrated their attention upon the aspect of choice implied by this definition, *i.e.* the direction of resource utilisation, particularly in relation to the decision-making behaviour of firms and individuals. This is the microeconomic approach which largely revolves round the price and output policies of firms and how resources would be attracted to or deflected from particular uses by fluctuating prices. An implicit assumption was that all resources would be fully utilised. The basis of this belief was to be found in J. B. Say's "law of markets."

2. Say's "law of markets." This law reasoned that the decision of individuals to work and produce is motivated only by the wish to acquire the produce of others. An increase in the output of the individual will then generate for him sufficient income to take from the market goods equivalent to those produced by his own efforts.

The fundamental premise is that *all* income will be spent upon either consumer goods or capital goods at a rate sufficient to guarantee the full employment of all resources.

Resources could remain unemployed in the short run but only because the supply price was too high. In the long run a fresh equilibrium price established at a lower level would ensure that they were once more fully utilised.

3. The depression of the 1930s. Whatever the validity of this classical analysis of the economic system it clearly provided only a partial explanation. It could give no account of the failure to utilise resources. In the period 1921–39 only

3

once did the proportion of insured persons unemployed fall below 10 per cent. In two years it was above 20 per cent and the overall average was in excess of 14 per cent. There was immense hardship, apart from which it was estimated that there was an annual loss of potential output of between £400 million and £500 million.

4. New economic thinking. Economic theory had now to provide an explanation and attention shifted from the direction of the demand for resources to the level of that demand. It was clear to some economists that at least in the short run demand might fall below that level necessary to maintain full employment. It followed that there was room for public policy designed to stabilise demand at an appropriate level.

The new macroeconomics was therefore concerned with analysing the relationship between certain fundamental variables expressed as aggregates, *i.e.* the volume of consumer and investment expenditures, the level of national income and employment and the volume of production.

Since the Second World War Government economic policies have centred upon the manipulation of these variables within the framework of macroeconomic analysis. For the theoretical foundations of this analysis we must turn to the *General Theory of Employment, Interest and Money* published by John Maynard Keynes in 1936.

THE BUSINESS CYCLE

5. A general theory. The weakness of classical economics was as we have seen that it was only able to explain the working of the economy in a particular situation, full employment. Keynes provided a "general theory" in the sense that it explained how the economy might function at *any* level of employment. Writing in a time of massive unemployment it was natural that his primary concern should be with this problem. However, it is often forgotten that he provided an explanation of the whole business cycle and had a good deal to say about the problem of over-full employment and inflation.

6. Industrial fluctuations. Variations in the level of economic activity can be observed to occur in different time series and from different causes.

(a) *The secular trend.* This is the long-term trend which in Western economies in the nineteenth and twentieth centuries has been one of growth with rising production and consumption.

(b) *Seasonal variations.* As the name suggests, for climatic reasons variations occur within the space of one year, *e.g.* in the building trade.

(c) *Erratic fluctuations.* In a wholly unpredictable way variations result from forces external to the economy, *e.g.* natural catastrophes or political upheavals.

(d) *Long waves.* Since 1822 it is possible to define six periods, each averaging twenty-five years' duration, in which the prevailing trends of prosperity and depression alternated.

(e) *The business or trade cycle.* Within each long wave there can be discerned between two and a half and three and a half business cycles comprising a regular alternation of prosperity and depression.

Government economic policy since 1945 has aimed to reduce and, hopefully, eliminate cyclical fluctuations, the ultimate objective being a smoothly rising growth curve. The degree of success is to be observed in the less pronounced booms and the less severe depressions, referred to nowadays as "recessions." On the other hand the periodicity of the cycle has increased and "stop-go" economic policies became subject to much criticism.

7. Phases of the business cycle. Four phases may be discerned:

(a) *The upswing.* A period of rising economic activity and prosperity. The general price level tends to rise.

(b) *The downturn.* The point of crisis at which expansion slows down or ceases.

(c) *The downswing.* A period of contraction. The general price level tends to fall.

(d) *The upturn.* The point of revival prior to the next upswing.

8. Manifestations of the business cycle. There are three principal criteria by which one may distinguish the phases of the cycle. They are the level of employment, the volume of production and the volume of consumption. At the outset it should be stressed that these indications need not point in the same direction. If they diverge then the considerations set out below must be set against each other in order to arrive at a conclusion.

9. Level of employment. Because of their far-reaching social and political implications there has been a tendency to accept unemployment figures as the principal if not the only indicator of the phases of the business cycle. The reliability of this indicator must therefore be assessed. It must first be made clear that unemployment springs from a variety of causes:

(a) *Seasonal unemployment.* This corresponds to seasonal variations in certain types of business activity.

(b) *Frictional unemployment.* This is "short-term" structural unemployment. Within any industry there are always those firms which are contracting while others are expanding. It follows that in the short run there will be unemployment as some men move from one firm to another.

(c) *Secular unemployment.* This is "long-term" structural unemployment. In a dynamic society technological change brings new industries while old industries become obsolescent. Unemployment results for those men whose skills are no longer in demand.

(d) *Cyclical unemployment.* The figures rise or fall according to the phase of the business cycle.

In the period between the wars the hard core of chronic unemployment was secular in character and associated with the regions in which there had been excessive specialisation in industries such as cotton, coal, iron, steel and heavy engineering. Superimposed was the huge mass of unemployment of cyclical origin. In such a period the economy may move into an upswing while there remains a considerable volume of unemployment for secular, seasonal and frictional reasons.

Moreover, if there is downward pressure on wage rates during the downswing, unemployment figures need not necessarily rise. The same number of men continue to be employed at lower wage levels. This was commonly the case in the nineteenth century and in recent years has manifested itself in trade-union pressure for work sharing as an alternative to redundancies.

On the other hand during an upswing it is possible for the level of unemployment to rise if increased output is due to the improved productivity of labour.

Finally, in utilising this criterion there remains the difficulty of defining full employment as a norm upon which to base policy measures. The choice of figure must ultimately be arbitrary. Judged by Government policies in the years 1945–66 it would seem to have been accepted as lying within the range $1 \cdot 2$–$1 \cdot 4$ per cent unemployed. Subsequently it appears that a figure of about $2 \cdot 4$ per cent has been considered more appropriate. It would therefore follow that a figure below this implies that the upswing has become too steep and inflationary pressures excessive.

10. Volume of production and consumption. We must next assess the validity of the other two indicators.

(a) *Volume of consumption.* It has been observed that during a downswing it is possible for a high level of employment to be maintained at the expense of lower wage rates. However, with lower earnings it is likely that expenditure on consumption will decline and this will be a more reliable index of the state of trade. Even so, it cannot be used in isolation.

(b) *Volume of production.* During a downswing the volume of consumption may for a time remain unaffected but expenditure on investment declines. In short, the nation is subsidising its standard of living by consuming capital. Conversely, in an upswing there may be a big increase in capital expenditure while consumption is little affected. The nation is adding to its capital.

11. Policy implications. The aim of economic policy will be to achieve continuous growth (*i.e.* eliminate the business cycle) at stable prices and with full employment. If the various manifestations of the business cycle point in the same direction there will be no doubt as to the phase of the cycle and the policy to pursue. Where they diverge it may be necessary to sacrifice one objective in order to achieve another.

For example, during 1970 the volume of production and consumption continued to expand, albeit marginally, but so did the level of unemployment and the general price level. If the unemployment figures had been taken as the principal indicator, measures to accelerate into an upswing would have followed. That this was not done implies that the principal concern of economic policy was for inflation.

ANALYSIS OF THE CAUSES OF THE BUSINESS CYCLE

12. Business-cycle theories. The causes of the business cycle are complex and it would be idle to claim that any single explanation is adequate or that the same explanation is equally valid for all countries or for every cycle. This is generally recognised by most writers on the subject and differences are usually of emphasis rather than of principle.

There are five groups of theories which may conveniently be placed under the following headings:

(a) Psychological theories.
(b) Monetary theories.
(c) Over-investment theories.
(d) Under-consumption theories.
(e) Keynesian theory.

It is a merit of the work of Keynes that he gives due consideration to these other theories and having allowed for their validity in certain circumstances goes on to offer his own explanation. We shall confine our attention to Keynesian theory since this has provided the foundation for practical economic policy-making since 1945.

13. Effective demand, national income and the level of employment. The "General Theory" centres upon the concept of effective demand which comprises total national expenditure upon consumer goods and services and upon capital goods. The crucial thing to remember is that spending generates income and employment while saving does not. What one man spends represents demand for another man's employment and constitutes his income. Expenditure and income are two aspects of the same thing. A third aspect will be the money value of the total volume of production since this equates with both total money expenditure and total money income. Whatever is spent upon production will be distributed in wages, rent, interest and profits.

From these propositions three important conclusions follow:

(a) *The key indicator is the national income figure.* Employment according to Keynes is a function of national income. If income is declining so is employment and vice versa.

NOTE: This was a valid enough assumption in a period of depression. An increase in business activity would be reflected in the use of more labour. The proposition becomes more questionable once a high level of employment has been attained and emphasis is placed upon increasing national income through improved productivity. A post-war phenomenon has been the periodic rise in unemployment at the same time as national income has continued to rise.

(b) *The production of goods and services of a given value generates sufficient income to purchase them in their entirety if we so wish.* However, if we fail to spend the whole of that income then some goods and services will cease to be produced. Income and employment will decline.

(c) *Total effective demand determines the levels of income and employment.* It follows that where the figure of national income shows decline the remedy is to be sought in supporting effective demand.

14. The impact of saving. All income is divided between individuals and institutions in the form of wages, interest, rent and profits.

A part of this income will be devoted to current expenditure upon consumption. The rest will be saved. If a given level of income and employment is to be maintained the *whole* of these savings *must* be devoted to investment, *i.e.* in the Keynesian sense, expenditure upon capital equipment.

In short, the level of effective demand will be determined by the interaction of the rate of saving and the rate of investment. However, saving and investment are distinct functions governed by different motives and normally carried out by two different groups of people. It would be wholly coincidental if "intentions" to save and invest were to agree. It is essentially because of a discrepancy in these intentions that instability in the level of effective demand arises.

15. The propensity to save. While some savings are corporate and their volume is directly related to a decision to invest, the greater part are the product of decisions by individuals to refrain from current consumption. These decisions are governed by three factors.

(a) *Psychological motivation.* A wide variety of personal considerations motivate individual savings, *e.g.* prudence of the desire to satisfy some ambition. It should be stressed that none of these motives will be in any way related to the investment requirements of the entrepreneur. However, they will be broadly influenced by the prevailing economic climate. Keynes remarked upon "the paradox of thrift." In the downswing of the cycle, a sense of insecurity increases the propensity to save which in itself contributes to the descent into depression. Conversely, during the upswing, while the mood is optimistic, the propensity to save declines, thereby contributing to inflationary pressures.

(b) *The rate of interest.* It was assumed by the classical economists that investment and saving would be equated by a fluctuating rate of interest. An increased demand for investment funds by the entrepreneur would be reflected in a higher interest rate. More savings would now be called forth. The evidence of this century suggests that while there is some correlation between the rate of interest and the propensity to save it is not nearly so strong as was once thought (*see* VII, **37**).

(c) *The level of income.* The principal determinant of the propensity to save will be the level of income. As income rises the marginal propensity to save rises to the point where saving ultimately becomes automatic.

It follows therefore that the marginal propensity to save of the upper-income groups is high and of the lower-income groups low. Conversely, the marginal propensity to consume of the upper-income groups is low and of the lower-income groups high.

If the intention is to regulate total demand by an adjustment of consumer expenditure a redistribution of income may be

accomplished in a way which affects the propensities to save
and consume.

16. The rate of investment. Investment manifests itself in
a demand for new capital goods in either the private or public
sector. In the Keynesian sense it does not include the
purchase of securities on the Stock Exchange since this
normally implies only the transfer of ownership of existing
capital.

The rate of investment depends upon the anticipation of
business-planners of a profitable return to their outlay. This
anticipation is governed by the "marginal efficiency of capital,"
the phrase Keynes employs to denote the relationship between the prospective yield of one more unit of investment and
the rate of interest which must be paid for its use.

In making his assessment of capital's marginal efficiency the
planner will take account of certain objective factors, *e.g.* the
size of the existing stock of capital of a particular kind.
Nevertheless, however sophisticated his techniques may be
his prediction of the future ultimately involves a guess. The
problem stems from the unreliability of this guesswork. In
advanced economies, Keynes asserted, forecasting recurrently
erred on the side of pessimism with the result that investment
fell short of what would have been justified had the future
been more clearly foreseen.

In order to compensate for this repeated shortfall in effective
demand there was scope for periodic injections of Government
expenditure, "pump-priming." While conceding that this
expenditure might on occasion be designed to stimulate
consumption Keynes argued that in the interest of long-term
development it was preferable that it should be expressed in
investment.

17. The multiplier. The significance of one unit of investment more or less is amplified when attention is given to
the operation of the multiplier.

The investment of a further £100 will certainly increase
income and employment in the capital-goods industries, but
it will also stimulate the propensity to consume of the income
recipients. If it is assumed that one-fifth is saved then £80
will be spent upon increased consumption. Income is now
increased in the consumer-goods industries and further

stimulus given to consumption. Still assuming a savings factor of one-fifth this will be of the order of £64. The multiplier gradually loses momentum due to the impact of saving until the total addition to effective demand has been £500 and to savings £100.

Seen in terms of the effect upon employment, at an average wage level of £10, the initial investment would give work to ten men. When the multiplier had run its course, employment would be increased by fifty men.

In the same way that the beneficial effect of an extra unit of investment is enhanced by the multiplier, the depressant effect of the withdrawal of investment is equally magnified. In any attempt to stabilise demand timing is therefore of vital importance. A lost unit of investment must be replaced before the multiplier can take effect.

18. Deflationary and inflationary gaps. We are led to conclude at this point that instability in the level of effective demand may be attributed to an apparent disequilibrium between saving and investment.

(a) *A deflationary gap* between saving and investment initiates the downswing of the cycle and is magnified by the operation of the multiplier. It may result from:

(i) *A decline in investment* unaccompanied by an increase in consumption.
(ii) *A decline in consumption* unaccompanied by an increase in investment.

Stabilising action calls for the support of effective demand.

(b) *An inflationary gap* emerges when the rate of investment exceeds the rate of saving. Total expenditure is now higher than necessary to maintain the economy at the previous level of activity and the cycle has turned into the upswing. It may result from:

(i) *Increased investment* unaccompanied by decreased consumption.
(ii) *Increased consumption* unaccompanied by decreased investment.

When resources are unemployed, stabilising action may not be required. The tendency for prices to rise consequent upon the increased pressure of demand may be largely offset by the increased flow of goods and services at the higher level of employment. Where resources are already fully employed, price inflation will be avoided only by improved productivity. If this is not forthcoming, stabilising action requires that effective demand should be curbed by restricting either consumption or investment or both.

19. Nature of the disequilibrium of saving and investment. Some economists have adhered to the view that cyclical fluctuations originate in a *real* disequilibrium between saving and investment. Keynes, however, insists that they must equate.

During the upswing the entrepreneur finances his increased investment on credit. At the higher level of income now generated and given a fixed propensity to save, a volume of savings sufficient to cover the increased investment is called forth.

Conversely, during the downswing a lower rate of investment reduces income. Savings must then be restricted to a level dictated by the rate of investment.

In short the position is not one in which investment waits upon saving. It is the rate of investment itself which determines the ability to save. The two must always equate but may do so at any level of economic activity.

20. Reconciliation of the two views of saving and investment. A reconciliation of the two views of saving and investment has been offered in the following terms. Any given period of production can be viewed from two positions:

(a) *The ex ante position.* At the beginning of any period of production society anticipates a certain level of income and plans consumption, investment and saving in a way which it hopes will fulfil this expectation. Since saving and investment plans are unco-ordinated it is unlikely that the two will equate.

(b) *The ex post position.* At the end of a period of production what *in fact* happened can be observed. Expenditure upon consumption and investment generated income sufficient to permit a volume of saving exactly equal to the volume of investment.

In the form of a simple equation:

Consumption   expenditure + investment   expenditure =
National income = consumption expenditure+savings.

It follows that if *ex post* investment (which equals *ex post* saving) differs from *ex ante* saving there is a gap between anticipation and realisation which, if inflationary, moves the economy into the upswing and, if deflationary, moves it into the downswing. The momentum is then increased by the operation of the multiplier.

21. Instruments of demand management. In its attempts to regulate the level of effective demand Government has at its disposal three types of control.

(a) *Direct controls.* Rationing, restrictions upon new capital issues, import licensing are some of the direct methods of demand management to which Government may resort in times of emergency. However, they are not methods which are compatible with the aspirations of a free society and in normal times will be used sparingly. Preference will therefore be given to the other two controls which are "indirect" in their effect.

(b) *Fiscal controls.* Although fundamentally a monetary economist Keynes came to the conclusion that the principal instrument of control should be fiscal. This was the weapon which would be most precise and immediate in its effects.

(c) *Monetary controls.* While a complementary monetary policy was considered necessary, it was seen in a subordinate role. Credit controls would affect the position in the long run but their impact was less certain, less immediate and less precise. It was only during the 1960s with the failure of fiscal policy adequately to control demand that interest in a more positive monetary policy was revived.

PROGRESS TEST 1

1. Distinguish between microeconomics and macroeconomics. **(1–4)**

2. Point out the main features of six types of industrial fluctuation. **(6)**

3. Distinguish between four types of unemployment. **(9)**

4. How reliable is the unemployment figure as an index of the phase of the business cycle? (**9**)

5. Reconcile the two interpretations of the relationship between the rates of saving and investment. (**10**)

6. Explain the importance of the concept of effective demand. (**13**)

7. What determines the level of effective demand? (**14**)

8. Explain the factors which influence the rate of saving. (**15**)

9. What determines the rate of investment? (**16**)

10. What is the significance of the multiplier? (**17**)

CHAPTER II

THE MANAGEMENT OF DEMAND

A PERSPECTIVE OF PUBLIC FINANCE

1. Objectives. The study of macroeconomics places emphasis upon the use of fiscal policy for the purpose of managing demand. Nevertheless, it should not be forgotten that there are other objectives.

Modern public finance may be said to have three aspects. It is:

    (*a*) *The instrument for the satisfaction of collective wants.*
    (*b*) *An instrument of social policy.*
    (*c*) *An instrument of economic policy.*

2. Satisfaction of collective wants. We should not lose sight of the primary purpose of public finance, which is to raise revenue for expenditure upon collective wants. It has always been considered appropriate that certain services should be provided by collective action in the public sector rather than in response to market forces in the private sector.

In the *laissez-faire* society of the eighteenth century the view was that such services should be limited to external and internal security, *i.e.* defence and the preservation of law and order. A changing view of society has subsequently brought a gradual extension of the public sector, most dramatically since 1945.

3. Definition of the public sector. In this segment of the economy the production of goods and services depends upon the decision of central or local government. In arriving at a decision, while reference will be made to the cost of production, social objectives will be paramount. Resources will be deployed in a way which would not be achieved by the free operation of the price mechanism, *e.g.* it is reasonable to assume that a far higher proportion of resources is devoted to education than would be the case if all education were provided by private enterprise.

4. Two types of public expenditure. In the public sector the State commands resources in two ways:

(*a*) *Exhaustive expenditure.* The State directly employs a vast number of people, *e.g.* civil servants, teachers, soldiers, etc. Indirectly it employs as many in the private sector in the production of goods and services for the satisfaction of collective wants, *e.g.* defence equipment, schools. Such expenditure is exhaustive in the sense that resources have been diverted as a result of Government decision from the use which free market forces would have determined.

(*b*) *Transfer expenditure.* When income is redistributed from tax-payer to beneficiary in the form of pensions, family allowances, etc., the recipient is free to dispose of his benefit in response to the pull of market forces.

5. Public enterprise. Since the late nineteenth century local and central government have extended their economic interests, providing goods and services in response to market forces and sometimes in competition with private enterprise, *e.g.* water-supplies, local transport, the B.B.C. The scope of public enterprise was greatly expanded after 1945 with the nationalisation of major industries.

At this point the frontier between public and private enterprise becomes indistinct. To the extent that public corporations follow pricing and output policies dictated by the market, their behaviour parallels that of privately owned companies and they lie *outside* a strictly defined public sector. To the extent that social and political considerations determine that they should provide a service even at the expense of a loss to be shouldered by the tax-payer, they fall *within* the public sector, *e.g.* the subsidisation of uneconomic British Rail services.

6. Public revenue. Government has three sources of income from which it may pay society's collective expenses.

(*a*) *Taxation.* Taxes are levied upon the income and expenditure of individuals and corporate bodies in both the private and public sectors.

(b) *Profits of public enterprise.* While public corporations are not generally required by their acts of incorporation to do more than pay their way, occasionally there are trading profits.

(c) *Borrowing.* Until 1945, this source of income was considered appropriate only in times of national emergency. Sound public finance required that the Budget should always be balanced. Subsequently it was seen that a deflationary gap could be closed most effectively by loan-financed public expenditure. Government borrowing therefore developed as a means of financing both short-term indebtedness on current account and long-term capital investment by public corporations and local authorities.

7. An instrument of social policy. The social objectives of public finance are open to debate and will vary from time to time. A first objective will be the preservation of society and for the exponents of *laissez-faire* philosophy the security of the State was the only legitimate sphere for intervention.

In the nineteenth and twentieth centuries the view gradually developed that society had an obligation to guarantee minimum standards of welfare to all its members. Public finance was then faced with the problem of determining the proportions in which individual contributions should be exacted and benefits allocated. The commonly agreed aim was to secure some reduction in the inequality of income and wealth. The structure of public revenue and expenditure is therefore designed to make a positive contribution to this objective.

8. The principle of progression in taxation. The older view of equity in taxation rested upon the "principle of proportionality." It was argued that if all contributed in the same proportion then income and wealth relationships between individuals remained undisturbed by taxation. When it was appreciated that this approach imposed a greater real burden upon the poor another principle was sought and progression was introduced into the British tax system in the Budget of 1893. Applied first to estate duty it subsequently became a feature of the income tax. Progressive taxation requires a more than proportionate contribution from those who are better able to pay.

It will be noted that apart from satisfying modern notions

of equity this principle provides a positive instrument for effecting a more equal distribution of income and wealth.

9. Public expenditure.

Public expenditure may be classified as:

(a) *Defence and environmental expenditure.* The benefits of public expenditure upon defence and the maintenance and improvement of the environment by both local and central government are enjoyed equally by all. No attempt is made to equate real net incomes.

(b) *Social service expenditure.* It is in the area of social service expenditure that there has been most growth since the war. Under this heading is included outlay upon education, national health, pensions, unemployment insurance, supplementary benefits, etc. While guaranteeing certain benefits to *all* citizens as of right, the intention is nevertheless to concentrate expenditure upon those most in need, *i.e.* to achieve a more equal distribution of real income.

10. An instrument of economic policy.

Public finance may be instrumental in the pursuit of economic policy.

(a) *Protection of industry.* Historically, customs duties were viewed not only as the principal source of revenue but also as a means of limiting foreign competition. Only in the mid nineteenth century did Britain embark upon a period of free trade. In 1932, free trade was abandoned and a protective tariff established. Since 1945, there has been close international co-operation aimed at restoring free trading conditions (*see* X, **19–33**). Nevertheless, in certain conditions a protective customs duty may still be considered legitimate (*see* X, **14–18**).

(b) *Support for private enterprise.* Expenditure may be of two types:

(i) *Common services.* Certain services are provided which are of general benefit to all firms, *e.g.* the Departments of Employment and Trade and Industry.

(ii) *Specific assistance.* Specific firms or industries may be singled out for support with investment grants, loans on favourable terms.

(c) *Development of public enterprise.* In developing a country's economic infrastructure certain industries may be considered so vital that it is felt that their services should be guaranteed by the State and not left to the uncertainties of market forces, *e.g.* railways, postal services.

(d) *Demand management.* It has been explained in Chapter I that since 1945 fiscal policy has been considered the most powerful instrument for the management of demand. Ideally it will be deployed in a way which secures the optimum utilisation of resources, continuous growth and stable balance of payments.

11. The reconciliation of objectives. It will be seen from the foregoing discussion that public finance has a variety of objectives which the Chancellor of the Exchequer must reconcile. Of paramount importance will be the need for a structure which encourages the most effective economic performance. Within this framework the detailed pattern of revenue and expenditure will seek to deploy resources between public and private sectors in a way which secures the most rapid attainment of social objectives. It is worth emphasising that, however desirable the social objectives, if the means of achieving them are inappropriate or the pace too fast the subsequent strain upon the economy may make those same objectives unobtainable. We shall therefore return to the use of public finance as an instrument of economic policy.

12. Economic policy aims. A system of public finance will seek to manage total effective demand in a way which is conducive to:

(a) *Full employment.*
(b) *Growth.*
(c) *Stable prices and a balance of payments equilibrium.*

In the present imperfect state of economic knowledge it may prove impossible to achieve these objectives simultaneously and socio-political considerations will establish priorities. The record would seem to indicate that during the post-war years the main concern was to stabilise demand at a level consistent with full employment, if necessary at the expense of some inflation and associated balance of payments problems and also at the cost of an unsatisfactory growth rate. A "stop-go" cycle of events emerged. During the upswing unemployment fell towards 1 per cent but demand continued to outstrip full employment output. The subsequent rise in prices and incomes induced an unfavourable balance of payments sufficient to warrant the restriction of demand by fiscal and monetary means and a mild recession ensued.

When unemployment began to rise towards 2 per cent reflationary measures were adopted which moved the economy into the next upswing.

After 1962, emphasis shifted to the management of demand in a way which would produce more rapid growth. The net result was to escalate the rate of inflation and produce more serious balance of payments crises in the middle years of the decade.

The devaluation of 1967 brought a further shift of emphasis. Priority was now given to a restraint of domestic demand sufficient to stabilise prices at a level consistent with a favourable balance of payments at the new rate of exchange. The incoming Conservative Government of 1970, despite a favourable balance of payments, placed still more emphasis upon the need to check inflation as a precondition for the long-run attainment of the other policy objectives.

We shall therefore examine in turn the possible variations in the structure of fiscal policy where priority is given to full employment, growth or stable prices.

STABILISATION OF DEMAND AT FULL EMPLOYMENT

13. The revenue and expenditure approaches. Total effective demand may be stabilised by varying the structure and volume of taxation or public expenditure. Both approaches will aim to influence consumption expenditure by altering the propensity to consume or investment expenditure by affecting the marginal efficiency of capital.

Adopting the revenue approach, taxes may be classified under two headings:

   (a) *Automatic stabilisers* (see **14** below).
   (b) *Policy-effected stabilisers* (see **15** below).

14. Automatic stabilisers. Certain fiscal devices automatically regulate the level of demand without the need for policy decisions. They include:

(a) *Unemployment insurance contributions.* In the upswing excess purchasing power is removed and contributions accumulate. Conversely, in the downswing the failure of demand is partially compensated by the payment of benefits.

(b) *Capital depreciation allowances.* Where allowances are based upon "initial" and not "replacement" cost, during the upswing more than true profit is taxed. The opposite is true during the downswing.

(c) *Capital gains taxation.* In an inflationary situation any given rate taxes more than the true gain. During the downswing, if there is a falling price level, then *if* tax is paid it will be on less than the true gain.

Automatic stabilisers have the advantage that they are continuously at work without the need for publicly announced changes in economic policy which in themselves may have an adverse effect upon business confidence. On the other hand they cannot be considered as powerful as decisions to change rates of taxation or to introduce new taxes or delete old ones.

15. Policy-effected stabilisers. It will be generally true that the manipulation of the tax structure is likely to be more effective in closing an inflationary gap than in countering deflation and unemployment. The argument is that higher taxes remove purchasing power which clearly cannot then be utilised. On the other hand while lower rates of tax will increase disposable net incomes there is no certainty of a corresponding rise in demand. The increase may be saved.

Disinflationary taxation may seek to check consumption or investment.

16. Restricting consumption expenditure. Taxes may be varied upon income or expenditure.

(a) *Income taxes.* It has been argued that higher rates of income tax are in fact inflationary, since they lead to more militant wage claims which if conceded are reflected in higher prices. For this proposition to be true there is an assumption that the consumer is able to pay the higher price and therefore that credit will always expand ahead of tax liability. It follows that higher income-tax rates should be supported by a sufficiently strict monetary policy if consumption expenditure is to be curbed.

A more widely held view of the effect of high income taxes relates to their possible disincentive influence, which may adversely affect the volume of production. It is argued that the tax structure should encourage earning and saving while penalising spending.

(b) *Expenditure taxes*. In practice, most reliance has been placed upon higher expenditure taxes designed to discourage consumption. Much use has been made of the "regulator," the power the Chancellor has to vary rates of purchase tax and excise duties by a maximum of 10 per cent between Budgets.

The argument against such taxes is that they are regressive. Little account is taken of "ability to pay," and while rates will be higher upon luxury goods the burden will inevitably fall more heavily upon the lower-income groups.

17. Restricting investment expenditure. Expenditure of any kind represents demand for limited resources. While it is clearly desirable that in the long run adequate resources should be directed to investment it is possible that in the short term investment may exceed the rate which the economy can comfortably sustain. In this case investment allowances may be made less favourable or an investment tax introduced, *e.g.* in Sweden an arrangement has worked where a tax upon investment was levied during the upswing of the cycle and the proceeds disbursed during the downswing.

18. Reflation. When unemployment figures begin to rise there is invariably political pressure for lower levels of taxation which it is hoped will stimulate demand. It has already been observed that there can be no certainty that an increase in net disposable income will increase the level of demand. Nevertheless, if expenditure taxes on the products of certain key industries are reduced a general expansionary effect will be anticipated provided that demand is elastic, *e.g.* a reduced purchase tax on motor vehicles may be expected to stimulate demand throughout that industry and also the general level of consumption in the areas in which the industry is located.

Similarly, it may be hoped to induce an "investment-led boom" by lowering the taxation of capital. If net profit margins are widened then not only will investment be encouraged but the liquidity of companies is improved. Funds are available for self-financed expansion.

On the other hand lower levels of direct personal taxation are unlikely to prove very expansionary. While it is possible that greater incentives may now exist the principal benefits will be derived by the upper-income groups who have a high propensity to save. Because of the progression in the tax system relatively little advantage accrues to the lower-income groups who have a high propensity to consume.

19. Varying the level of public expenditure. Variations in taxation depend very largely for their effect upon the uncertain responses of the private sector. A much more positive result may be expected from decisions to increase or diminish public spending.

Two factors are of importance:

(a) *The multiplier.* It should be remembered that the consequence of an addition or a withdrawal of a unit of public investment will be magnified by the operation of the multiplier.

(b) *Timing.* Precision in the management of demand depends upon appropriate timing. This implies intervention which forestalls the multiplier. A criticism of the application of these techniques has been that all too frequently Government has acted too late, *e.g.* expansionary measures have been adopted when the economy has already moved into the upswing, thus inducing unwanted inflationary pressures. Certain practical difficulties obstruct the correct timing of intervention:

(i) *Delayed information.* There is, inevitably, delay in the preparation of statistics upon which policy decisions will be based.

(ii) *Planning time.* A decision having been made there will be an interval before plans to increase or scale down expenditure can be completed.

(iii) *Implementation of plans.* For wholly practical

reasons fresh work cannot be started nor existing work stopped without warning.

(*iv*) *The operating time of the multiplier.* Even when the variation in public expenditure has begun to bite there will be a time-lag before the impact on demand has worked its way through the whole economy.

Decisions to change the level of public expenditure may be applied through four channels (*see* **20–23** below).

20. Direct central Government expenditure. The great expansion of the public sector since the Second World War has made it easier for Government to have a direct influence on the rate of investment. All the nationalised industries have investment programmes, the pace of which can be regulated in accordance with the needs of demand management.

21. Local authority expenditure. Since most local authority investment is heavily dependent upon Government financial support, it is possible to regulate the rate at which plans for schools, roads, urban renewal, etc., are implemented.

22. Private investment. It may be possible to influence investment decisions in the private sector with the inducement of a system of cash grants. Government agrees to pay in cash a proportion of the total cost of investment. Such a scheme offers the advantage of selectivity both in the industries and in the regions in which the incentives are to apply.

23. Private consumption. Transfer payments in the form of family allowances, pensions and other social security benefits are made to those who may be expected to spend rather than save.

For socio-political reasons it is unlikely that any attempt would be made to curtail demand (*i.e.* pursue disinflationary policies) by reducing benefits. On the other hand there may be scope for a more prudent administration of social security in a way which ensures that only those in real need receive benefit.

As a means of providing stimulus for expansion it is certain that the level of consumer demand will be increased by raising benefits and this course of action may be followed if it is not at the expense of the desired rate of investment.

POLICIES FOR ECONOMIC GROWTH

24. Objectives. It has been observed that during the 1960s although the goal of full employment had been achieved there was growing dissatisfaction with the growth rate which had tended to centre upon a figure of about 2 per cent per annum. This compared very unfavourably with most advanced industrial nations and it was felt that the economy should be able to sustain a real expansion of about 4 per cent per annum. Recognition of the greater priority now given to growth policies was implied by the establishment in 1962 of the National Economic Development Council (N.E.D.C.) (*see* XIII, **11**), the creation of a new Department of Economic Affairs (1964) which placed emphasis upon expansion and the publication in 1965 of a National Plan for growth.

25. Determinants of the growth rate. The rate at which the economy grows depends upon:

(a) *The availability of labour and capital.*
(b) *The efficiency with which labour and capital are utilised.*

Ideally, the structure of public finance will be disposed in a way which is most conducive to improvement under both headings. It should be stressed, however, that in an essentially private-enterprise economy Government can only attempt to create the right conditions for expansion. It cannot guarantee that growth occurs.

26. The availability of labour and capital. In the first place the growth rate is governed by the availability of labour and capital of the right quality at the right place at the right time.

(a) *Labour.* Under this heading falls labour of all kinds, skilled and unskilled, managerial and entrepreneurial. Its availability hinges upon:

(i) *Size and structure of population.* Absolute size and rate of increase of population together with its distribution between age groups and sexes are factors governing the flow of labour on to the market.

(ii) *Geographical and occupational mobility.* These are considerations which determine whether labour is of the right kind and in the right place. Implicit is the need for movement not only between occupations or industries or even firms but also movement between jobs within the same firm, *i.e.* adaptability to new working methods and procedures.

They are in turn influenced by a country's cultural attitudes and social and economic institutions, *e.g.* class and sex prejudices, the educational system, the trade-union structure.

(*b*) *Capital.* The creation of capital equipment of the right kind to assist in further production depends upon:

(*i*) *Rate of saving.* Factors governing the rate of saving have already been considered (*see* I, **15**). However, the saver now requires some inducement to surrender his liquidity by investing in some tangible asset.

(*ii*) *Rate of investment* (*see* I, **16**). Before the entrepreneur will invest he must anticipate sufficient net profit to recompense both himself and those whose savings he utilises.

(*iii*) *Research.* It should not be forgotten that the purpose of all production is consumption. The creation of capital is not in itself an objective and if it is to assist in satisfying future demand it must be of the right kind. To this end there should be adequate market research to produce a reasonable prediction of demand. Secondly, there should be adequate technological research to ensure that the most productive capital equipment is created.

27. Efficient use of labour and capital. To maximise the productivity of labour and capital it is necessary that they should be both fully employed and combined in the optimum proportion appropriate to any given stage of technology. This accomplished, expansion is then limited by technological and organisational change which permits the progressive substitution of capital for labour. Implicit is the need for flexibility in the deployment of the factors of production.

28. Flexible deployment of labour. Post-war experience suggests that there is a conflict between the objectives of full employment and mobility. When the economy is run at a high level of demand, the balance of industrial power shifts from management to labour. The employee resists change which dislocates his own economic life and which may offer no immediate recompense. He is supported by trade unions which are not disposed to accept redundancies. For the sake of industrial peace the employer continues to use his labour force uneconomically and there is a strong tendency towards overmanning. He is able to hand on higher costs in higher prices since demand continues to be sustained at a sufficiently high level.

This conflict has led some economists, notably Professor Paish, to conclude that it is necessary to run the economy with a higher margin of unused resources, e.g. 2·4 per cent unemployment.

29. Flexible deployment of capital. Ideally, it is desirable to have investment which is immediately responsive to the needs of new technologies and new markets. In practice it is very difficult to achieve this sensitivity. Much investment is of a highly specialised nature, large in scale and undertaken well in advance of the demand for the consumer goods at which it is directed. A decision to construct a steel-mill in a particular location cannot be easily reversed although technological or market changes may invalidate the premises upon which the decision was based.

The best that can be said is that sudden and large-scale changes in the direction and volume of investment should be avoided.

30. A tax structure to improve the availability of labour. It may be possible to vary the incidence and the weight of taxation in a way which improves the availability of labour.

(a) *Direct personal taxation.* The disincentive effects of a complicated and steeply progressive system of income tax and surtax have been the subject of recent discussion but the conclusions must remain imprecise. Nevertheless, the strategy of the changes in the tax structure proposed by the Chancellor in March 1971 is based upon the assumption that simpler and lower direct taxation will provide an incentive to work harder. The changes included:

(i) An immediate lowering of standard-rate income tax with an increase in child allowance coupled with considerably improved earned-income relief for surtax-payers.

(ii) The substitution in 1973 of a single graduated personal tax for existing income tax and surtax. It was argued that the complicated earned income relief had a built-in disincentive since few people understood it and most consequently over-estimated their marginal tax liability.

(b) *Indirect taxation.* In general it may be thought that direct taxation which penalises earnings is likely to be more disincentive than indirect taxation whose incidence is upon spending. Moreover, if the incidence of this taxation is upon those luxury goods which are complementary to improved leisure pursuits there may be some incentive to work harder in order to attain them.

On the other hand expenditure taxes may offend in two ways:

(i) *They are regressive,* bearing no relationship to taxable capacity.

(ii) *They must be selective* and therefore distort the normal pattern of consumer choice by discriminating arbitrarily against certain goods and services. On the basis of this objection, the Government is committed to the substitution in 1973 of a broad-based non-discriminatory Value Added Tax (V.A.T.) for the existing Selective Employment and Purchase Taxes.

31. A public expenditure structure to improve the availability of labour. Public expenditure may be directed in two ways to the improvement of labour's availability:

(a) *Personal direct transfers.* The level of pensions, sickness, supplementary and unemployment benefits may or may not influence retirements or returns to work. However, the decision of the 1970 Conservative administration to disqualify the first three days of sickness from benefit is based on the view that currently many days' work are unjustifiably lost. Similarly, administrative adjustments in the payment of supplementary benefits have been made with a view to speedier settlement of strike action, *e.g.* in the case of the 1971 Post Office strike a considerably larger sum was paid to strikers' families in supplementary benefits than was paid to the strikers themselves from the union's small emergency fund.

(b) *Improvement of the economic infrastructure.* It is from expenditure in this field that the most positive long-term results will be expected although they will not be quantifiable. An effective education service coupled with adequate retraining facilities will improve the quality, the adaptability and the mobility of the labour force. An efficient health service will reduce the number of days lost through sickness and extend the working life of the population. Expenditure upon housing and communications may be expected to improve geographical mobility.

32. A tax structure to improve the availability of capital.

The taxation of profits must have regard to the need to leave sufficient incentive to the saver to surrender his liquidity and to the entrepreneur to invest (*see* **26** (*b*)).

(*a*) *Taxation of company profits.* When costs rise more rapidly than the general price level, profits may be squeezed to a degree which is incompatible with the desired rate of investment. Capital cannot be renewed from the reduced volume of retained company profits. There is no incentive to raise fresh equity capital for the purpose of expansion. In such a situation there is a strong argument for the reduction of profits taxation, *e.g.* the decision to reduce Corporation Tax in 1970 followed by the halving of S.E.T. in 1971 was aimed at widening profit margins.

Assuming that companies have ample profits they may be induced to reinvest by favourable allowances which can be offset against tax liability, *e.g.* variable capital depreciation allowances.

(*b*) *Taxation of investment income.* British taxation normally discriminates against distributed profits in the hope that companies will retain a larger proportion in order to finance their own capital requirements. There is further discrimination against dividend income upon which the recipient pays a higher rate than he does on earned income. It may be anticipated that beyond a certain point the incentive to the individual investor is removed and fresh capital will not be forthcoming. It is from this point of view that a reform of the structure of Corporation Tax and of the degree of discrimination against unearned income was foreshadowed in the 1971 Budget.

The principal point is that if the net return to risk capital falls below a certain level the willingness to undertake risk upon which change and growth ultimately depend will be inhibited.

33. Public expenditure and the supply of capital. Saving and investment may be encouraged by:

(a) *Cash grants* to firms on the condition of further investment, *e.g.* the Investment Incentives scheme of 1966. The objection to this method is that it distorts market forces and may encourage investment which is not genuinely profitable. The scheme was abandoned in 1970.

(b) *Support to local authorities* for the purpose of improving the local economic environment may encourage private investment.

(c) *Investment programmes of public corporations.* The Government is in a powerful position to force saving and investment by increasing taxation and devoting the proceeds to investment in the nationalised industries.

34. Financial policy and the optimum deployment of labour and capital. It has been observed (*see* **27** above) that the efficient use of labour and capital involves their combination in optimum proportions in the wake of changing technologies and markets. While the principal instrument will be "productivity bargaining" between management and labour, public finance may provide a context which is conducive to such improvements.

(a) *Structure of taxation.* The object will be to influence the labour/capital cost ratio in a way which promotes the substitution of capital for labour.

The criticism has been levelled that compared with our European competitors it has been *artificially* cheaper to employ more labour rather than more capital. For example, the proportion of the social insurance contribution borne by the State is considerably higher in the U.K. than elsewhere. Moreover, food subsidies and the pricing policies of the nationalised industries weighted in favour of the consumer all tend to relieve the employer of the *full* cost of labour. On the other hand, the taxation of capital in the U.K. has tended to be severe compared with European countries.

The cost ratio may be reversed by tax changes, *e.g.* a general payroll tax, the proceeds of which are used to relieve the burden of capital taxation.

(b) *Structure of public expenditure.* There are a number

of directions in which public funds may be used to secure a better utilisation of labour and capital:

(i) *Housing.* Support for private and municipal building programmes may be expected to contribute to labour mobility.

(ii) *Adequate unemployment benefits* when coupled with redundancy payments may relieve the resistance to the redundancies which inevitably follow change.

(iii) *Education and training* when soundly based will improve skills and aptitudes which in turn will increase mobility.

(iv) *Government-sponsored research and development* which encourages selective investment of the most productive kind.

THE STABILISATION OF PRICES

35. The nature of the problem. The stabilisation of prices has been an economic policy objective for two main reasons:

(a) *Arbitrary redistribution of incomes.* In a period of rapid inflation there is a redistribution of "real" income from those whose money incomes are fixed to those whose money incomes respond to price change; from weak and badly organised labour to strong and militant trade unionists; from lenders to borrowers.

(b) *Imbalance in foreign payments.* As inflation progresses export prices lose their competitive edge while the high domestic price level invites an increase in imports. A balance of payments crisis ensues necessitating restrictive policies which retard growth and increase unemployment.

36. A majority view of the causes of inflation. During the 1960s the most widely held view of the cause of inflation has rested upon the connection between a high pressure of demand in a tight labour market and rising costs and prices which in turn gave a further twist to the wage/price spiral.

(a) *Demand in the labour market.* It was argued by A. W. Phillips that there exists a positive relationship between the rate of change of wages and the demand for labour which in turn is inversely related to the percentage rate of unemployment. It then follows that the rate at which wage rates change will be determined by the unemployment percentage. (See A. W. Phillips, "The Relation Between Unemployment and the Rate of Change of Money Wage Rates in the United Kingdom, 1861–1957." *Economica*, vol. 25, November 1958.)

(*b*) *Inflated wage costs.* Since wages are a major cost in all forms of production and since all firms in an industry are likely to accede to a wage increase agreed by one there will be a squeeze on profit margins and a strong incentive to raise prices.

(*c*) *Wage/price spiral.* The general rise in prices which was initiated by an excessively low unemployment percentage now gives rise to further wage demands and inflation gathers momentum.

37. Disinflationary policies. If the foregoing explanation of inflation is accepted there are three possible courses of action.

(*a*) *A general restriction of demand* (*see* **38–42** below).

(*b*) *Regional development* (*see* **43** below).

(*c*) *Incomes policy* (*see* **44–49** below).

38. A general restriction of demand. The fiscal measures appropriate to a reduction of the pressure of demand have been considered (*see* **13–23** above). The intention will be to stabilise the economy at a higher level of unemployment.

Three objections arise:

(*a*) *Social cost.* There are obvious social objections to policies deliberately designed to raise unemployment.

(*b*) *Loss of potential output.* At current prices a rise of $0 \cdot 2$ per cent in the rate of unemployment may be associated with a loss of production of about £400 million.

(*c*) *The phenomenon of inflation and rising unemployment.* In the post-war years the fiscal weapon has been regularly used to check the rate of inflation and this has generally been achieved at about 2 per cent unemployment. However, by 1970, despite severely restrictive taxation the rate of inflation had escalated to $8\frac{1}{2}$ per cent at the same time as unemployment rose to 3 per cent, its highest point since the 1930s. The implication was that to contain inflation by a further restriction of demand would result in unemployment of a wholly unacceptable level.

The failure of fiscal policy to produce the required results during the 1960s gave added influence to the arguments of the monetary economists.

39. "Inflation is always and everywhere a monetary phenomenon." (*See* VII, 42–50.) Professor Friedman argues that there is a consistent although imprecise and delayed relationship between the growth of the money supply and the growth of money incomes. This relationship can be observed in economies as diverse as those of Japan, India, Israel, Canada and the U.S.A.

About six to nine months after a change in the rate of money growth there will be a change in the rate of growth of nominal incomes and also of physical output. After a further six months there will be some impact upon prices. "That is why it is a long road to hoe to stop an inflation that has been allowed to start. It cannot be stopped overnight."

Thus in the short run the effect of monetary change is upon output and negligibly upon prices. Overall, however, when thinking of the very long term, output depends upon real factors such as enterprise, thrift, ingenuity and industrial structure while prices are determined by the rate of money growth. (See Milton Friedman, *The Counter-revolution in Monetary Theory*. Occasional Paper 33, I.E.A., December 1970.)

40. Relationship between money supply, income and effective demand. The monetarist argument continues that the initial effect of a change in the money supply is not upon incomes but upon the price of existing assets such as bonds, equities, houses and other physical capital.

An increase in the money supply increases cash balances relative to other assets. The holders of excess cash now attempt to adjust their position by acquiring other assets but since one man's purchase is another man's sale, total liquidity remains unaffected. However, the increased rate of purchases tends to raise the price of assets and to reduce interest rates. Lower interest rates encourage spending on new assets and also on current services. In this way prices are given an upward tilt.

41. Money supply and interest rates. An important feature of the monetarist case is that a change in monetary growth will affect interest rates at first in one way but later in another way.

Rapid growth in the money supply at first lowers interest rates but as spending, price inflation and the demand for loans are stimulated, interest rates rise. Thus countries such as Brazil and Chile with the highest rates of monetary growth and price inflation have also the highest interest rates. On the other hand, countries such as West Germany and Switzerland which have had slow monetary growth have also the lowest rates of interest.

It is for this reason that the monetarists view "monetary aggregates" (the quantity of money) as the principal criterion of monetary policy rather than interest rates, which they regard as misleading.

This view was accepted by the U.S. Federal Reserve in January 1970.

42. Policy implications. The view of many monetary economists including Professor Friedman is that while the money supply should be the central feature of monetary policy so little is understood of the precise relationships between money, prices and output that it should not be used as an instrument of fine tuning. Rather do they favour a stable (*e.g.* 5 per cent per annum) rate of monetary growth which in the long term will permit economic expansion without an unacceptable degree of inflation.

In the short term fiscal and other means should be used *gradually* to contain and then de-escalate the rate of inflation.

We are therefore led to conclude that if the monetarist rather than the neo-Keynesian view is accepted, at least in the long term, less reliance must be placed upon fiscal policy and more upon monetary policy as a means of containing the growth of demand.

43. Regional development. The distribution of unemployment is by no means even and many areas of the country, *e.g.* Merseyside, Cumberland, have figures well above the national average. It is argued that inflation may be relieved by regional policies which increase unemployment in areas where there is excessive demand for labour at the same time as unemployment is decreased in the depressed areas. Thus unemployment is simply "transferred," the national figure remaining the same.

Financial incentives (*e.g.* favourable tax treatment, discriminatory investment grants) can be built into the fiscal system in an attempt to achieve this objective but the results will be unpredictable.

INCOMES POLICY

44. "Moral persuasion." The principal purpose of incomes policy has been to solve the problem of how to avoid inflation at full employment. In attempting to achieve restraint in prices and incomes, emphasis has been placed upon voluntary co-operation although some form of Government intervention has usually proved necessary. The policy may take the form of a short-term emergency measure to deal with a balance of payments crisis or a long-term attempt to establish more orderly economic relationships.

45. Chronology of U.K. incomes policy. There have been four attempts to establish policies in restraint of prices and incomes.

(*a*) *1948.* Following the 1947 balance of payments crisis, the Government applied its remaining wartime powers to check price rises at the same time as it secured the co-operation of the trade unions in postponing wage claims. This policy met with some success until the 1949 devaluation brought inflationary pressures which forced the unions to abandon restraint.

(*b*) *1956.* The Government asked for a voluntary and temporary "wage pause" but was unsuccessful in gaining union co-operation. An independent and purely advisory body, the Council on Productivity, Prices and Incomes, was then set up but met with little success.

(*c*) *1961.* A pay pause was initiated, followed in 1962 by the setting up of a National Incomes Commission (N.I.C.) to review pay claims, and the publication of "guiding lights" for wages and salaries. Without union support, N.I.C. proved uninfluential.

(*d*) *1964.* A "declaration of intent" on productivity, prices and incomes was signed by employers, unions and

Government as a pre-condition of economic policies which would permit more rapid growth. Finally, the machinery of a full-scale incomes policy was provided in 1965 with the establishment of a National Board for Prices and Incomes (N.B.P.I. or P.I.B.) which replaced N.I.C. and was to review price and pay increases. Its criteria were set out in a White Paper, *Prices and Incomes Policy.* A norm for wage increases was established at 3–3½ per cent.

Later in 1965 an "early warning system" was set up by which Government was to be notified in advance of any proposed increases in wages or prices.

In July 1966, the Government introduced a wage and price freeze for six months to be followed by a six-month period of "severe restraint." Statutory power was given to this decision by the *Prices and Incomes Act* of August 1966, which was to have force for exactly twelve months.

The Government indicated its intention to return to a voluntary incomes policy in a White Paper, *Prices and Incomes Policy after 30 June 1967.* The P.I.B. would again rely on the criteria set out in the 1965 White Paper with the main difference that the norm would now be zero and that there should be a minimum twelve-month period between wage increases.

In April 1968, a further White Paper outlined the Government's intentions for 1968 and 1969. A ceiling of 3½ per cent per annum was set for wages, salaries and dividends and twelve months were to elapse between the dates of successive settlements.

In 1970, the incoming Conservative Government declared its lack of confidence in a formal incomes policy and announced that the P.I.B. would be dismantled.

46. Incomes policy criteria. During its lifetime the P.I.B. evolved certain operational criteria within the broad framework established by legislation.

(a) *Shortage of labour.* It was not considered justifiable to raise wage levels, particularly in labour-intensive industries, as a means of attracting more staff. Rather should employers concern themselves with improving the productivity of the existing work force.

(b) *Comparability*.   The "principle of parity" with work-ers employed in similar jobs became during the 1960s an increasingly popular basis for wage claims.   However, it is a very loose principle and capable of almost infinite exten-sion, *e.g.* the 1971 national Ford strike was in support of pay parity with the highest-paid Midlands car workers.   Mean-while, on Merseyside, all factory pay claims have tended to have some eye to parity with local Ford workers.   The P.I.B. disapproved of this principle.

(c) *Job evaluation*.   The Board was generally sympathetic to job-evaluation systems which increased wage differentials within a firm or industry when they had been excessively narrowed by external pressures.

(d) *Rising cost of living*.   Since a prices and incomes policy was concerned with stabilising prices it followed that a rise in the general price level should not automatically signal a general rise in wages.   This could only perpetuate the wage/price spiral.

(e) *The low paid*.   A secondary objective of an incomes policy will be to secure some redistribution of income in favour of the lower paid and this case has generally been viewed as an exception when a standstill or norm has been imposed on other incomes.   The practical difficulty which the P.I.B. acknowledged was deciding who in fact were the low paid.   Moreover, there is inevitably resistance to any narrowing of differentials.   Any gain secured by the lower paid is likely to herald further claims by the higher paid.

(f) *Productivity*.   The principal reason approved by the Board for pay increases in excess of a given norm was the case where it could be clearly demonstrated in accordance with fairly tightly prescribed rules that there would be an increase in labour's productivity.

47. Implementation of criteria.   The voluntary acceptance of criteria for a prices and incomes policy has hinged upon three factors:

(a) *National emergency*.   When the nation has been made aware of an economic crisis as in 1966, there has been a greater willingness, at least in the short run, to accept wage restraint.

(b) *The influence on their members of trade unions and*

employers' organisations. While employers and union leaders may agree to an incomes policy there is no guarantee that "wage drift," the product of plant-level bargaining, may not destroy the restraining influence of national agreements. Moreover, since the number of unofficial strikes during the 1960s far exceeded those which were official there is little evidence that the trade unions can deter a dissatisfied membership.

(c) *Political party in power.* Only Labour Governments have had any success in securing the co-operation of the unions in implementing an incomes policy.

48. Prospects for a future incomes policy. While the devotees of an incomes policy will claim that the arrangements made after 1964 were not given a long enough trial, the evidence of all post-war experiments is not encouraging. It suggests that whenever wages are temporarily restrained there is subsequently an even greater pressure for increases. This was particularly noticeable in the run-up to the 1970 general election when the Government appeared to slacken the reins with the result that wage claims rapidly escalated to levels far beyond what could be justified on the grounds of keeping abreast of inflation. It appeared that the union leadership, as in 1950, was unable to resist the pressure from the rank-and-file membership, a pressure augmented by the inflationary effects of the 1967 devaluation. The "theory of adaptive expectations" seemed now to be substantiated. The nation, having finally adjusted its expectations to one of continuing inflation, was not only allowing for past price rises in formulating its wage claims but was also trying to anticipate them. Wage claims so based make further price rises inevitable.

49. The Industrial Relations Act, 1971. Having abandoned a formal incomes policy the 1970 Conservative Government pinned its faith on a general resistance to wage claims in the public sector in the hope of a gradual de-escalation towards 3–4 per cent which would be transmitted to the private sector. In the absence of other measures, there has so far been little impact upon the level of private-sector settlements.

In the long term, the hope is that legislation for the reform of industrial relations will produce a more stable climate within which reasonable wage bargains will be struck and observed.

PROGRESS TEST 2

1. In what senses may public finance be employed as an instrument of social policy? (**7, 8, 9**)

2. Point out four areas in which public finance may be employed in support of economic policy. (**10**)

3. At what policy objectives will "demand management" be aimed? (**12**)

4. What do you understand by an "automatic stabiliser"? (**14**)

5. Compare income taxes and expenditure taxes as means of restricting consumption. (**16**)

6. Is it ever justifiable to restrict investment? (**17**)

7. What practical difficulties are encountered in using public expenditure as an instrument of demand management? (**19**)

8. Through which agencies can central government expenditure be channelled? (**20–23**)

9. Analyse the determinants of the economic growth rate. (**25–29**)

10. Compare the effectiveness of direct and indirect taxes as means of improving the availability of labour. (**30**)

11. Suggest how taxes may be varied to improve the flow of capital. (**32**)

12. How might public expenditure improve the rates of saving and investment? (**33**)

13. How might financial policy improve the labour/capital cost ratio? (**34**)

14. Explain the generally held view of the causes of inflation. (**36**)

15. How would you modify this view if you held the monetarist view of inflation? (**39–42**)

16. What do you understand by "incomes policy"? (**44**)

17. What operational criteria were evolved by the P.I.B. for the application of an incomes policy? (**46**)

18. Do you consider that an incomes policy has any future in the U.K.? (**47–49**)

CHAPTER III

THE MACHINERY OF DEMAND MANAGEMENT

THE POLICY-MAKING ORGANISATION

1. The Treasury. The modern Treasury originated in 1714 when the medieval office of Treasurer to the Crown was "put into commission," *i.e.* a number of Lords Commissioners shared the office as a Board of Treasury. The Prime Minister is the First Lord of the Treasury and the Chancellor of the Exchequer is the Second Lord with the special responsibility of placing before Parliament the Government's financial policy.

2. Treasury responsibilities. Since the powers and responsibilities of the Treasury are not defined by statute it is difficult to delineate the scope of its work with precision.

Traditionally, its first and central task is to raise money to finance Government expenditure but in the twentieth century the Treasury's influence has extended into many other fields determined by the interests and personal stature of its Permanent Secretaries. In the inter-war period there was a total rejection of the idea that Government expenditure could relieve the problem of unemployment and the principal preoccupation lay with the Treasury's function in managing the Civil Service.

During the war, Government intervention in the economy resulted in the formation of the Central Statistical Office and the Economic Section of the Cabinet Office, both of which played a major part in the co-ordination of the work of departments with economic interests under the general direction of the Lord President of the Council. In 1947, the latter's economic responsibilities were taken over by a new Ministry of Economic Affairs under Sir Stafford Cripps. When six weeks later he moved to the Treasury he took with him his new economic functions. By 1950, any post-war notions of detailed central economic planning had been abandoned and Cripps himself stated that "the Budget itself can be described as the most important control and the most important instrument for influencing economic policy."

Keynesian doctrine had been accepted and the Treasury was to provide the machinery for its implementation. Apart from the period 1964–69, the lifespan of a revived Department of Economic Affairs, these macroeconomic functions have remained with the Treasury.

3. The other economic Departments. The Treasury has never been the only Department with economic interests although the division of functions between other Ministries has varied very frequently. Nevertheless, these functions have remained basically the same and include trade-union relations, regional policy, local government, housing, public works, power, transport, commercial, industrial and incomes policy.

In 1971, four large Ministries cover these responsibilities. They are the Department of Trade and Industry, the Department of the Environment, the Department of Employment and the Department of Health and Social Security.

Attached to the Cabinet Office is an institution of great importance, the Central Statistical Office. It is responsible for collating and presenting figures for the national income, the balance of payments and factors influencing the money supply.

4. The problem of co-ordination. The Treasury lies at the centre of the economics Ministries and exercises control through its responsibility for Government spending and for demand management. However, the range of economic problems is so great that it would be impossible for the Chancellor alone to co-ordinate the work of the various Departments.

The attempt is made to overcome this problem through a series of inter-departmental committees. Since the war there has always been one main economic policy committee (currently known as the "Steering Committee on Economic Policy") attended by the Prime Minister, the Chancellor and the principal economic Ministers. This is paralleled by an official committee of Permanent Secretaries. Additionally, there are numerous special committees dealing with specific issues such as environmental planning and regional policy.

5. Treasury organisation. In view of the range of Treasury responsibilities the Chancellor is supported not only by a Permanent Secretary but also by three Ministers each responsible for an aspect of the Department's work.

(*a*) *Finance.* This group is responsible for Government borrowing and lending, the balance of payments and international financial negotiations.

(*b*) *National Economy.* This section is concerned with demand management (*i.e.* fiscal policy), economic assessment and industrial and incomes policy.

(*c*) *Public Sector.* This group is concerned with control of all central Government expenditure.

NOTE: The old responsibility for management of the Civil Service has been transferred to a new Department.

6. The position of the Bank of England. The Bank occupies the somewhat anomalous role of an independent institution which sees itself as the City's representative in Whitehall and yet which behaves very much like a Government Department, making known the views of Whitehall to the City.

The Treasury's Finance Group provides the main Government links with the Bank through highly confidential meetings of senior officials.

It should be noted that the Treasury has no direct links with either domestic or foreign financial markets. The Bank operates on its behalf.

7. International financial relations. In the post-war world it has not been possible to determine domestic economic policy without reference to its implications for other countries. There are seven important international financial organisations at which the U.K. viewpoint is represented by delegations normally composed of Treasury and Bank officials.

(*a*) *International Monetary Fund* (*see* XII, **30–39**).

(*b*) *The Group of Ten* (*see* XII, **37**).

(*c*) *Organisation for Economic Co-operation and Development* (*see* X, **40**).

(*d*) *Working Party Three.* This is a sub-committee of O.E.C.D., made up of the Group of Ten less Belgium but with the addition of Switzerland, which meets in Basle. **Its** function is to exercise surveillance over members' domestic policies in respect of demand management and the balance of payments.

(*e*) *Bank for International Settlements.* Formed in 1930 for the purpose of facilitating German war reparations it became an instrument for co-operation between European central bankers.

(*f*) *International Bank for Reconstruction and Development* (*see* XII, **41**).

(*g*) *International Development Association* (*see* XII, **42**).

8. The Treasury Economic Service. Professional economists are spread throughout the three Treasury groups although the majority are concentrated in the National Economy Section. This vitally important group subdivides into four.

(*a*) *Economic assessment.* Short- and medium-term forecasting.

(*b*) *National economy* (*general*). Advice and briefing on any economic topic.

(*c*) *Fiscal policy.* The co-ordination of the Budget.

(*d*) *Industrial and incomes policy.* Prices and incomes movements, monopolies and mergers, investment, consultations with unions and employers through the medium of the National Economic Development Council.

9. Economic forecasts. The most important function of the Treasury economist is to provide forecasts upon which economic policy can be based.

(*a*) *Spot assessments.* Since 1967, the Treasury has published a monthly economic report containing current data on the most important variables such as employment, output, imports and exports.

(*b*) *Short-term forecasts.* In February, June and October, the Treasury in conjunction with the other economics Ministries prepares a National Income Forecast for the following year together with a Balance of Payments Forecast.

These are essentially predictions of business-cycle movements made on the assumption of no change in Government policy.

(c) *Medium-term forecasts.* These are made annually during the summer and normally for a five-year period. They are based on the assumption that Government policy will determine the level of activity and take account of underlying growth trends in population and productivity. From this prediction of the increase in future output an assessment can be made of the required allocation between consumption and investment in both private and public sectors. Guidelines are thus established for demand management.

THE FORMULATION OF THE BUDGET JUDGMENT

10. The Budget and the financial year. For the purpose of the Budget Report and Financial Statement, the financial year begins on 1st April and ends on 31st March. (For the purpose of income-tax assessment, the year begins on 6th April and ends on 5th April.)

The Chancellor will normally make his Budget speech in April after the close of the old financial year. In it he gives a brief review of the previous twelve months' expenditure, but the vital part of his statement is concerned with his tax proposals for the coming year.

Since the object of a modern Budget is not only to raise revenue but also to regulate the nation's spending, it has become conventional to build the speech round a theme, *e.g.* the 1971 Budget was both mildly reflationary and concerned with the long-term benefits which would flow from reform of the tax structure.

11. Financial Statement and Budget Report. When opening the Budget the Chancellor lays before the House the Financial Statement and Budget Report. This comprises four sections:

(a) *The economic background to the Budget.* A review of developments and trends during the previous year.

(b) *Public sector transactions.* The accounts of the public sector as a whole, they comprise the current and capital account transactions of the central Government (including the Consolidated and National Loans Funds, the National Insurance Fund) and of local authorities and nationalised

industries.   Provisional figures are given for the previous
year's out-turn and estimates made for the following year.

NOTE: These accounts rather than those of central Government alone are considered of vital importance in assessing
the impact of the public sector upon the economy (*see* IV,
14–21).

(*c*) *Central Government transactions.*   All central Government receipts are paid into a central account, the Consolidated
Fund, and all payments are made from this fund.   This
section is a record of these transactions for the previous
year and an estimate of transactions for the forthcoming
year.

(*d*) *Annex.*   Details are given of the Chancellor's proposed
tax changes which are intended to produce the estimated
revenue and to achieve the economic objectives outlined in
his speech.

12. Preliminary estimates.   In February of each year,
Government Departments first send into the Treasury their
preliminary forecasts of their expenditure for the next financial year but one.   At about the same time the Inland Revenue and Customs and Excise Departments send in their
revenue forecasts.   Revisions are made during the spring and
in the early summer the Treasury Accountant is able to prepare
his first Exchequer Prospects Table.   This outlines revenue
and expenditure for the coming year and is submitted to the
Budget Committee in July.

13. The Treasury Budget Committee.   The Committee
meets continuously from July until March under the chairmanship of the Permanent Secretary.   It comprises the Heads
of the Public Sector and Finance Groups, senior Treasury
economists, the chairmen of the Inland Revenue and Customs
and Excise Departments and is attended by the Deputy
Governor of the Bank of England.

In July it has at its disposal the summer National Income
Forecast and the preliminary Exchequer Prospects Table, on
the basis of which its primary concern at this stage is the
possible need for the use of the regulator during the summer.

14. The Queen's Speech.   Parliament reassembles in the
autumn and is opened by the Queen's Speech in which the

Government's legislative programme is outlined and some idea given of the revenue necessary to implement it.

Meanwhile, early in October, the Budget Committee has already agreed figures for public investment in schools, hospitals, roads, etc. It has also discussed the need for an autumn "mini-budget" in the light of what has so far transpired during the year.

15. Autumn National Income Forecast. In November the autumn Forecast predicts the way in which demand and output will grow in relation to productive capacity and the way in which the balance of payments will respond, both on the assumption that no change is made in the forthcoming Budget. A basis is thus given for an assessment of the sort of changes which will be desirable.

16. Firm estimates of revenue and expenditure. By early December Government Departments have sent into the Treasury firm expenditure estimates and the Revenue Departments have sent revised revenue estimates. The Treasury Accountant is then able to revise his Exchequer Prospects Table by the end of the month.

By the end of January the Treasury has approved the estimates of the spending Departments and in February they are introduced into Parliament for debate on the allocated "supply days."

Once the estimates have been approved by the Treasury, the Chancellor receives his first recommendations from the Budget Committee and from then on plays an active part in its deliberations. At this stage the "Budget judgment" begins to take shape and by mid February the Chancellor is receiving advice on the precise size of the deficit or surplus at which he should aim.

17. The Budget outline. During February and early March the main outline of the Budget has been agreed and much of the detail of the tax proposals has been firmly formulated. In the case of indirect taxation, it is necessary to agree changes well in advance since they are effective from Budget day. Since income-tax changes are not immediately applicable changes can be made up to about a week beforehand.

18. The Budget speech. By mid March, the main Budget judgment will have been made and the remaining weeks are occupied in the preparation of the Budget speech. A provisional outline is drawn up by the Chancellor's Principal Private Secretary and sections contributed by experts in the Treasury and other Departments. The Chancellor adds his own ideas on presentation and vets the various drafts until one is finalised. On the morning of the Budget, the Treasury Accountant checks the speaking copy of the speech to ensure that all figures are correct.

THE CONTROL OF PUBLIC EXPENDITURE

19. Consolidated Fund Standing Services and supply services. Each year Parliament reviews certain recurrent items of expenditure but is obliged to sanction them. They are known as the "Consolidated Fund Standing Services" and include interest payments on the National Debt, Royal Household expenses, judges' salaries and post-war credits. These standing commitments are agreed without much discussion by means of a "financial resolution."

All other annual current expenditure comes under the heading of "supply services" and falls into two groups. "Civil supply" comprises eleven classes of expenditure corresponding to the work of different Ministries or groups of Ministries. Secondly, there is the "defence budget."

20. Summary of procedure for supply services. Supply services are "voted" annually by the House of Commons. The procedure passes through five stages:

(*a*) The spending Departments submit estimates of their proposed expenditure to the Treasury which approves, rejects or modifies them.

(*b*) The Crown submits the estimates for the consideration of Parliament.

(*c*) The House of Commons debates the estimates and "votes" sums for agreed purposes.

(*d*) The House authorises drawings upon the Consolidated Fund to meet agreed expenditure.

(*e*) In order to ensure that all drawings are utilised only for agreed purposes an *Appropriation Act* is passed.

At each stage there is opportunity for control and the whole procedure is underwritten by House of Commons Standing Order No. 78.

21. Standing Order No. 78. This famous Standing Order dates back to 1713. "This House will receive no petition for any sum relating to public service or proceed upon any motion for a grant or charge upon the public revenue, whether payable out of the Consolidated Fund or out of money to be provided by Parliament, unless recommended from the Crown."

The Government alone has the power to propose expenditure, a factor which militates in favour of coherent and effective financial planning. It follows that the Government alone is responsible for the success of the plan to Parliament and the electorate.

22. Treasury control. The spending Departments have always viewed the Treasury as a body whose primary concern is to restrain expenditure. The Treasury's authority to do so rests ultimately with the influence of the Chancellor in Cabinet, for it is here that his decisions may be overridden.

Subject to this proviso the Treasury's power is based upon two rules:

(*a*) Since 1861, it has been formally agreed that in the light of Standing Order No. 78, proposed departmental expenditure should first be sanctioned by the Treasury. When reviewing the estimates the Treasury attempts in a commonsense way to produce a balance between competing demands so that the country is given the best value for money.

(*b*) Since 1924 it has been agreed that no proposal for increased expenditure can be circulated in Cabinet without prior discussion with the Treasury.

It can thus be seen that the Treasury is in a very powerful position to exert pressure at the stage where the estimates are first submitted.

23. Parliamentary debate of the estimates. Twenty-nine "supply days" are set aside for discussion of the estimates between February and the end of July. The Opposition are free to choose the estimates which will be debated but will be concerned to challenge the Government's overall strategy rather than to achieve detailed economies. In July or August an *Appropriation Act* is passed which authorises the Treasury to make advances to the Departments from the Consolidated Fund.

24. Committee on Expenditure. This Committee has now superseded the Select Committee on Estimates which had been appointed annually since 1921. The intention is for an inter-party committee to examine the estimates in more detail than is possible on the floor of the House.

Select Committees have performed a useful function in subjecting departmental administrations to external criticism, *e.g.* a Select Committee was responsible for a highly critical examination of Treasury control methods in 1957–58 which led to the Plowden Report on Public Expenditure (*see* **28** below).

25. Exchequer and Audit Department Act, 1921. This Act requires that each Department to which supply grants have been provided should prepare "accounts of appropriation" by a given date. The Departments and not the Treasury are therefore responsible for their own day-to-day spending but must show that public funds have been utilised only for purposes designated by Parliament.

26. Comptroller and Auditor-General. The appropriation accounts are submitted for auditing to the office of the Comptroller and Auditor-General. The office has a staff of over 500 divided into eight divisions, each responsible for auditing the accounts of a group of Departments.

Their function is not only to verify the technical accuracy of the accounts but also to look for waste and inefficiency.

27. Public Accounts Committee. The verified accounts are placed before the House of Commons in January and are referred to the Public Accounts Committee. This very powerful body comprises fifteen members with an Opposition M.P. as chairman. It scrutinises the accounts and publishes a report upon which the Treasury must take action.

LONG-RANGE PLANNING AND CONTROL

28. The Treasury and forward planning. We have so far
considered the methods by which during the course of the
financial year public expenditure is regulated. However, it
had long been apparent that twelve months was far too short
a period for the effective planning and control of expenditure,
e.g. current expenditure on the building of a teacher-training
college must be viewed in the light of continued expenditure
over a number of years before there is any benefit in an increased supply of teachers.

The present approach to forward planning derives from the
report of a 1961 committee under the chairmanship of Lord
Plowden which fostered the concept of a five-year programme
rolled forward at the end of every financial year.

29. The Plowden approach in practice. In 1961, the first
comprehensive survey was made of the anticipated total of
public expenditure in all sectors set against an estimate of the
probable growth of national income. At this stage the
surveys were forecasts rather than instruments of policy but,
from 1965, the Cabinet began to make positive decisions on the
portion of anticipated national income to be appropriated for
use in the public sector.

The first survey to be published was in 1963 followed by a
second in 1966. In 1969, a White Paper, *Public Expenditure
1968–9 to 1973–4*, began a regular annual series of such surveys.

In practice the Treasury maintains that in any five-year
programme the third year is the earliest at which major
changes may be made without serious dislocation. Plans for
the fourth and fifth years are viewed as provisional

30. Public Expenditure Survey Committee (P.E.S.C.). Each
summer an inter-departmental committee makes a survey of
public expenditure intentions costed on the basis of the previous year's projections. To this is added the best available
estimates of total private-sector expenditure and the grand
total is set against the anticipated growth of national income.
If it exceeds the expected growth rate then the conclusion is
that the total claim on real resources is too heavy and there
will have to be a cut-back in public expenditure or a general
increase in taxation.

31. Appraisal of public expenditure surveys. During the
1960s the inaccuracy of public expenditure surveys stemmed
from the recurrent tendency to underestimate future costs.
From 1963 to 1968 the percentage increase in public expenditure regularly exceeded that which had been planned. Only
in 1968–69 was the annual increase brought under control and
subsequently held within the limits planned. However, for a
variety of technical reasons, the tendency to underestimate
the growth of public expenditure remains.

(a) *The problem of forward projections at constant cost.*
Certain public sector activities (*e.g.* education) do not lend
themselves to measurable productivity increases which can
offset the effects of inflation. It follows that not only will
the expansion of such services need to be borne by an
expansion of G.N.P. but also that the maintenance of
existing services at inflated prices is also a charge upon
growth. In short, the share of public expenditure in
G.N.P. increases with inflation. Forward projections must
therefore take account of this difficulty.

(b) *The problem of changed expenditure classifications.* An
example of this difficulty is found in the change from
investment allowances to investment grants in 1966 and
back to accelerated capital depreciation allowances in 1970.
While grants are classed as expenditure, allowances are
treated as offsets against revenue. Although the net effect
may be the same, for accounting purposes the abolition of
grants reduces public expenditure. In calculating percentage rates of increase of public expenditure it is therefore
necessary to make allowance for such changes.

(c) *The problem of a standardised system of costing.*
Plans may be costed for different purposes employing
different sets of definitions and therefore producing different
results. None of these may be of value in checking the
actual cost of the completed work. The Treasury is
currently engaged in standardising definitions so that they
may be used equally for forecasting, operational control and
checking results.

(d) *The problem of public expenditure not wholly within the
control of central Government.* The Supply Estimates represent only about half of total public expenditure. Local
authorities control about a quarter and while central

Government is in a position to influence their capital expenditure there remains a good deal of autonomy in respect of current expenditure.

32. The problem of demand management. One major problem not amenable to treatment by improved accounting methods remains unresolved. This concerns the extent to which public expenditure may be expected to play its part in the regulation of total demand without wasteful disruption of existing programmes. The theoretical solution of a "bank" of projects which can be advanced or slowed down as occasion demands has still to be achieved in practice.

PROGRESS TEST 3

1. Explain the relationship of the Treasury to the other economic Departments. (**2–4**)

2. What are the three main divisions of the Treasury? (**5**)

3. Explain the nature of Treasury economic forecasts. (**9**)

4. Outline the contents of the Financial Statement and Budget Report. (**11**)

5. What are the "preliminary estimates"? (**12**)

6. What is the importance of the autumn National Income Forecast? (**15**)

7. What do you understand by the "Budget judgment"? (**16**)

8. What are the Consolidated Fund Standing Services? (**19**)

9. What is the significance of Standing Order No. 78? (**21**)

10. Describe the function of the Comptroller and Auditor-General's Department. (**26**)

11. What is the function of the Public Accounts Committee? (**27**)

12. In what way is the Treasury concerned with long-range economic planning? (**28**)

13. Explain the operation of P.E.S.C. (**30**)

14. What practical problems arise in respect of long-range planning? (**31**)

CHAPTER IV

THE NATIONAL DEBT

PRINCIPAL FEATURES OF THE U.K. NATIONAL DEBT

1. Nature. On occasion Government may not find it convenient to finance its expenditure wholly from taxation and may supplement its revenue by borrowing, normally from its own citizens. It should therefore be noted that while the term "National" Debt is the one in common usage it is misleading since it suggests a debt owed by the nation to the rest of the world. Since the bulk of the Debt is held by U.K. residents it is more appropriate to think of it as the sum owed by citizens collectively (*i.e.* the Government) to citizens individually, in short the Government Debt.

2. Size. On 31st March 1970, the National Debt totalled £32,366 million. For the purpose of this figure the debt is defined as the amount payable in sterling as shown in the *Consolidated Fund and National Loans Fund Accounts 1969–70* together with stocks issued by the nationalised industries and guaranteed by H.M. Government. These amount to £1,520 million of the total. Additionally there is an overseas debt repayable in external currencies of £2,234 million. The greater part of this is attributable to the post-war North American loan, raised for reconstruction purposes, the repayment of which began in 1952.

3. Structure.

TABLE I. CLASSIFICATION OF THE NATIONAL DEBT, MARCH 1970

	£m.	% of total
Marketable debt:		
Funded debt	21,240	66
Floating debt	4,561	14
Non-marketable debt:	6,565	20

(*Source: B.E.Q.B.*)

54

(a) *Funded debt.* Strictly speaking the phrase "funded debt" applies only to those stocks for which no redemption date has been set. The most important example of debt incurred on these terms is $3\frac{1}{2}$ per cent War Loan (1952 or after). The Government is under no obligation to repay although it was at liberty to do so at any time after 1952.

Used in the broader sense, the phrase includes dated stock, *i.e.* all other Government and Government-guaranteed stocks. They are of varying maturities and are publicly quoted. A single repayment date may be set or there may be two dates, after the earlier of which Government can repay if it wishes and on the second of which it must repay.

Prior to the First World War, Government borrowed only against undated stock. Subsequently dated stock came to be the principal component of the National Debt.

(b) *Floating debt.* Government requires to borrow regularly on a short-term basis in order to accommodate the uneven influx of tax revenue to the fairly even flow of departmental expenditure. This it does by borrowing against Treasury bills which are of two types, "tap" and "tender." Tap bills represent lending by Government Departments back to the Treasury. Bills payable after ninety-one days are offered for tender every Friday on the London Discount Market (*see* VIII, **3–13**).

(c) *Non-marketable debt.* The biggest part of non-marketable debt is in the form of securities which are not publicly quoted and which have no redemption date set, although normally the holder is able to claim repayment after giving a period of notice. Included are national savings certificates, defence bonds, national development bonds, British savings bonds, premium savings bonds, national savings stamps and the contractual savings schemes of the Department for National Savings and the Trustee Savings Banks.

Other non-marketable-debt instruments include tax reserve certificates, annuities and Ways and Means Advances. The last item represents the only method by which the Bank of England lends directly to Government, lending which is on a very short-term basis.

4. Distribution of the National Debt, 1970. The National Debt is held in six categories:

(*a*) *U.K. official holdings.* Government Departments or agencies themselves held £8,942 million or 28 per cent of the total. About a half of this was in the hands of the National Debt Commissioners who administer the funds through which is invested money deposited with the National Savings Bank and the Trustee Savings Bank, together with the proceeds of national insurance contributions.

A third was held by the Bank of England Issue Department as the backing for the note issue (*see* VII, **10–12**), and the remainder by the Exchange Equalisation Account, the Bank of England Banking Department and Government Departments with a temporary surplus of funds.

About 56 per cent of official holdings were in stocks, 35 per cent in Treasury bills and 9 per cent in non-marketable debt.

(*b*) *Public bodies.* A small amount of debt, £217 million, was owned by public corporations other than the Bank of England and by local authorities.

(*c*) *Banking sector.* About 8 per cent, £2,465 million, was held by the banking sector which includes the deposit banks, the National Giro, the accepting houses, overseas and other banks and the discount market.

(*d*) *Other financial institutions.* Rather less than one-fifth, £5,825 million, was in the hands of the insurance companies (the biggest institutional investors), pension funds, building societies, unit and investment trusts and the special investment accounts of the Trustee Savings and National Savings Banks. These holdings were concentrated almost entirely in stocks with more than five years to maturity.

(*e*) *Overseas residents.* Some £5,253 million was held overseas, of which £2,267 million was owned by central monetary institutions and £1,960 million by international organisations. These figures reflect both the investment of overseas countries' official sterling reserves and the sterling counterpart invested in Treasury bills of £650 million of drawings by the U.K. on special aid facilities.

Of the holdings of international organisations, £1,845 million was non-marketable in the form of non-interest-bearing notes arising partly from U.K. drawings from the I.M.F. and partly from subscriptions to I.M.F. and the International Development Association (I.D.A.).

(*f*) *Other holders.* These include various non-corporate bodies' private funds and trusts, industrial and commercial companies and friendly societies. Of the total of £9,664 million in this category, £7,050 million, rather less than a quarter of the total debt, was in private hands.

THE BURDEN OF THE DEBT

5. International comparisons. Because of differences in structure and size of public sectors and of variations in definitions of National Debt, it is not easy to make accurate international comparisons. However, broad comparisons may be made by assessing the weight of debt as a percentage of gross national product.

TABLE II. THE NATIONAL DEBT AS A PERCENTAGE OF G.N.P.

	Total National Debt % G.N.P.	*National Debt excluding official holdings and I.M.F. notes as* % G.N.P.
Canada	37	29
France	18	13
Italy	61	54
Japan	10	4
The Netherlands	35	20
U.K.	*89*	*59*
U.S.A.	46	29
West Germany	30	19

It is apparent that the U.K. has a substantially heavier burden of debt than similar advanced countries. This is to be explained primarily by the huge cost of two world wars. Elsewhere, countries either incurred less war debt in relation to their resources or had its burden eroded by inflation or currency reorganisation.

6. Real burden of the external Debt. It has been observed that £5,253 million of the total Debt is held overseas. To the extent that interest payments are made abroad and principal repaid there are implications for the balance of payments.

Goods and services must be diverted to foreign use without any compensatory imports. Alternatively, if foreign demand for the debtor nation's goods is inelastic, there will have to be a corresponding reduction in the volume of imports. Either way there will be a real loss to the debtor nation's standard of living.

7. Real burden of the internal Debt. It has been stressed that by far the greater part of the Debt is owned internally. It follows that no increase or decrease in the size of the Debt can make the country as a whole either poorer or richer. Payment of interest or repayment of principal involves simply a transfer from tax-payer to security-holder. To the extent that the debtor (*i.e.* tax-payer) is worse off, the creditor (*i.e.* security-holder) is better off.

If all securities were evenly distributed throughout the community and all tax-payers made an equal contribution to the cost of servicing the Debt, the real burden would be nil since for every interest receipt of £1, the recipient would make a tax contribution of £1.

In practice, the ownership of the Debt is not evenly distributed and a real burden arises to the extent that the cost of debt servicing involves a transfer from tax-payer to security-holder which increases the inequality of incomes. Despite the fact that a broad cross-section of the community may benefit from an interest in that part of the Debt represented by national savings and the holdings of the institutional investors, on balance it is likely that the greater part of the benefits will be directed towards the upper-income groups whose propensity to save will be correspondingly increased. Conversely, as a result of their tax contributions, the propensity to consume of the lower-income groups will be reduced, *i.e.* they must accept a real cut in living standards.

8. Indirect effects of Debt charges. Annually, substantial sums must be raised in taxation for the purpose of servicing the Debt. The level of this taxation will have implications for the management of the economy as a whole.

(*a*) *Incentives.* It may be argued that the extra volume of taxation can reduce the incentive to work of the tax-payer while that of the security-holder is reduced by his unearned income receipts.

(*b*) *Demand management.* More significantly, redistribution of income will influence both the level of total effective demand and its structure.

PRINCIPLES OF DEBT MANAGEMENT

9. Objectives. The aims of Debt management policy will be threefold:

(*a*) To minimise the real burden (*see* **10–13** below).

(*b*) In any fiscal year to budget for a surplus or a deficit (*i.e.* decrease or increase the Debt) in line with the broad aims of economic policy (*see* **14–21** below).

(*c*) To manage the size and composition of the Debt in a way which accords with the needs of monetary policy (*see* VII, **33–38**).

10. Repudiation or repayment. It can be argued that if the cost of servicing a national debt becomes excessively irksome it is always open to Government to repudiate its obligations. This course is unlikely to be followed if only on the practical grounds that further borrowing would be extremely difficult.

Repayment involves the consideration that over a given period, long or short, repayments of principal must be added to current interest payments. If a substantial portion of the Debt is held externally then throughout the period extra surpluses would have to be earned in the balance of payments. This would probably necessitate policies which were disruptive of the natural flow of international trade.

To the extent that the Debt is held internally there will be a further redistribution of income from poorer to richer. Moreover, the effects would be strongly deflationary since the repeated Budget surpluses required would be more restrictive than the expansionary effects of the funds released.

The conclusion must be that the sheer size of the Debt today precludes any serious consideration of its total repayment. Reduction of the burden must be sought elsewhere.

11. Conversions. If economic conditions permit, it may be possible for Government to refinance (*i.e.* convert) debt incurred at high interest rates by borrowing afresh at lower rates.

In the twentieth century there have been two notably successful conversions. In 1932, in a period in which the prevailing economic conditions called for a policy of very low interest rates, £2,000 million War Loan was converted from 5 to 3½ per cent giving an annual saving to the tax-payer of £30 million, one-tenth of the total Debt charge at that time.

Similarly, in the period 1945–47, the Chancellor, who for economic reasons was pursuing a cheap money policy, forced down interest rates and achieved a number of conversions which resulted in a total annual saving of £38 million.

However, the inflationary conditions of modern times offer little prospect for conversion to lower interest rates. The opposite is in fact the case and in recent years the cost of servicing the Debt has been on a strongly rising trend.

Paradoxically, despite this gloomy picture the cost to the tax-payer has been on a downward trend due to the increasingly important offset of Government interest receipts.

12. The significance of Government interest receipts.

TABLE III. CENTRAL GOVERNMENT PAYMENTS AND RECEIPTS OF INTEREST

| | (£ million) | | | | |
	1965	1966	1967	1968	1969
Payments	973	1,041	1,110	1,244	1,287
Receipts from:					
Local authorities	142	171	203	235	281
Public corporations	313	385	414	523	595
Other lending	115	117	119	104	99

(*Source: B.E.Q.B.*, March 1971.)

In 1969–70, while the total National Debt fell by over £1,100 million, the cost of servicing it rose by £70 million. Nevertheless, the table shows that the net cost to the tax-payer is on a falling trend due to a rising proportion of the cost being met from interest on loans.

Since the war, central Government loans to local authorities and nationalised industries have risen from an insignificant level to over £15,000 million by 1970. This increase has exceeded the rise of £11,000 million over the same period in the size of the National Debt itself and indicates that on balance £4,000 million from Budget surpluses has been devoted to investment in the public sector.

It would seem that to an increasing extent the National Debt is becoming backed by income-earning tangible assets such as transport, power-stations and housing and that in the long run it may become largely self-servicing.

13. The significance of inflation and devaluation. It may be noted in passing that inflation erodes both the real value of the Debt and the real burden of servicing it. When debt is redeemed, repayment is made in depreciated currency. For the purpose of meeting service charges, a smaller proportion of money incomes is now required.

Secondly, when overseas investors have purchased sterling debt with currency converted at a given rate of exchange a devaluation leaves them with assets which are now worth less in terms of that currency.

BUDGETING FOR A SURPLUS OR A DEFICIT

14. The Budget judgment and the National Debt. Tradition-ally, the first precept of sound public finance was a balanced Budget. The principle of the private sector that income must always meet expenditure was equally applied in the public sector except in times of emergency.

Originating in 1694, the modern National Debt expanded during the eighteenth century as a result of wars which it proved impossible to finance from current tax revenue. In the intervals of peace, Chancellors were always concerned to find means of redeeming debt. The relative calm of the nineteenth century permitted some reduction by 1914 of the £850 million which had been outstanding at the end of the Napoleonic Wars. Two world wars then increased the Debt to £24,000 million. We can thus see that until 1945 deficits were incurred only in wartime or as a result of the miscalcula-tion of the estimates.

After the war, having accepted the Keynesian technique for the management of demand, it was seen that in a deflationary situation it might be desirable deliberately to plan a deficit. Conversely, in an inflationary situation, a planned surplus will be indicated. We have seen in the preceding chapter the machinery which enables the Chancellor to arrive at his "judgment." In 1971, the Chancellor was persuaded that the economy required some measure of reflation. He therefore budgeted for a total public-sector deficit of £378 million which compares with the £170 million surplus which would have been produced on existing policies.

15. The complications of the long-term capital account.

The Chancellor's task in planning a surplus or deficit with any accuracy has been made immensely more complicated by the extent to which the Exchequer has been involved in "below the line expenditure" to provide long-term capital to local authorities and nationalised industries.

When local authorities are unable or unwilling to obtain capital from the market they do so from the Exchequer through the Public Works Loans Board. From 1956 until April 1968, the nationalised industries sought all their investment requirements from the Exchequer.

An *ad hoc* system developed in which surpluses produced on current account were carried forward to the capital account (below the line). The investment needs of the public sector were then met and the Exchequer was left with a "net borrowing requirement." In short, the Chancellor borrowed from the market on behalf of the whole public sector.

NOTE: It therefore follows that when the Chancellor estimates the effect upon demand of a projected Budget surplus or deficit he will be concerned not simply with the impact of the current account of Central Government but rather with the combined current and capital accounts of the public sector as a whole.

Some economists have levelled the criticism that on this broader view budgetary control during the 1960s was too loose and that here lies the principal explanation of inflation. Not only were there massive overall deficits (despite record current account surpluses) when the correct application of the Keynesian technique called for an overall surplus, but the resulting increase in the National Debt was badly financed.

16. Summary of Exchequer Accounts, 1961–67.

TABLE IV. AGGREGATE INCOME AND EXPENDITURE OF
CENTRAL GOVERNMENT, 1961–67

Income		(£ *million*)
Current account receipts	54,551	
Capital account receipts	3,698	
		58,249
Expenditure		
Current account expenditure	50,746	
Capital depreciation and transfers	2,012	
Stockbuilding, new buildings, etc.	1,678	
		54,436
Central Government surplus		3,813
Long-term loans to:		
Private sector	228	
Local authorities	1,086	
Public corporations	4,051	
Overseas governments	230	
Overseas private industry	−17	
International lending organisations	42	
Purchase of company shares	33	
		5,653
Cumulative overall deficit		1,840

(*Source: Financial Statistics.*)

The first stage of the argument is that repeatedly Chancellors raised the levels of taxation ostensibly to counter inflation by curtailing demand, but that the proceeds and more besides were swallowed up primarily in the investment programmes of the nationalised industries and local authorities. Total effective demand, far from being restrained, was in fact increased and the Chancellor was left during the period with a borrowing requirement of £1,840 million.

The critics then argue that the impact of this deficit would not necessarily have been inflationary had it been financed "legitimately." The implication is that if Government requires £1,840 million over and above its current revenue it should sell fresh bonds on the market. In this way £1,840 million will be transferred from the private sector and total effective demand within the economy will be unchanged. However, one of the problems of Debt management in the 1960s was the weakness of the gilt-edged market. Increasingly, investors turned from fixed-interest securities to equities as a hedge against inflation. During the period there was in fact a net redemption of marketable debt of the order of £451 million. Non-marketable debt increased by £452 million giving a net increase in "genuine" borrowing from the private sector of only £1 million. It is then argued that the remaining £1,839 million was provided by "creating new money."

17. Finance of central Government borrowing, 1961–67.

TABLE V. SOURCE OF FINANCE

		£m.
Sale of gold and convertible currencies		365
Overseas borrowing		648
Increase in note issue		756
Genuine borrowing from private sector		
Marketable debt	−451	
Non-marketable debt	452	1
Net increase of Exchequer debt to Bank of England		70
Total		£1,840

It is argued that the deficit was in fact financed by the injection of new money into the economy and that total effective demand was therefore expanded with inflationary results.

(a) *Sale of gold and convertible currencies.* The country's gold and foreign currency reserves are all held in the Exchange Equalisation Account. It has been observed (*see* **4**(*a*) above) that the Account is one of the official holders of the National Debt. When it sells gold and foreign currency to finance a deficit in the balance of payments the sterling proceeds which automatically accrue are invested in Government securities.

(b) *Overseas borrowing.* Similarly, the proceeds of overseas borrowing are credited to the Exchange Equalisation Account. When utilised there results a flow of sterling to the Account which is *invested in Government debt.*

(c) *Increase in the note issue.* The note issue will be increased in response to demand from the general public (*see* VI, **32**). The Issue Department of the Bank of England then acquires bonds to back the notes.

(*d*) *Borrowing from the private sector*. It has been observed that loans from the private sector increased by only £1 million during the period.

(*e*) *Increase in debt to the Bank of England*. The additional £70 million represents an increase in the Government's credit by this amount.

18. Conclusion. The conclusion to the foregoing argument must be that a major element of the modern National Debt is attributable to the capital requirements of the public sector and that these must be managed wisely if public finance is to be an effective instrument of demand management.

In his 1967 Budget statement the Chancellor asked: "Is it necessarily the best arrangement that so much of the borrowing requirement of local authorities and public corporations is financed in the first instance by the Exchequer? The present arrangements have grown up as a series of *ad hoc* responses to particular situations over a long period of years. I think the time has come to take stock of the suitability of the present arrangements in the contemporary world and I have therefore put a review in hand."

The result of this review was the foundation, on the 1st April 1968, of the National Loans Fund.

19. The National Loans Fund. The Act which set up the Fund amended the law relating to Government borrowing and lending. It confined the Exchequer to the ordinary revenue and expenditure transactions of central Government met from Parliamentary votes.

Government borrowing and lending for local authorities and nationalised industries would be dealt with separately through the medium of the Fund. Exchequer surpluses at the end of the year would be transferred to the Fund. Similarly, any Exchequer deficit would be met from the Fund.

The Treasury's borrowing powers which were previously covered by a variety of statutes were framed into a single set of provisions and all future Treasury borrowing was to be for the account of the Fund.

20. Appraisal. Whether in the long run the National Loans Fund provides an effective answer to the problem of establishing stricter control over total Government expenditure depends largely upon the Treasury confining its borrowing activities to the sale of marketable and non-marketable debt to the private sector. The large and unpredictable flows of sterling in and out of the Exchange Equalisation Account which result from variations in the reserves and changes in the U.K.'s overseas indebtedness must be dealt with separately from the Government's domestic borrowing and lending.

21. Debt management and monetary policy. It was noted in **9**(c) above that the National Debt must be managed in a way which accords with the needs of monetary policy. The rate at which the Debt increases or decreases and its distribution between different types of security and different categories of holder all have vital significance for monetary management. A study of the National Debt therefore provides a link between the fields of public finance and the monetary system. This subject we now go on to examine in Part Two.

PROGRESS TEST 4

1. Define the National Debt. **(1, 2)**
2. Analyse the composition of the National Debt. **(3)**
3. Compare the real burden of the internally and externally held portions of the Debt. **(6–7)**
4. In managing the Debt, what principles will the Bank of England observe? **(9)**
5. What possibilities exist for an active attempt to reduce the burden of the Debt? **(10, 11, 13)**
6. What reasons have we to suppose that in due course the Debt may become self-servicing? **(12)**
7. Why is the National Debt so vast? **(14)**
8. Explain the significance of the "net borrowing requirement." **(15)**
9. Why may it be argued that Government financial policy during the 1960s aggravated the problem of inflation? **(16)**
10. How can it be argued that a good deal of Government borrowing during the 1960s was "illegitimate"? **(16, 17)**
11. Describe the way in which the National Loans Fund functions. **(19)**
12. Will the National Loans Fund solve the problem of establishing more effective control over public-sector expenditure? **(20)**

PART TWO

THE MONETARY SYSTEM

CHAPTER V

THE FUNCTIONS, CHARACTERISTICS AND EVOLUTION OF MONEY

THE FUNCTIONS OF MONEY

1. A fully planned economy without money. Provided that society is willing to surrender all individual choice to State-planning agencies it is possible to operate an economy without money. This has been demonstrated, for example, in the early days of the Soviet Union. The State determines the relative quantities of different lines of production while distribution is effected by a system of rationing which accords with prevailing notions of social justice. The weakness of such a system lies on the side of distribution once the economy has been raised above subsistence level. What principles of social justice, for example, would govern the allocation of grand pianos or croquet mallets?

2. A free economy without money. In a free economy the only alternative to the use of money is a system of barter such as that which largely prevailed in medieval England. There are, however, three major disadvantages:

(*a*) *Individual wants rarely coincide.* "Rather than there being a coincidence of wants there is likely to be a want of coincidence." It is unlikely that the baker's need for a pair of shoes will be timed to coincide with the shoemaker's need for a loaf of bread.

(*b*) *Adjustment of quantities of goods bartered.* It is unlikely that the shoemaker will want simultaneously the number of loaves of bread for which a pair of shoes would exchange.

(*c*) *Multiple exchange ratios.* It is necessary to establish separate exchange ratios between any one item and all other goods which enter into trade. There is no common denominator.

While barter may work in a simple society, it is clear that it would be inoperable in an advanced industrial economy practising a high degree of specialisation. What now becomes necessary is a "medium of exchange."

3. The functions of money. From the foregoing argument it may be deduced that money has certain functions:

(a) *A medium of exchange.* The most important function of money is to serve as the one universally acceptable denominator against which all men are willing to exchange their goods and services. It acts as the lubricant which promotes the smooth functioning of a market economy based upon division of labour not only between trades but also between processes. From this central function of money stem four others.

(b) *Extension of individual choice.* The distribution difficulty of the fully planned economy is overcome when the individual works for units of purchasing power which he can use at his discretion.

(c) *Standard unit of account.* Money cannot properly be said to be a measure of value since, unlike measures of weight or size, its own value varies. However, it does overcome the difficulty of multiple exchange ratios encountered in the barter system. It is the common denominator to which all trade items may be related.

(d) *A store of value.* Individual saving in an economy without money implies the setting aside of goods for future use. The self-evident disadvantage is that many goods are perishable and services cannot be stored. The use of money, however, enables purchasing power to be stored for use at a date determined by the individual.

It should be noted, nevertheless, that money fulfils this function imperfectly inasmuch as its purchasing power varies. The depreciation in the value of money since 1945 is not compensated by the interest paid on bank deposits after allowance has been made for the taxation of unearned income.

(e) *A means of deferred payment.* The extent to which money is capable of storing value gives it a final function. It is instrumental to credit transactions. Without money, present borrowing of goods and services would imply repayment in kind. Money enables general purchasing power to be utilised now and repaid later.

It should be noted that inflation will favour the debtor inasmuch as he will repay money whose purchasing power is less. Conversely a deflationary situation will favour the creditor.

THE EVOLUTION AND CHARACTERISTICS OF MONEY

4. Commodity money. The earliest forms of money were commodities held in high regard by the societies which used them. At first sight it would therefore seem that a prime characteristic of money is its intrinsic desirability. However, we shall shortly see that this is not so. Nevertheless, it should be emphasised that a quality common to all money has been relative scarcity. If the scarcity is too great, too little value is attached to it for it to continue in this role.

Additionally, early forms of commodity money enjoyed one or more other advantages, *e.g.* in the eastern Mediterranean, olive oil was easily divisible; in western Europe, iron was durable. The most universally acceptable of all commodity moneys, however, came to be gold. It had the foregoing qualities and was also portable. Second only to gold was silver. Initially, quantities of these metals were weighed in order to make payment, but from these it was only a short step to a standard coin of known weight and fineness guaranteed by the imprint of the State.

5. Paper money. Modern deposit banking began to develop in Britain for the first time in the sixteenth and seventeenth centuries in the hands of London goldsmiths. It was their practice to issue "warehouse receipts" for gold deposited with them and these receipts circulated freely as money, guaranteed by the good name of the goldsmith. In the 1680s, Francis Childs is credited with the introduction of the first true banknotes, receipts for gold but in standard denominations.

However, paper was seen only as a claim upon real money, gold, until 1931. The Bank of England's promise to pay the bearer on demand was a guarantee of immediate convertibility and apart from two major periods, 1797–1821 and 1914–25, this convertibility was maintained.

During the nineteenth century, it is doubtful, except in periods of national emergency, whether inconvertible paper money would have circulated freely. In the periods 1815–21 and 1918–25 there was considerable public agitation for the restoration of convertibility, but in 1931 the link between paper and gold was finally severed. Paper appeared for the first time in its own right as true money. This leads us to an important conclusion about the nature of money. Its principal characteristic is not its intrinsic desirability but its "acceptability." Paradoxically, this acceptability can be explained only be a general confidence that everyone will accept it. This confidence will be governed by the degree of political and economic stability. For example, where there is hyper-inflation, it is likely that paper money will cease to circulate and there will be a reversion to commodity money. This was partially demonstrated in post-1945 Germany when American cigarettes circulated as money. Our attention is therefore redirected to the first characteristic of money which has been noted. If it is to be acceptable, there must be a relative scarcity.

6. Limitation of the supply of paper money. When the sixteenth-century goldsmiths first issued receipts for gold deposits there was naturally a strict relationship between the quantity of gold and the paper circulated. However, as public confidence developed in the goldsmith's ability to pay he felt safe in increasing the amount of paper, ensuring only that he maintained an adequate ratio to gold to enable him to meet day-to-day claims for conversion. The danger of this practice was a loss of public confidence which would lead to a run on the bank with all note-holders anxious to convert paper to gold. Many small banks were forced out of business in this way. The 1844 *Bank Charter Act* aimed to exclude this danger. The sole right of note issue was gradually to be vested in the Bank of England. The Bank was to be permitted a small "fiduciary issue" of £14 million only partially backed by gold. Every note issued in excess of this amount had to be fully covered. England was placed firmly on the gold standard and had in consequence an inflexible money supply.

The *Currency and Banknotes Act* of 1913 introduced for the first time Treasury notes in denominations of £1 and 10 shillings. (The smallest denomination banknote had been and remained £5.) During the period 1914–18 the Treasury note issue was increased without gold cover and a considerable inflation resulted. Deflationary policies after 1920 sought to restore full convertibility and a large number of Treasury notes were withdrawn. The *Gold Standard Act* of 1925 established partial convertibility (gold could be purchased from the Issue Department in minimum quantities of 400 Troy ounces) but by 1928 it became apparent that further deflation of the note issue was undesirable. With many Treasury notes still in circulation it was decided to substitute for them £1 and 10 shilling Bank of England notes. This required legislation to permit a corresponding increase in the Bank's fiduciary issue and the *Currency and Banknotes Act* of 1928, was enacted. The fiduciary issue was established at £260 million but could be increased with Treasury approval over a maximum period of two years. After that the approval of Parliament had to be sought. Subsequently, the *Currency and Banknotes Act* of 1954 confirmed the general position. The fiduciary issue was set at £1,575 million and could only be increased with Treasury consent and with the ultimate approval of Parliament. In practice such approval has come to be a formality.

NOTE: The legal position governing the note issue is thus determined by the Acts of 1844, 1928 and 1954. The Bank of England retains the power to increase its notes against gold cover but since no notes have been backed in this way since August, 1970 this power is of no real significance. In practice, the Bank of England authorities in conjunction with the Treasury determine whether an increase is desirable and Parliamentary approval is given automatically.

7. Bank deposit money. The final stage in the evolution of money is to be seen in its appearance as a bank deposit, a figure on a ledger which can be transferred through the instrument of the cheque. Cheques were known in seventeenth-century England but their use was given considerable stimulus by the 1844 *Bank Charter Act*. It will be recalled that this Act rigidly limited the money supply and this in a period of rapid industrial and commercial expansion. Growth might well have been hampered by this restriction had it not been for an increasing willingness to settle business transactions with the cheque.

It should be noted, however, that it is not the cheque itself which is money but the deposit upon which it is drawn. The cheque will of course be valid only if such a deposit exists and the payee may not know this to be the case. Nevertheless, the cheque would appear to be increasingly acceptable, the majority of transactions involving payment of any size being settled in this way. In recent years the banks have attempted to extend their business by popularising current accounts. Many wage and salary payments are made either by cheque or bank transfer while the consumer, assisted by his banker's card (an instrument which certifies any cheque up to a value of £30 or £50), has made ever-greater use of his cheque-book even for relatively small payments. Moreover, the increased use of credit cards, credit accounts and hire purchase accounts which are settled regularly by cheque or banker's order suggests that cash will continue to play a proportionately smaller part and will finally become the "small change" of the monetary system.

8. The difficulty of a precise definition of the money supply. It has been shown that conventionally money has come to be defined as coin, notes and bank deposits. However, should deposits of *all* types with *all* financial institutions be included within this definition? In recent years there has been a good deal of discussion of this question.

In 1970 the Bank of England concluded that it is possible to select different types of deposits to form various totals which can each be described as the stock of money. "There are, however, no clear rules for deciding which of these totals is most appropriate: there can be alternative definitions of the stock of money, encompassing a wider or narrower set of components."

9. Three Bank of England definitions. Bank calculations of the money stock conform to three definitions, M1, M2 and M3.

(a) *M1.* This narrow definition is restricted to notes and coin in circulation with the public plus sterling current accounts held by the private sector. The basis of this definition is that if money comprises those assets which perform the function of a medium of exchange then it consists of cash plus the accounts upon which cheques can be drawn, *i.e.* current accounts only.

(b) *M2.* To the items covered by M1 are added private-sector sterling deposit accounts. It is argued that the distinction between current and deposit accounts as monetary assets is not clear cut. In practice a deposit account holder may be able to draw a cheque on his current account even when it contains insufficient funds. However, it is possible to make a somewhat arbitrary distinction between deposit accounts with deposit banks and discount houses and those held with other banks. In the case of the former, deposits are held at seven days' notice, a constraint rarely enforced. In the case of the latter, funds are less easily withdrawn *and are not therefore included in M2.*

(c) *M3.* This definition is still broader. To M2 are added private sector non-sterling accounts with *all* banks, sterling-deposit accounts with non-clearing banks and all public-sector deposits. The justification for this wider concept is that for some purposes it is preferable to have broader rather than narrower definitions, *e.g.* analyses of bank lending and the expansion of domestic credit.

TABLE VI

MONEY STOCK, SEPTEMBER 1971

£ *millions*

M1	£10,131
M2	£16,042
M3	£19,108

(*Source: B.E.Q.B.*)

PROGRESS TEST 5

1. Why may money be viewed as essential to an advanced economy? (**1–3**)

2. Explain why "acceptability" is the most important characteristic of money. (**5**)

CHAPTER VI

THE COMMERCIAL BANKS

STRUCTURE OF BRITISH BANKING

1. Classification. Over the past 400 years the British banking system has developed as one of the most highly specialised financial centres in the world. It has created a complex and sophisticated market for both short-term and long-term finance on an international scale, a business which is of value not only to Britain as a source of overseas earnings but also to overseas countries as a source of investment funds and trade credit. The system may be classified under six main headings.

(*a*) *The central bank.* At the centre of the system stands the Bank of England. It fulfils a unique role to which attention is given in the following chapter.

(*b*) *The commercial banks* are sometimes referred to as the "joint-stock banks." They are for the most part limited liability companies, subject to the appropriate company law and operated for the profit of their shareholders. They include:

- (*i*) The London clearing banks.
- (*ii*) The Scottish and Northern Irish banks.
- (*iii*) British overseas and foreign banks with London offices.

(*c*) *The discount houses.* The London Discount Market Association comprises eleven houses. They have a specialised function in the provision of short-term finance (*see* **VIII, 3–13**).

(*d*) *The merchant banks.* Used loosely, this term is often applied to a variety of financial institutions. In a specific sense it includes:

(*i*) *Accepting houses.* The basic business is the "acceptance credit" through which a considerable part of Britain's overseas trade is financed (*see* VIII, **14–22**).

(*ii*) *Issuing houses.* They are concerned with raising credit for borrowers at home and abroad and, where appropriate, organising a market in bonds and shares against which funds are raised (*see* VIII, **43**).

(*e*) *The savings banks.* Independently operated savings banks where small savings could be deposited to earn a rate of interest arose in Britain in the early nineteenth century. To afford greater security to depositors, legislation in 1817 brought them under the supervision of the National Debt Commissioners. Management remained in the hands of local trustees – hence Trustee Savings Banks.

In order to bring savings facilities within reach of the whole community legislation in 1861 led to the foundation of the Post Office Savings Bank (*see* VIII, **39**).

(*f*) *The National Giro.* The National Giro was set up in 1969 in the belief that by providing facilities for current account payments it would very quickly be in a position to compete on even terms with the commercial banks. So far it has not proved a great success and there would seem to be some question as to its continuance. In March 1971, its total current and deposit accounts amounted to only £54 million.

2. Evolution of the London clearing banks. It has been observed that in Britain the first indigenous banking was developed in the sixteenth and seventeenth centuries by goldsmiths who issued paper money against the security of gold deposits (*see* V, **5**). They also established rudimentary current accounts, cheque and bill-discounting facilities. An Act of 1707 imposed certain legal restrictions which delayed the development of joint-stock banking in England except for the Bank of England itself. Scotland did not suffer this legal impediment and joint-stock banking developed on a sound basis at an earlier date.

The result was a system of banking based upon private partnership which persisted until 1826. In that year the *Country Bankers Act* permitted the formation of joint-stock banks *with* note-issuing powers outside a sixty-five mile radius of London. In 1833 a further Act allowed joint-stock banks *without* note-issuing powers within that radius. The *Bank Charter Act* of 1844 denied all new banks the power to issue notes but the development of the cheque diminished the significance of this restriction (*see* VII, **3**). An Act of 1862 extended the privilege of limited liability to banking companies and the last obstacle to the growth of large-scale joint-stock banking was removed.

The following sixty years were a period of expansion, take-overs and amalgamations in which was established a national system of branch banking. In 1919, the formation of the British Bankers' Association promoted consultation and co-operation between its fifty-six members. Included in this membership were fourteen English, five Scottish and three Northern Ireland commercial banks.

Eighty per cent of British banking business is concentrated in the six members of the London Bankers' Clearing House (*see* VI, **7**). Until 1968 there were eleven which included Midland Bank Ltd.; Barclays Bank Ltd.; Lloyds Bank Ltd.; Westminster Bank Ltd.; National Provincial Bank Ltd.; District Bank Ltd.; Martins Bank Ltd.; Williams Deacon's Bank Ltd.; National Bank Ltd.; Coutts & Co.; Glyn Mills & Co. Mergers have caused the gradual loss of a separate identity of Martins following its fusion with Barclays and of District following its amalgamation with National Provincial and Westminster to form the National Westminster. Williams Deacon's merged with Glyn Mills to form Williams and Glyn's.

3. Scottish banks. Scottish banking business is concentrated in four banks with head offices and some 1,700 branches in Scotland. These banks retain the power of note issue which, apart from a small fiduciary issue, is made against the cover of Bank of England notes. The advantage is largely a matter of advertisement.

Total deposits in November 1971 amounted to £1,180 million.

4. Northern Irish banks. There are three native banks with head offices and some 500 branches in Northern Ireland. Like the Scottish banks they issue their own notes. Additionally, a number of other banks with head offices in Dublin, Cork and London have branches in Northern Ireland. In October 1971, total deposits amounted to £282 million.

5. British overseas banks. There are thirty-two members of the British Overseas Banks Association with head offices in London or the Commonwealth and branches overseas. The Association comprises four groups: African, Australasian, Canadian and Eastern. They act as exchange-dealers and finance monetary transactions between Britain and these areas and between third parties. They also employ funds in London primarily in the money market. They therefore provide a mechanism whereby British short-term investment funds can be rapidly employed in all parts of the world and conversely foreign funds employed in Britain. The bulk of their London deposit liabilities do in fact originate overseas. In recent years their business has expanded rapidly, from £2,300 million at the end of 1967 to £6,367 million in October 1971.

6. Foreign banks. By far the most important are the American banks which due to increased U.S. investment in Europe have experienced a dramatic expansion of their business. At the end of 1971 deposits totalled £13,134 million. In a similar way other foreign banks by virtue of their trading connections and special knowledge are able to provide for their own nationals a unique service in London. In 1971 their deposits amounted to £2,720 million.

A number of these banks fulfil all the functions of the domestic banks but by unwritten agreement do not attempt to compete with them.

7. Functions of the clearing banks. The description "London clearing banks" is applied to the six members of the London Bankers' Clearing House, the place where their representatives meet to settle inter-bank indebtedness. These banks account for the greater part of the normal commercial banking business of England and Wales although in the last decade there has been a considerable expansion of the business of the non-clearing banks.

8. Deposits. The basic service from which all others stem is the provision of facilities for current and time deposit accounts.

(a) *Current accounts.* In November 1971 current accounts totalled £6,312 million covering personal and business deposits. The banks are enabled to exercise their principal function, the transfer of money, through the use of the current account in conjunction with:

(*i*) *The cheque system.* A cheque is an instruction to a bank to make payment of a specified sum to a third party.

(*ii*) *Bank Giro credit.* The expense of separate cheques and postages can be avoided by the completion of Bank Giro credit forms in favour of a number of payees and payment to the bank of the total amount either in cash or with a single cheque.

(*iii*) *The standing order.* This method of money transfer is designed for regular payments of fixed amount, *e.g.* mortgage or hire-purchase instalments. It is a standing instruction to the bank to pay a certain sum regularly upon a specified date.

(*iv*) *Direct debit.* A second method of automatic payment is the direct debit which differs from the standing order in which the "payer" gives his bank the necessary standing instruction. In this case it is the "payee" who originates the payment.

(*b*) *Deposit accounts and savings accounts.* In November 1971 they totalled £5,386 million. They differ from current accounts in two respects:

(*i*) *Interest.* These accounts yield interest.

(*ii*) *Limitation of withdrawal.* Funds may be withdrawn only after an agreed period of nitice has been given. In practice there is often flexibility in the application of this rule.

9. Advances. The second most important banking service and the one which is most profitable to the banks themselves is the provision of personal and business overdraft facilities against security. This security may take the form of something tangible and marketable, *e.g.* share certificates, savings certificates, title-deeds, insurance policies. Sometimes the proven integrity, business ability and prospects of the borrower are sufficient.

Rates of interest until September 1971, were geared to a formula, normally a fixed margin above Bank Rate subject to a minimum. The majority of customers paid 1 to 2 per cent above Bank Rate, the biggest and most credit-worthy about $\frac{1}{2}$ per cent. Since 1971 the banks have pursued independent policies in respect of interest rates.

The provision of working capital for industry and commerce is based upon the assumption that the loan will be self-liquidating, *i.e.* as the firm's income grows, so it is enabled to repay the loan which has made its activities possible. Traditionally, the banks have financed agriculture with short-term advances of a seasonal nature. In industry, banks may be prepared to make longer-term loans for, say two to three years for the purchase of machinery and buildings. In commerce there has been in the last decade a considerable expansion in the finance of export contracts.

Advances in November 1971 stood at £6,554 million.

10. Security facilities. Bank strong-rooms are available to customers for the safe-keeping of valuables and night-safe facilities allow customers to deposit money overnight after banking hours for payment into their accounts the following morning.

11. Investment-advice and services. Banks will give advice on the investment of savings and through their own stockbrokers will make purchases and sales, their charges being paid out of the normal broking commission. Arrangements can be made for dividends to be paid directly into bank accounts or for the banks to detach coupons from bearer bonds and present them for payment. They will also act for their customers in applying for allotments arising from fresh capital issues and pay calls as they are made.

12. Income tax services. Most banks will advise or undertake to act on behalf of individuals in the preparation of income-tax returns, the checking of coding and notices of assessment and the making of claims for tax overpaid.

13. Executor and trustee services. Most banks have either an executor and trustee department or an affiliated company to deal with this branch of business. A bank may be nominated as an executor and, if necessary, a trustee of an estate after death. The advantages are professional expertise in handling a variety of assets, complete impartiality and continuity of administration.

14. Foreign travel. The banks will provide their customers with foreign currency, travellers' cheques which can be encashed at corresponding banks overseas or, for larger sums, letters of credit, any part of which the traveller can draw upon as required.

15. Remitting money abroad. Individuals may remit money abroad by two methods:

(*a*) *Bank draft.* This is a banker's cheque, often expressed in sterling but made payable in a foreign currency. The customer pays his bank in sterling at the current rate of exchange. The cheque will be honoured upon presentation at the foreign bank.

(*b*) *Cable transfer.* A credit is cabled by the payer's bank to the payee's bank.

16. Export finance. The larger commercial banks have special departments which specialise in the finance of foreign trade. They are assisted by banks affiliated to them overseas, or alternatively have arrangements with foreign banks which act as correspondents.

In the seller's market of the immediate post-war years international indebtedness was often settled on the basis of "cash on delivery" or even "cash with order." Increasing competition between the industrial nations has meant that price and quality are not always the deciding factors. The credit terms which the exporter is able to offer will often be decisive in winning an order. The banks have been encouraged, even in periods of domestic credit restraint, to afford short-, medium- and longer-term export finance.

17. Short-term finance. The most usual method of settlement for exported goods is the "bill of exchange." The exporter draws a bill on the overseas buyer, attaches shipping documents to it and hands it to his own bank for collection. The documents are then forwarded to a bank in the buyer's country and handed over against payment or acceptance, the proceeds then being transmitted to the exporter through the two banks. The bill may be payable at sight or at a fixed future date, normally a maximum of six months forward. In the latter case the drawee "accepts" the bill, *i.e.* agrees to pay when the bill is due. In both cases, however, the exporter must wait before the proceeds are credited to his account. The banks can help either by purchasing the bill or by making an advance against its security, the exporter's working capital thereby being immediately received. An interest charge and a collection commission are charged.

Bank finance is given against approved bills, approval being contingent upon:

(*a*) The financial standing of the drawee.

(*b*) Absence of restrictions upon money transfers from the country in which payment is to be made.

(*c*) The bill having a maximum of six months to run to maturity.

If the above conditions are not satisfied the banks may still provide finance if the Export Credits Guarantee Department provides suitable cover.

18. Export Credits Guarantee Department. This department of the Department of Trade and Industry provides extensive insurance cover against the risk of default by the foreign buyer whether his failure to pay results from insolvency or delay or from the political risk of exchange control restrictions being imposed in the buyer's country. The Department operates on commercial principles and charges an insurance premium.

19. Medium-term finance. This is offered by the banks to assist exporters in granting credit terms in excess of two years. Terms for each transaction are calculated on an individual basis but all are subject to the availability of E.C.G.D. cover.

20. Long-term finance. This is available from individual banks or banks in consortium for sums in excess of £2 million where repayment is spread over five to fifteen years. Such a loan would again be underwritten by the E.C.G.D. The unusual feature of such long-term finance is that it is provided by the banks direct to the overseas buyer. The British exporter can therefore be paid on a cash basis.

THE LENDING ACTIVITIES OF THE
LONDON CLEARING BANKS

TABLE VII. COMBINED BALANCE SHEET, LONDON CLEARING BANKS,
JULY AND OCTOBER 1971

Liabilities	(£ *millions*)			
Gross deposits				
	July		*October*	
Current accounts	6,001		6,304	
Deposit accounts	4,859		5,186	
Other accounts	353		398	
Total	11,213		11,888	
Assets		*% deposits*		*% deposits*
Coin, notes and balances with the Bank of England	912	8·1	843	7·1
Money at call and short notice	1,446		1,527	
Treasury bills	202		135	
U.K. commercial bills	489		590	
Other bills	537		530	
Total liquid assets	3,586	32	—	
Reserve assets	—	—	1,777	*Reserve ratio 16·5%*
Special deposits	383		—	
Investments	1,234	11	1,991	16·7
Advances and other accounts	5,989	53·4	6,206	52·2

(*Source: B.E.Q.B.*)

21. Comments on balance sheet. An examination of the balance sheet will show:

(*a*) A picture of the main lending activities of the clearing banks.

(*b*) The principles governing these activities prior to 16th September 1971, and after that date when new arrangements were implemented.

22. Gross deposit liabilities. These comprise current accounts, deposit accounts and other accounts which include credit items in the course of transmission, contingency reserves and other internal accounts. The economic significance of these liabilities is that they constitute the principal element of the money supply. The post-war period has seen a

D

striking expansion of total deposits from £4,692 million in 1945 to over £12,000 million at the end of 1971.

23. Liquid reserves. The banks must steer a middle course between two conflicting considerations. On the one hand they are in business to make loans and if these are increased so are their profits. On the other hand they must hold a sufficient reserve in cash or assets which are readily convertible to cash in order to meet day-to-day withdrawals.

Until 16th September 1971, the London clearing banks *voluntarily* observed two liquidity rules, the 8 per cent cash ratio and the 28 per cent liquidity ratio. On that date these rules were abandoned in favour of a single but *obligatory* 12½ per cent reserve ratio.

24. The old liquidity rules. Experience and prudence had established:

(*a*) *A minimum 8 per cent cash ratio.* This comprised cash in the tills of branches up and down the country together with balances at the Bank of England to settle inter-bank indebtedness at the clearing house. In July 1971 this ratio was 8·1 per cent of deposit liabilities.

(*b*) *A minimum 28 per cent liquidity ratio.* In order to insure himself against an abnormally high demand for cash the banker holds a proportion of his assets in a form which, while yielding an income, can easily be realised without loss. His *total* liquid assets prior to the change of rules comprised the first five items in the balance sheet, *viz.* coin, notes and balances with the Bank of England; money at call and short notice; U.K. Treasury bills; U.K. commercial bills; other bills. In July 1971 liquid assets totalled £3,586 million, 32 per cent of deposit liabilities.

In the event of pressure upon bank cash the easiest course of action for the banker is to recall his very short-term loans (money at call) from the discount market. Secondly, the liquidity of Treasury bills, commercial and other bills is only slightly less than that of money at call. The banks arrange their portfolios so that bills fall due in fairly even sums each week. Cash can therefore be made good by refraining from further purchases. Moreover, the bills are in any case negotiable on the discount market.

25. The 12½ per cent reserve ratio. In May 1971 the Bank of England published proposals for new arrangements which it hoped would lead to a more effective monetary policy (*see* VII, **51**). After discussion with the banking associations and agreement on points of detail the arrangements were implemented on the 16th September. They established a uniform minimum reserve ratio of 12½ per cent of *"eligible liabilities"* for *all* banks (defined as deposit-taking institutions).

(*a*) *Eligible liabilities.* These are defined as the sterling deposit liabilities of the banking system as a whole with the exception of those deposits which are originally made for a minimum period of two years. Also included are net liabilities in currencies other than sterling.

(*b*) *Eligible reserve assets.* These are more strictly defined than the old "liquid assets" and it will be noted from the balance sheet that, while the latter would have totalled £3,625 million in October, *eligible reserve assets* amounted to only £1,777 million. Reserve assets comprise:

(*i*) Balances at the Bank of England. Cash in banks' tills does *not* count as a reserve asset.

(*ii*) British Government and Northern Ireland Government Treasury bills.

(*iii*) Company tax reserve certificates.

(*iv*) Money at call with the London money market.

(*v*) British Government stocks and nationalised industries' stocks guaranteed by H.M. Government, *with one year or less to maturity*.

(*vi*) Local authority bills eligible for rediscount at the Bank of England, *i.e.* those with an original maturity of less than six months.

(*vii*) Commercial bills eligible for rediscount at the Bank of England *up to a maximum of 2 per cent of total eligible liabilities*.

Other than the limitation upon commercial bills there are no restrictions upon the distribution of funds between the seven categories of asset. However, the London clearing banks have agreed to maintain a minimum 1½ per cent of eligible liabilities in cash balances with the Bank of England, partly to facilitate the clearing system and partly to assist the Bank of England's operations in the money markets.

26. Special deposits with the Bank of England. This item appeared in the balance sheet for the first time in 1960. The Bank of England has the power to call upon the banks to deposit a specified sum in cash, thus reducing bank liquidity and the power to expand credit (*see* VII, **39**). With the introduction of the new reserve arrangement existing special deposits were repaid.

27. Investments. These are made up almost wholly of British Government securities, some Commonwealth Government and local authority bonds and some fixed interest securities of public companies. All of these securities are marketable and therefore in one sense liquid. However, they are illiquid to the extent that sale on the stock exchange before maturity may involve a capital loss. The bankers' portfolios are so arranged that a proportion of their investment matures each year and the greater part of it within ten years.

The banks do not aim to maintain any fixed percentage of investments, this being the residual item after the demand for advances, the most lucrative asset, has been satisfied.

28. Advances. These assets are the most illiquid, the most risky and the most profitable. A fairly substantial proportion of overdrafts may in normal circumstances be for personal or professional purposes but by far the greater part are for business purposes.

In 1971 bank advances were distributed as follows:

(*a*)	Manufacturing industry	39·1%
(*b*)	Construction	5·4%
(*c*)	Agriculture	5·9%
(*d*)	Finance	13·9%
(*e*)	Distributive trades	10·1%
(*f*)	Professional	6·9%
(*g*)	Personal	12·6%
(*h*)	Other	6·1%

THE CLEARING BANKS AND THE SUPPLY OF MONEY

29. Significance of the London clearing banks. The difficulties of a precise definition of the money stock have already been observed (*see* V, **8** and **9**). However, if the conventional M2 definition is adopted, in September 1971 the supply of money amounted to £16,042 million. Of this £3,454 million comprised notes and coin in circulation with the public. At the same time the gross deposits of the London clearing banks stood at £11,391 million, the principal constitutent of the money supply.

30. The creation of deposits. To a very small extent new deposits are created when notes are deposited at the banks rather than remaining in circulation. *The greater part of the new deposits are, however, created at the initiative of the banks themselves.* This occurs whenever a bank makes a loan. Loans may be made to:

(*a*) *The public sector.* Loans to Government whether in the form of purchases of securities or Treasury bills or in advances to the discount houses for the financing of Treasury bills will all result in the creation of fresh deposits immediately the proceeds are spent; *e.g.* Government funds raised in this way may be used to pay a civil engineer for road construction work. They then appear as an addition to his bank account.

(*b*) *The private sector.* Similarly, advances to private customers or purchases of commercial bills result in an expansion of deposits when the proceeds are spent.

It will be noted that in neither case do the banks hand out notes over the counter. If they purchase bills or securities they do so with a cheque drawn upon themselves. If they grant an overdraft, the borrower uses his cheque-book to make payments from an account which now shows a debit balance. The banks can create deposits in this way up to the point where their reserve assets bear a minimum $12\frac{1}{2}$ per cent ratio to eligible deposit liabilities.

EXAMPLE

Liabilities		*Assets*
Deposits	*Reserve assets*	*Investments & advances*
£50	£12.50	£37.50

In this position the banks are considerably "under-lent" since they are holding a reserve ratio of 25 per cent. They have capacity to increase their lending under the heading of investments and advances.

Deposits	*Reserved Assets*	*Investments & advances*
£100	£12.50	£87.50

In the second position more "deposit or ledger money" has been created and deposit liabilities have risen to £100. The banks are now said to be "fully lent," since their reserves bear the minimum 12½ per cent ratio to deposit liabilities.

31. Restrictions upon the creation of deposits. The clearing banks do not have unlimited power to create money as has been demonstrated in the preceding example. The reserve assets rule imposes one restriction and this will be given further consideration (*see* **34–38**). Other limitations arise from the availability of collateral security, the necessity for all banks to observe a common lending policy and, most important of all, the controls which are imposed by monetary policy (*see* VII, **51–55**).

32. Availability of collateral security. For a loan transaction to be completed it is necessary for the borrower to provide satisfactory security to the banker. Share certificates, insurance policies and title-deeds are examples of such security although in practice there may be some flexibility in what individual bankers accept. However, since collateral securities are themselves limited in supply, this limitation must exercise some restrictive effect upon the creation of deposits.

33. A common lending policy. The banks must move broadly in line in determining the level at which they will lend. Since there are now four big banks the probability is that three-quarters of any loans made by one will be expressed in fresh deposits for customers of the other three and only one-quarter as fresh deposits for its own customers. If all four banks are lending at the same rate, then their deposits will grow in line and their inter-indebtedness at the clearing house will roughly cancel out.

If, however, one bank adopts a more liberal lending policy than the others it will find that its cash balances at the Bank of England are gradually depleted as it settles its greater indebtedness with the other banks. In order to maintain its liquidity it must now drop back into line and restrict its lending.

DIFFERING VIEWS OF THE SIGNIFICANCE OF LIQUID ASSETS

34. Cash base theory of deposit determination. So long as the country adhered to a gold standard it was held that the chief limitation on the power of the banks to create credit was the need to maintain a given ratio between cash reserves and deposits. The note issue was tied to gold and if gold flowed out of the country the cash available to the banking system was correspondingly diminished. The credit based upon it had therefore to be contracted. After the link with gold was severed it gradually became apparent that while an increase in cash could still form the base for an expansion of bank deposits it might itself be increased *in consequence* of an increase in bank deposits. The banks can always make good their cash reserves by recalling money from the discount market. The latter can make good its funds by exercising its privilege of borrowing from the Bank of England (*see* VIII, **6**). The Bank of England, in turn, should it find its note reserves dropping below a certain level, can appeal to the Treasury for permission to increase the note issue (*see* V, **6**). What now seemed to be of greater importance was the maintenance of the minimum liquidity ratio.

35. Liquid assets theory of deposit determination. In its simplest version this theory is analogous to the cash base theory. Assuming that the only liquid assets were Treasury bills and that these were all held by the Bank of England, the clearing banks and the discount houses (the last being financed by money at call or short notice from the clearing banks), then any variation in the supply of Treasury bills would be reflected in the volume of liquid assets held by the banks. This would be followed by a corresponding variation in the volume of deposits based upon those assets.

Some credence could have been attached to this view in the period after 1945 when Treasury bills formed by far the greatest portion of available liquid assets.

36. A more sophisticated version. Evidence offered to the Radcliffe Committee on the Working of the Monetary System (1959) suggested a more elaborate explanation. The authorities were interested not only in controlling the Treasury bill supply but also in stabilising Treasury bill rate at a level acceptable to their own borrowing requirements. If it became necessary to borrow more on Treasury bills then the discount houses would increase their money at call and short notice from the clearing banks. When Government spent the proceeds there would be an increase in the level of bank deposits.

At this higher level the banks' liquidity would still be satisfied since liquid assets would have expanded under the heading of money at call. On the other hand cash reserves would have remained unchanged and therefore their ratio to deposits would have fallen below the minimum 8 per cent. In order to restore the ratio the banks would now have to recall money from the discount market, which in turn would be "forced into the Bank" to borrow at the penal Bank rate. Treasury bill rate would now tend to move up for as long as money remained tight. If this situation were to be forestalled, the Bank would have to enter the market of its own volition to relieve the shortage of cash. In these circumstances the banks would be enabled to continue to take advantage of the increase in their liquid assets.

From the preceding argument it may be deduced that if the authorities wished to restrict the volume of bank deposits they could follow one of two courses of action:

(a) *Reduce the supply of Treasury bills and stabilise their rate of discount.* The assumption was that at a constant rate of interest the demand for bills outside the banking sector would remain unchanged. The supply of liquid assets to the banking system would consequently diminish together with the deposits based upon them.

(b) *Stabilise the supply of Treasury bills and raise their rate of discount.* The assumption is now that the demand for bills by buyers outside the banking sector will increase. Their availability to the banks will correspondingly diminish.

Neither deduction was borne out by experience. Despite the reduction during the 1950s and 1960s in the supply of

Treasury bills together with an increase in Treasury bill rate, deposits continued to expand rapidly.

37. Modification of the liquid assets theory. That the banks were able to maintain the volume of their liquid assets despite the reduction in the supply of Treasury bills is explained by their increased holdings of commercial and other bills and money at call and short notice. Thus the emphasis in the early 1960s on the view that the principal means of curtailing the money supply lay in the disciplined control of Government short-term borrowing gave way to the view that if the *total* supply of liquid assets to the banking system could be controlled then the power of the banks to create deposits could also be controlled. The Bank, however, disputed its ability to implement a policy based on this view inasmuch as one consequence would be a pattern of interest rates inconsistent with its duty to minimise the cost of servicing the National Debt. The Bank's case will be explained later (*see* VII, **38**).

38. Conclusions. From the foregoing discussion it may be concluded that the cash ratio and liquid assets ratio theories were in themselves an insufficient explanation of the determination of the volume of bank deposits. Account had also to be taken of interest rate policy in respect of National Debt servicing.

The fresh arrangements for the control of credit introduced at the end of 1971 had three implications.

(*a*) *A single reserve ratio.* That the banks no longer observe a minimum cash ratio leads us to the conclusion that the cash base is not now seen as a constraint upon deposit determination.

(*b*) *Strictly defined reserve assets.* An attempt to deal with the difficulty of controlling the supply of liquid assets to the banking system is made by restricting the eligibility of those assets which may be treated as reserves, particularly in respect of commercial bills.

(*c*) *More flexible interest rates.* The Bank intends to be less inhibited by its National Debt servicing obligations and is prepared to place more reliance upon changing interest rates as a determinant of the rate of bank lending.

These conclusions will be explored more fully in the next chapter.

PROGRESS TEST 6

1. What types of bank are found in the U.K.? (**1**)

2. What do you understand by the expression "clearing banks"? (**2**)

3. In terms of business volume, how important are the banks in Scotland and Northern Ireland compared with the London clearing banks? (**2–4**)

4. Explain the principal function of the British overseas banks. (**5**)

5. Point out the most striking feature of the U.S. banks in London. (**6**)

6. List the principal services provided by the commercial banks. (**8–20**)

7. Why is the banks' interest in export finance of especial economic significance? (**16**)

8. Explain the function of the Export Credits Guarantee Department. (**18**)

9. List the assets of the London clearing banks and compare their importance in the balance sheet. (**21**)

10. Assess the relative importance of the two liquidity rules. (**23**)

11. Why are advances the asset of greatest interest to the banks? (**25**)

12. Define the "money supply." (**27**)

13. Explain the way in which the banks themselves are able to create both their own assets and liabilities. (**28**)

14. Why are the banks unable to expand their assets and liabilities without limit? (**30, 31**)

15 Is it true that the cash reserves of the banks are the principal determinant of the volume of deposits? (**32**)

16. Explain the importance of liquid assets to the volume of deposits. (**33–36**)

17. What impact do the non-clearing banks have on the money supply? (**37, 38**)

CHAPTER VII

THE BANK OF ENGLAND

HISTORY

1. Foundation. The Governor and Company of the Bank of England was incorporated in 1694 by an Act of Parliament which granted a Royal Charter. It was the result of pressure in the City for a larger institution which could offer greater security and lower interest rates than the existing private banks. The privilege of a Royal Charter was offered in return for a loan to the Government of £1,200,000 against an annuity of £100,000.

2. The early work of the Bank. In the eighteenth century, the Bank accepted deposits and made advances against security. It discounted approved bills of exchange and later undertook the circulation of Exchequer bills and the issue of Government securities. In 1751 it took over the management of the National Debt.

3. The Bank Charter Act, 1844. The unique position of the Bank was advanced a stage further by this Act which decreed that no new banks would have the power to issue notes while existing banks would have this power curtailed. The result was that in due course the Bank of England became the only note-issuing bank in England and Wales. The Act also granted a fiduciary issue to the Bank, all notes in excess of which had to be backed by gold.

It was also established that the Bank should be divided into two departments, the Issue Department and the Banking Department, the object being to enable the same institution to carry out the duties of a central note-issuing authority at the same time as it engaged in normal commercial banking. The two functions did not prove to be entirely complementary with the result that commercial activities have almost completely disappeared, being gradually replaced by central banking functions.

4. Growth of central banking functions.   The establishment of the Exchange Equalisation Account in 1932 following the departure from the gold standard, the introduction of exchange control in 1939 and the great increase in Government expenditure throughout this century all added to the special responsibilities of the Bank.   The position was formally acknowledged in 1946 with the Act of nationalisation.

5. The Bank of England Act, 1946.   The Bank was taken out of private ownership and the capital stock vested in the Treasury.   Power was expressly given to the Treasury to issue such directives to the Bank as seemed to accord with the public interest.   In fact there has never been occasion to use this power since the Bank has simply continued its pre-nationalisation practice of meeting the Government's requirements in respect of monetary policy without resort to statutory intervention.

The Radcliffe Committee found that the Bank remained a separate entity but that through a number of committees continuous consultation with the Treasury was maintained, views and advice being exchanged and policy determined.   It is this series of liaison bodies that we refer to as "the monetary authorities."

ADMINISTRATION OF THE BANK

6. The Court of Directors.   The Crown appoints a governor, deputy governor and sixteen directors to the Court which controls the Bank.   There may be four working or executive directors with the remainder in a part-time capacity drawn from banking, commerce, shipping, industry and the trade unions.

7. The committees.   The policy body which examines the work of all the other committees is the Committee of Treasury made up of seven members of the Court including the governor and deputy governor.

The other standing committees are:

(a) *The Debden Committee* which supervises the Bank printing works at Debden.

(b) *The Audit Committee.*

(c) *The Committee to Consider the Securities of Certain Funds* which supervises the investment of the Banking Department.

(d) *The Committee on Bank Premises.*

(e) *The Staff Committee.*

(f) *The Charitable Appeals Committee.*

(g) *The Committee on Permanent Control of Expenditure.*

8. The departments. There are eight departments each subdivided into a number of offices covering various aspects of the Bank's work.

(a) *The Accountant's Department* maintains registers of stock on behalf of the U.K. Government, Commonwealth Governments, nationalised industries and some local authorities and issues dividend warrants.

(b) *The Cashier's Department* deals with the note issue, the Exchange Equalisation Account, and all banking operations. Under the last heading come dealings with the discount market and in securities.

(c) *The Economic Intelligence Department* is concerned with collating and interpreting financial and economic information.

(d) *The Overseas Department* is responsible for relations with foreign central banks and international financial bodies.

(e) *The Audit Department.*

(f) *The Secretary's Department.*

(g) *The Establishment Department.*

(h) *The Printing Works.*

THE BANK RETURN

9. Significance. Like the balance sheet of the commercial banks the Bank Return gives an insight into the operations of the Bank of England. For accounting purposes the twofold division into Issue Department and Banking Department has continued to be observed since 1844.

10. Issue Department (selected items), November 1971.

TABLE VIII. BANK RETURN, ISSUE DEPARTMENT

Liabilities	£m.	Assets	£m.
Notes issued:		Government debt	11
In circulation	3,696	Other Government	
In Banking Department	29	securities	3,277
		Other assets including coin other than gold	437
Total	£3,725	Total	£3,725

(*Source: B.E.Q.B.*)

11. Issue Department liabilities.

It will be observed that liabilities consist entirely of notes, either in circulation or in reserve with the Banking Department.

12. Issue Department assets.

Assets are made up of:

(*a*) *Government debt.* Direct lending by the Bank to Government which ceased in 1844 but continued to be shown as a separate item in the Bank Return.

(*b*) *Other Government securities.* This is by far the most important group of assets and any increase in the note issue implies an equivalent increase in Government securities. This is to say that whenever the note issue is expanded the Issue Department receives interest-bearing securities in exchange.

(*c*) *Other assets.* Included in this category are certain eligible bills and coin other than gold coin.

NOTE: It will be seen that the note issue is almost entirely fiduciary.

13. Banking Department (selected items), November 1971.

TABLE IX. BANK RETURN, BANKING DEPARTMENT

Liabilities	£m.	Assets	£m.
Capital	15	Government securities	411
Deposits:			
Public	18	Advances and other accounts	29
Bankers	231		
Reserves and other accounts	335	Premises, equipment and other securities	129
Special	---	Notes and coin	30
Total	£599	Total	£599

(*Source: B.E.Q.B.*)

14. Public deposits. These are the balances of the branches of Government and include the accounts of the Exchequer, the Paymaster-General, the Revenue Departments, the National Debt Commissioners and the National and Trustee Savings Banks.

It will be noted that the balance is relatively small. This is deliberately so since the accumulation of large public deposits in consequence, say, of substantial tax payments would correspondingly reduce bankers' deposits.

The reverse would be true when Government is making payments to society. Alternating shortages and excesses of cash would cause wide fluctuations in the short-term rate of interest and since the Government is the largest short-term borrower it desires an orderly and stable money market (*see* VII, **25** below).

15. Bankers' deposits. The Bank of England is the bankers' bank and stands in much the same relationship to the clearing banks as the latter do to their customers. The clearing banks are enabled to make payments to each other or to the Exchequer by cheques drawn on their accounts and they can draw out the notes and coin that they require.

(*a*) *The clearing.* Net indebtedness between banks which can be settled only in cash is regulated through an adjustment in the bankers' balances at the Bank of England. Settlement at local clearings is carried out through the provincial branches of the Bank of England.

(*b*) *Cash and coin.* In the same way that the individual may draw notes or coin from his bank so the clearing banks can draw upon their accounts at the Bank of England. At holiday-times when the public's demand for cash rises, the banks are able to meet requirements by drawing upon these balances.

NOTE: We shall see later that bankers' deposits are important to the implementation of monetary policy. In the same way that the banks are able to vary the volume of their total deposits the Bank of England is in a position to vary the volume of bankers' deposits and therefore, at least theoretically, the credit which is related to them.

16. Reserves and other accounts. These include unallocated profits together with the accounts of overseas central banks maintained in London to assist in settling trade indebtedness, accounts of overseas Governments and the few remaining private accounts. The Bank of England does not compete with the commercial banks and will not therefore accept fresh private business. However, a number of old-established firms continue to enjoy the banking facilities which they have always had.

17. Special deposits. This item corresponds to the asset which appears in the combined balance sheet of the commercial banks. It has been noted that the banks can be called upon to deposit a percentage of their own total deposits with the Bank of England as a means of reducing their liquidity and hence restricting their power to create deposits.

18. Government securities. Included here are Treasury bills and longer-dated securities (bonds) and Ways and Means Advances to the Exchequer to cover a temporary need for funds. This occurs normally when at the end of the day the Exchequer balances are run down and the Government needs to borrow only until the following day. Since July 1971, Treasury bills discounted for customers appear under this heading.

19. Advances and other accounts. These fall into two groups:

(a) *Private customers.* Advances on private accounts.

(b) *Discount market.* The Bank discounts bills for the discount market and also makes advances against bills as collateral security. In so doing it carries out its function as "lender of last resort." If for any reason the commercial banks recall money from the market (money at call and short notice) the discount houses in order to meet their obligations may now be "forced into the Bank" to borrow at Bank Rate. Since this rate is in excess of discount rates they are put under penalty and there will be a restriction of business until the market can get out of the Bank.

If the Bank wishes to avoid this situation it will operate "at the back door," acquiring bills approaching maturity from the commercial banks and enabling them again to increase their lending to the discount houses.

These operations are vital to the control of the monetary system and further consideration will be given to them (*see* **36** below).

20. Premises, equipment and other securities. These are non-Government securities and include commercial bills acquired from time to time in order to test their quality and discourage the circulation of bills of which the Bank does not approve. Also included are shares and debentures in certain institutions established in the 1930s to stimulate industrial activity and in the 1940s to promote post-war industrial and commercial reconstruction. Since July 1971, premises and equipment have been added to this heading.

21. Notes and coin. It will be observed that this item is insufficient to cover the total balances of the commercial banks held with the Bank of England. If therefore there is an unduly high demand for cash by the banks consequent upon an increased demand by the general public the Bank of England's reserve will be depleted. If it falls below a certain level, the machinery will be set in motion for an increase in the fiduciary issue (*see* V, **6**). This level is known as the "proportion," the ratio between cash reserves and total assets, and is somewhat similar to the cash ratio of the commercial banks.

THE BANK OF ENGLAND'S DOMESTIC BUSINESS

22. The bankers' bank. It has been noted that the commercial bankers maintain cash balances with the Bank of England in order to facilitate the operation of the clearing and from which they replenish their supplies of notes and coin.

Beyond routine banking business exists a close relationship maintained by constant contacts through organisations such as the Committee of London Clearing Bankers and the British Bankers' Association. There are regular meetings between the governor and deputy governor of the Bank and the chairman and deputy chairman of the Committee of London Clearing Bankers as well as meetings at a lower level between bank executives and Bank of England senior officials. Both operational and policy matters are discussed. In this way the Bank becomes the channel of communication between Government and the banking system and the means whereby the Chancellor can make his wishes known without resort to the statutory powers which exist but which have never been used.

The *Bank of England Act*, 1946, gave power to the Bank to request information from and make recommendations to bankers. If authorised by the Treasury it also empowered the Bank to issue directions to any banker for the purpose of securing that effect is given to any such request or recommendation. Recent developments would, however, seem to cast doubt upon the effectiveness of this clause (*see* **40** below).

23. Banker to the discount houses. The 11 discount houses which make up the London Discount Market Association all maintain working balances at the Bank but unlike the clearing banks enjoy the unique privilege of being allowed to borrow. Each house maintains a Loan Account at the Discount Office of the Bank of England where, if it is unable to meet its commitments, it can always raise cash either by rediscounting approved bills or by borrowing against eligible security. The Bank, however, dictates its own terms, specifically with reference to the interest charged which is known as "Bank Rate." Since this is in excess of "Treasury bill rate" (the rate at which the market discounts Treasury bills) and well in excess of "money rate" (the rate at which the market borrows from the clearing banks to finance its operations), the discount houses will use the Bank only as "the lender of last resort."

Nevertheless, this borrowing facility is vital to the functioning of the monetary system. The clearing banks are enabled to maintain minimal cash reserves in the certain knowledge that when necessary money can be recalled from the discount houses which in turn will always be able to repay by resorting to the Bank of England.

24. Banker to the Government. The Bank's unique position among financial institutions stems from its historic relationship with Government.

Of first importance is the Exchequer account, the Government's central bank balance which together with certain subsidiary accounts is held at the Bank of England. The Bank also arranges to meet the Government's borrowing requirements either through Ways and Means Advances or through short-term securities (Treasury bills) and long-term bonds whether for cash or conversion.

25. Treasury bills. The Treasury offers a certain quantity of Treasury bills for sale by tender every Friday. These bills are normally for ninety-one days and do not yield any set rate of interest. Instead, offers are made at a price less than redemption value, *i.e.* the bills are discounted. It is the Bank of England which opens the tenders, makes the allotments, issues the bills and credits the proceeds to the Exchequer account. Bills are allotted to the highest bidders among applications from the discount houses; the Bank of England itself, acting on behalf of foreign central banks; the London branches of overseas banks and British banks acting on behalf of institutional investors. (By agreement with the discount houses the clearing banks do not compete on their own behalf at the weekly tender but make their purchases of bills from the discount houses after the bills have run at least a week.)

The Bank of England also pays bills as they mature.

It has been observed earlier (*see* **14** above) that the Bank seeks to avoid alternating shortages and excesses of cash in the money market which would cause fluctuations in short-term interest rates. To this end it operates almost daily in the market, putting cash out by buying Treasury bills or taking cash in by selling. This is one aspect of the Bank's "open market operations" and is carried out through a firm of discount brokers known as "the special buyer." The Bank does not itself deal directly with the market.

26. Issues of stock. The Bank also carries out continuous open market operations in long-term securities. It advises the Government on new issues and conversions, publishes prospectuses, receives applications and allots the bonds.

On the day that a new issue is made, it is not anticipated that the public will take up the whole amount. Arrangements are therefore made for the balance to be bought by the "departments," which effectively means the Issue Department of the Bank. These bonds are then gradually released to the market through the "Government broker," a firm of stockbrokers acting on behalf of the Bank.

The Bank is also a regular buyer of the stock which next matures so that on the redemption date the number of bonds remaining in the hands of the public is considerably reduced.

It therefore follows that whether the Bank is releasing a new issue or redeeming or refinancing existing debt, cash movements between the public and private sectors are smoothed out over a period of months.

Through these open market operations the Bank seeks to establish an orderly gilt-edged market which is consistent with the wise management of the National Debt. If security prices are falling (*i.e.* interest rates rising) the Bank may intervene more actively as a buyer in order to check the trend. Similarly, as a seller, if the Bank has always "on tap" at least one medium- and one long-dated stock, the rate at which it releases them to the market will have a major influence upon the price and therefore the yield of gilt-edged securities.

THE BANK OF ENGLAND'S EXTERNAL BUSINESS

27. Five tasks. There are five tasks which the Bank must perform in its dealings outside the U.K.

(*a*) The operation of the Exchange Equalisation Account.
(*b*) The management of foreign exchange control.
(*c*) Monetary relations with the sterling area.
(*d*) Monetary relations with foreign central banks.
(*e*) Participation in international financial institutions.

28. The Exchange Equalisation Account. After the gold standard was abandoned in 1931 there no longer existed a common denominator which would automatically relate the exchange values of two paper currencies. In order to avoid the fluctuations which would have resulted from the determination of exchange rates solely by market forces the *Finance Act* of 1932 set up the Exchange Equalisation Account. Gold was transferred from the Issue Department and these funds, placed under the control of the Treasury, were to be utilised in stabilising the foreign exchange markets.

An excess supply of sterling which resulted in a depreciation in its exchange value was checked by the purchase of sterling with gold or foreign currencies. Conversely, an appreciation in the exchange rate was checked by the sale of sterling for gold or foreign currencies.

In 1939, the balance of the gold held by the Issue Department was transferred to the Account which ever since has been the sole depository of the nation's gold and foreign currency reserves.

The *Finance Act* of 1946 widened the scope of the Account to include the conservation or disposition in the national interest of the means of making payments abroad.

The Bank of England manages the Account in accordance with the terms of Britain's membership of the International Monetary Fund. Currently this means that the exchange rate of sterling must be held within the limits of $2·54 and $2·66.

NOTE: When the Bank enters the foreign exchange markets to buy sterling with gold or foreign currencies the proceeds are lent to the Exchequer against "tap" Treasury bills. Conversely, when sterling is sold it becomes necessary to call in loans, with the result that the Exchequer has to borrow from other sources.

29. Foreign exchange control. Exchange control was introduced in 1939 and given a peacetime form in the *Exchange Control Act* of 1947. The Treasury was given extensive powers of control over the conversion of sterling to foreign currencies and over the disposal of the foreign currency receipts of U.K. residents.

Control policy varies and is agreed between the Treasury and the Bank of England and administered by the latter.

Some 120 banks have been appointed authorised dealers in foreign exchange and they are allowed a certain latitude according to the policy in force to deal freely with applications for foreign currencies.

30. The sterling area. Sterling has two important international roles:

(a) *A world trading currency.* A considerable part of world trade is invoiced and financed in sterling and many overseas banks maintain trading balances in London.

(b) *A world reserve currency.* Many countries find it convenient to hold reserves in sterling in London where it earns a rate of interest rather than in gold. Those countries which hold the bulk of their reserves in this way are members of "the sterling area."

Close liaison on operational and policy matters is necessary between the Bank of England and the monetary authorities of sterling area countries. These include gold and foreign currency sales within the area in order that members may make payments to countries outside the area. They also include discussion of the management of the overseas sterling countries' holdings of British Government securities.

31. Foreign central banks. The Bank of England provides banking services, *e.g.* the management of sterling holdings, for many foreign central banks. These banks provide reciprocal services.

In recent years this relationship has developed beyond a narrow banking connection to the point where there are regular exchanges of views and information. The link is especially strong with the U.S. Federal Reserve System, the Bank of Canada and the European central banks.

32. International financial institutions. The Bank of England takes an active part in the work of a number of international bodies and in some cases provides the representative of the U.K.

(a) *Bank for International Settlements.* The Bank of England as the country's central bank is a member in its own right. Post-war, the B.I.S. has been primarily concerned with the acceptance from European central banks of short-term deposits of gold and dollars and the granting of short-term credits.

(b) *The International Monetary Fund (see* XII, **31–41**). The Bank works in conjunction with the Treasury in making preparations for I.M.F. proceedings.

The Bank also makes a substantial contribution to the work of:

(c) *The International Bank for Reconstruction and Development (see* XII, **43**).

(d) *The Organisation for Economic Co-operation and Development (see* X, **40**).

THE BANK'S ROLE IN THE IMPLEMENTATION OF MONETARY POLICY

33. Instrument of Government. The Bank of England is the institution through which Government seeks to impose a monetary policy which will influence the level of economic activity and the balance of payments. Making use of its central position in the banking and financial system the Bank attempts to regulate the volume of credit, the level of interest rates and the external demand for sterling.

34. The traditional methods of control. The methods by which the Bank of England has traditionally implemented monetary policy are:

(a) *Bank Rate.*
(b) *Open market operations.*

35. Bank Rate. This is the minimum rate at which the Bank of England as lender of last resort will rediscount eligible securities for the discount houses. It is the key interest rate since all other rates are directly or indirectly related to it, *e.g.* bank deposit rates, overdraft rates, bill rates, building-society rates.

It was argued that Bank Rate by making money cheap or dear to borrow could influence the level of business activity. If interest rates rose some activities which had been profitable would now be unprofitable and would therefore cease. The volume of bank loans and hence deposits would correspondingly contract. The opposite would be true if interest rates fell.

Bank Rate is made effective by open market operations.

36. Open market operations. The Bank of England sets out to regulate the lending capacity of the commercial banks by influencing their cash balances.

If the Bank goes on to the open market to purchase Government securities from the general public it must pay with cheques drawn upon itself. When these cheques are paid into the commercial banks, the Bank of England will have an adverse balance at the Clearing House. This can be settled only by crediting the cash balances of the commercial banks, *i.e.* bankers' deposits will increase. We have seen that these deposits are treated as part of the banks' reserve assets. Since this has now been enlarged the banks will be able to pursue a more liberal lending policy and deposits will grow.

Conversely, if the Bank enters the market to sell, cheques drawn on the commercial banks in favour of the Bank of England will result in a reduction of bankers' deposits and a curtailment of their ability to lend. The immediate effect will be the recall of money from the discount market in order to make good cash ratios. The discount houses will now be compelled to borrow from the Bank of England and Bank Rate is "made effective" at least at the short end of the market. In due course this rise in short-term interest rates will work its way through to medium- and long-term lending rates.

NOTE: This process can be speeded quite independently of what is happening to net cash movements. The Bank in its capacity as manager of the National Debt can alter the maturity distribution of marketable debt held by the private sector and thus influence the structure of interest rates throughout the market.

37. Appraisal of the effectiveness of Bank Rate. It was orininally thought that, of the two instruments of monetary policy, Bank Rate was the more powerful. Open market operations were employed only in support to make Bank Rate effective. During the 1930s, however, it became apparent that low interest rates were not giving the stimulus to business activity which might have been expected. Confidence in traditional monetary policy was therefore diminished with the result that in 1931 it was completely abandoned for the following twenty years.

In the absence of any more constructive ideas the authorities opted for cheap money in the hope that economic recovery might eventually occur. This lack of confidence seemed to be borne out by the failure of the economy to respond to interest rates as low as 2 per cent. It seemed apparent that the businessman would not borrow no matter how low the rate of interest if he were not confident of a profitable return.

Similarly, it can be argued that a rate of interest as high as 10 per cent will not discourage the potential borrower if he is confident of a 20 per cent return. This view would seem to find support in the very high interest rates which have been paid for loans outside the banking system during the period in the late 1960s when the banks have been under severe credit restraint.

It may therefore be concluded that a policy of dear or cheap money is not in itself sufficient to discourage or encourage business activity. The effect of interest rates is more deep rooted as we shall shortly see. Taken at face value variations in Bank Rate have primarily a psychological effect. They are an indication to domestic borrowers and to overseas bankers and monetary authorities of the Government's serious intention to check inflation.

38. Appraisal of the effectiveness of open market operations. The effectiveness of open market operations depends upon adherence by the banks to a fixed liquidity ratio. If the volume of liquid assets is in excess of the minimum 28 per cent then there is spare lending capacity and the Bank can sell securities on the open market without forcing the commercial banks to restrict their investments or advances.

Moreover, when engaging in open market operations in support of monetary policy the Bank has been inhibited by its duties in respect of the management of the National Debt. When the Bank enters the market to sell securities in an attempt to reduce the cash reserves of the banks its sales will depress gilt-edged prices; *i.e.* interest rates rise and Government long-term borrowing becomes dearer. In fact, after 1960, the Bank increasingly intervened in the market to *buy* securities in order to hold up prices even though this course of action conflicted with the needs of a restrictive monetary policy. Similarly if the Bank enters the money market to sell Treasury bills it must accept that short-term interest rates will rise and Government borrowing become more costly. In any case open market operations in Treasury bills will curb the power of the banks to create deposits only to the extent that:

(a) higher interest rates discourage the drawing of *commercial* bills and so restrict the *total* supply of liquid assets to the banking system *or* (*b*) investors outside the banking system are tempted by higher interest rates to increase their bill holdings and so reduce the supply of liquid assets to the banks.

It has been observed earlier that these propositions were not borne out by experience (*see* VI, **36**).

The weakness of the traditional instruments of monetary policy was recognised by increasing reliance upon two new weapons, *Special deposits* and the *Treasury directive*.

39. Special deposits. From time to time the banks have been called upon to make Special deposits with the Bank of England. They are calculated as a percentage of total bank deposits, cannot be treated as part of the cash balances but do yield interest, in normal circumstances the current Treasury bill rate.

The object of the Special deposit scheme was to restrict the liquidity of the banks, thereby putting a brake upon lending where the traditional instruments of monetary policy had failed.

All the evidence of the 1960s would suggest that this scheme has been unsuccessful. When Special deposits are called for the banks will raise cash by selling either bills or securities. It is likely that they will choose the latter, thus maintaining their liquid assets and leaving total deposits undisturbed. This likelihood is reinforced by the fact that the conventional liquid assets are cushioned by the banks' portfolio of bonds with early maturities. Even if liquid assets are realised it is probable that they can be quickly replaced. In neither case then will total deposits be affected and it is highly unlikely moreover that the cash for Special deposits will be found by any restriction of advances. In fact advances, the most lucrative asset, may well be increased to compensate for any loss sustained in holding Special deposits rather than other assets.

Lack of confidence in the scheme and to some extent in the efficacy of the traditional monetary instruments would seem to be indicated by the heavy reliance in the late 1960s upon Treasury directives.

40. The Treasury directive. There have been two types of directive issued to the commercial banks.

(a) *Qualitative.* The first directives in 1951 and 1952 advised the banks to restrict their advances to those activities which were in the national interest.

(b) *Quantitative.* The general instruction which became standard practice in the 1960s to restrict *all* advances (with a few exceptions such as firms engaged in export trade) to a specified level.

Even the quantitative directive did not prove entirely successful in containing the expansion of deposits since the banks have protested that it was impossible to comply fully with the Treasury's instruction and still honour their commitments to their customers.

41. The external effects of Bank Rate. It has been noted that the Bank has a role not only in implementing domestic monetary policy but also in regulating the overseas demand for sterling.

In the first place a rise in Bank Rate makes it relatively more profitable to hold funds in London rather than in overseas financial centres. Secondly, and more fundamentally a rise in Bank Rate is seen as a symbol of the Government's determination to take stern measures to check inflation. It is an indication that the authorities will deflate rather than devalue and that overseas holders of sterling can therefore have confidence. In this way any potential outflow of funds may be forestalled.

THE RADCLIFFE COMMITTEE AND THE CONCEPT OF GENERAL LIQUIDITY

42. General liquidity and the money supply. The Radcliffe Committee maintained that it was insufficient for monetary policy to rely upon methods designed to control the supply of money in the conventional sense. Traditionally, time deposits as well as current accounts have been considered along with notes to form the money stock. However, if time deposits with the banks could be included, why not Post Office savings accounts, building-society deposits, insurance policies, etc.? What was of importance was the "total liquidity picture" of which the conventional money stock formed the most liquid part.

The Committee's conclusions followed the following steps (see *Report*, paras. 381–97).

43. Purpose of monetary measures. In conjunction with other measures the objectives are the implementation of employment policy, economic growth and stability in the internal and external value of sterling. Control is sought through the determination of the pressure of total demand. When unemployment is rising and prices are falling demand is increased and vice versa.

44. The two monetary weapons. There are two instruments of control which the Committee described as:

(*a*) *The interest-incentive effect.* It was argued that in recent years there has been little evidence of the presence of any interest-incentive effect. Theoretically, the willingness of merchants to hold stocks will be influenced by short rates of interest and the volume of long-term capital investment by long rates of interest (*see* **37** above). Only partially distinct from this instrument (since movements in interest rates play a central part in determining it) is:

(*b*) *The general liquidity effect.* Interest rates may or may not influence willingness to borrow. What is certain is that "if the money for financing the project cannot be got on any tolerable terms at all, that is the end of the matter."

45. Traditional view of the importance of the money supply. It has been a commonly held view that the quantities which are relevant to the level of demand are the flow of money incomes and the quantity of money, *i.e.* notes plus bank deposits. It therefore follows that if the central bank is both able and willing to control the supply of money allowing it to increase only in step with the expansion of the economy the objectives of monetary policy can be achieved.

To a greater or lesser degree, all exponents of this view agree that control of the money supply is a central objective. The Radcliffe Committee was of a different opinion.

46. Radcliffe Committee view. The supply of money was important but only as part of the wider structure of liquidity in the economy. The decision to spend is governed not only by whether the spender has cash in the bank but by whether he has saleable assets or can borrow on the strength of future cash receipts. The ability to borrow depends upon the structure of the borrower's assets and the current resources (*i.e.* liquidity) of the financial institutions which will provide him with present purchasing power.

There is therefore no systematic relationship between present spending and the existing quantity of money.

NOTE: Viewed theoretically it is perfectly possible for the volume of spending to increase without any increase in the quantity of money. Money simply changes hands more rapidly, *i.e.* the velocity of circulation increases.

47. Unity of the market for loanable funds. The Committee emphasised that there is no firm division between "the market in credit" and "the market in capital." By their very nature certain financial institutions will specialise in certain forms of lending but not exclusively. Equally, borrowers will raise funds regularly from specific sources but if thwarted will turn elsewhere. Thus the small businessman who is denied a bank overdraft may run down his cash, mortgage his house, obtain longer trade credit terms, realise an insurance policy or turn to the increasing number of institutions outside the banks which will provide finance.

It is therefore insufficient to pursue a monetary policy aimed at restricting the power of the commercial banks to create deposit money.

48. Importance of the structure of interest rates. Short of a complex of direct controls upon all forms of lending the authorities must rely upon influencing the structure of interest rates throughout the market. This it may do through Bank Rate and by its open market operations in securities which influence capital values and hence yields. If an appropriate structure of interest rates can be established then potential lenders and borrowers will be drawn to a particular distribution of their assets. Their liquidity having been established it will now be difficult or easy for spending to take place. Any desired variation in the structure of their liquidity may now be induced by variations in the structure of interest rates.

The Committee believed, however, that the general interest rate policy of the authorities would be slow in producing positive results. In an emergency situation they therefore advocated measures which would strike directly at the liquidity of spenders, *e.g.* control of capital issues, bank advances and consumer credit.

49. A controversial area of monetary theory. The stages of the argument may be summarised in the following way:

(*a*) There exists no systematic link between the supply of money and the level of demand since there are no means of limiting the velocity of circulation.

(*b*) It is useless therefore to concentrate upon limiting the money supply.

(*c*) A general reliance may be placed upon the structure of interest rates which will help determine the general liquidity of the economy.

(*d*) In emergency, specific measures may be employed directly to restrict liquidity.

This extreme viewpoint became less popular during the 1960s. Academic interest in the significance of the money stock has centred upon the work of the Chicago school of economists led by Milton Friedman. Their growing influence has been reflected in U.S. Government policy and more recently it has become evident that the U.K. monetary authorities also attach considerable importance to the control of the money supply (*see* VII, **50, 53, 54**).

50. Domestic credit expansion. In May 1969 the Chancellor of the Exchequer reaffirmed the importance which the Government attached to monetary policy in general and to the achievement of a satisfactory rate of domestic credit expansion (D.C.E.) in particular.

The concept of D.C.E. springs from the belief that any consideration given to the growth of the money supply, certainly in the U.K., must take account of the external position. If the balance of payments is in deficit the money supply will decline. Foreign expenditure will in the first place be financed by the running down of bank balances as people purchase foreign exchange. The banks will then make good their foreign currency holdings by purchases from the Exchange Equalisation Account against sterling. The proceeds will be used by the Bank of England to redeem Government debt held by the banking system. In this way deposits decline or grow less quickly than they would otherwise have done. The opposite will be true in the case of an external surplus.

It therefore follows that when there is an external deficit the resulting decline in the rate of growth of the money stock is not an adequate measure of the effectiveness of current monetary policy. For this reason the concept of D.C.E. has been evolved as a monetary indicator to be used in addition to the rate of change of the money supply.

A FRESH APPROACH TO MONETARY POLICY

51. Competition and credit control. In his 1971 Budget speech, the Chancellor declared his interest in exploring new techniques which would stimulate inter-bank competition and at the same time make credit control more effective without reliance upon direct quantitative controls, *i.e.* Treasury directives.

The essence of the new approach is found in para. 5 of the Bank of England's paper *Competition and Credit Control* of May 1971:

> "The techniques of monetary policy now proposed would involve less reliance on *particular* methods of influencing bank and finance house lending and more reliance on changes in interest rates, supported by calls for special deposits on the basis of a reserve ratio across the whole of the banking system. There would be similar arrangements for deposit taking finance houses."

The intention clearly is to revert to a primary reliance upon moving interest rates as the instrument of monetary policy with the reserve ratio and special deposits serving as a supporting mechanism and applicable not only to the clearing banks but to all banks and finance houses defined as deposit taking institutions.

The Bank had two basic motives in advocating a **new** approach:

(a) *Commercial considerations.*
(b) *The weaknesses of existing monetary policy.*

52. Commercial considerations. Increasing reliance upon Treasury directives imposing loan ceilings during the 1960s amounted to enforced market sharing between the banks. Moreover, these restrictions artificially encouraged the development of financial institutions whose activities, although differing only marginally from those of the banks, were not defined as banks and were not therefore subject to Treasury directives. These considerations in conjunction with the collective agreements of the clearing banks on deposit and lending rates both distorted and diminished the effects of competition, stultifying innovation and making the banking system less responsive to the changing needs of its customers.

At the same time as loan ceilings were removed the clearing banks abandoned their collective agreements on interest rates. This was necessary not only for the improvement of competition but also for the effectiveness of an approach to monetary policy founded upon a greater flexibility of interest rates.

53. Reappraisal of monetary policy. It has been noted that the conclusions of the Radcliffe Committee which influenced the formulation of policy during the greater part of the 1960s have been subject to continuous critical scrutiny by economists and also to the test of a prolonged period in which it proved necessary to exercise stringent controls (*see* VII, **42–49**).

(*a*) *Money supply*. Largely because research indicates that the velocity of circulation is fairly stable the money supply has been reinstated as more than just one of a whole range of liquid assets. It is now seen as an important indicator of the impact of monetary policy.

(*b*) *Interest rates*. Research has also led to the conclusion that interest rates can play a greater role in influencing the behaviour of the economy than was accepted by the Radcliffe Committee.

(*c*) *Loan ceilings*. In recommending that in emergency the authorities should resort to direct controls, the Radcliffe Committee could not foresee the need which emerged during the 1960s for a prolonged period of restriction. The undesirability of loan ceilings as a means of achieving this has already been shown (*see* **52** above).

The decision to depend once more upon changing interest

rates had implications for the practices which the Bank had developed after 1960 in its open market operations both in gilt-edged and in money.

54. The gilt-edged market. It has been noted that throughout the last decade the Bank's operations in gilt-edged securities were concerned primarily with the stabilisation of the market to ease the problems of National Debt financing rather than with the needs of a restrictive monetary policy (*see* VII, **38**). It was further noted that a weakness of the Special deposits scheme was the inclination of the banks to meet calls by selling securities rather than liquid assets (*see* VII, **39**).

In May 1971 the Bank announced and put into effect a different policy in respect of its gilt-edged dealings. Since that date it has no longer been prepared "to respond to requests to buy stock outright except in the case of stocks with one year or less to run to maturity." In other words the Bank was no longer willing to support gilt-edged prices and was prepared to let interest rates rise.

This conclusion was reached because the Bank had decided that its "operations in the gilt-edged market should pay more regard to their quantitative effects on the monetary aggregates and less regard to the behaviour of interest rates."

This change in practice was clearly aimed at assisting the effectiveness of a *restrictive* monetary policy. However, for the new arrangements to be complete, allowance had to be made for open market operations in support of an *expansionary* monetary policy. For this reason the Bank reserved the right to purchase stock with *more* than one year to run at its discretion.

55. The money market. The structure of the Bank's dealings with the discount market remains basically unchanged but a major modification of technique was introduced in September 1971. Until that time the discount houses agreed prices between themselves not only for the weekly Treasury bill tender but also for subsequent dealings in long bills. The Bank in its day-to-day operations in bills was then prepared to deal in line with the market's prices. Its influence on those prices was thus restricted to its actions *at the tender* when it might force the market to borrow at the penal Bank Rate.

The new arrangements provided not only for the abandonment of the syndicated tender (the collective pricing agreement of the discount houses) but also that the Bank would now be free *day by day* to determine the price at which it would be prepared to deal in Treasury bills. The Bank thus acquired a greater flexibility in influencing short-term interest rates. The implications for the role of Bank Rate had still to be determined but it was clear that the decline in its central importance to monetary policy was continuing.

56. Abolition of Bank Rate, 9th October, 1972. Over some 250 years Bank Rate had evolved three functions. It was the "prime rate" to which certain other rates, e.g. bank overdraft and deposit rates, were directly related. However, after September, 1971, the banks determined their own base rates separately and independently. Secondly, it served as an economic signal of the Chancellor's view of the economy and during the 1960's this was viewed by many as its principal role. More recently its value in this respect seemed doubtful since the Chancellor might wish to *raise* Bank Rate to *encourage* foreign confidence while not wishing to *discourage* the domestic economy. Thirdly, it retained its traditional function as a means of controlling the discount market. However, as has just been shown, after 1971 the Bank had greater flexibility in influencing market rates directly. Moreover, during 1972 there developed a situation in which the market could theoretically borrow at Bank Rate, a supposedly penal rate, while the *actual* market rate for money lay above.

These anomalies were resolved with the abolition of Bank Rate and the substitution of *"the minimum lending rate"*. The latter differs in being a product rather than a cause of money market rates since it is calculated by taking the last Treasury bill rate, adding $\frac{1}{2}\%$ and rounding up to the next quarter point.

57. Reserve ratios and Special deposits. The nature of the new reserve assets requirements has already been examined (*see* VI, **25**). The stricter definition of these assets which places emphasis upon public sector debt gives the authorities greater power to influence bank liquidity and hence the ability to create credit. The Special deposits scheme is retained to support this mechanism and in view of the Bank's new gilt-edged market policy may be expected to work more effectively than in the past (*see* VII, **39**).

PROGRESS TEST 7

1. Why may the Bank of England be described as a "central bank"? **(1–5)**

2. Describe the organisation of the Bank. **(6–8)**

3. What is the nature of the assets which back the note issue? **(12)**

4. Why are public deposits at the Bank surprisingly small? **(14)**

5. What essential purpose do Bankers' deposits serve? **(15)**

6. What are "Special deposits"? **(17)**

7. Explain the phrase "lender of last resort." **(19)**

8. What is the "proportion"? **(21)**

9. List the three key rates of interest in the money market. **(23)**

10. How are Treasury bills issued? **(25)**

11. Who is the "special buyer"? **(25)**

12. How does the Bank attempt to establish an orderly gilt-edged market? **(26)**

13. What is the Exchange Equalisation Account? **(28)**

14. Describe the two international roles of sterling. **(30)**

15. Define Bank Rate. **(35)**

16. Explain the use of open market operations in making Bank Rate effective. **(36)**

17. Are borrowers always especially sensitive to interest rates? **(37)**

18. What problem inhibits the Bank in employing open market operations to pursue its monetary policy? **(38)**

19. How effective has the Special deposit scheme been? **(39)**

20. What are Treasury directives? **(40)**

21. What was the main Radcliffe criticism of traditional monetary policy? **(42–47)**

22. Outline the main conclusions of the Radcliffe Committee. **(48)**

23. Explain the principal differences in the application of monetary policy which would result from the adoption of the Bank's 1971 proposals. **(53)**

CHAPTER VIII

THE MARKET IN LOANABLE FUNDS

STRUCTURE OF THE MARKET

1. The markets in credit and capital. Britain has a highly developed market in loanable funds with a large and diverse number of financial institutions serving as intermediaries between borrowers and lenders. Continuing growth in both number and variety is economically significant in contributing to the better allocation of scarce resources.

The part played by the banks in providing loans has already been examined. We turn next to those other institutions whose work is complementary.

It has been observed that there is an underlying unity in the market for all loanable funds (*see* VII, **47**). Nevertheless, it is possible to make a fairly clear distinction between short-term lending (the market in credit) and long-term lending (the market in capital). The distinction rests upon the period of the loan and the purpose to which it is put.

(*a*) *The credit or money market*. Money is advanced chiefly by the commercial banks on terms ranging from "call" to "short notice" to finance trade transactions and Government borrowing normally over a maximum period of three months.

(*b*) *The capital market*. Loans may be for periods as short as three months (*e.g.* in the case of some bank advances to industry) but normally will be for much longer periods or even of indefinite duration. Thus industry meets its fixed capital requirements through the issue of debentures for which a repayment date is set or of share capital destined for permanent employment. Similarly, Government borrows against securities dated ten, twenty or thirty years hence or against undated stock.

2. The financial institutions.

The organisation of the market can be seen from the diagram.

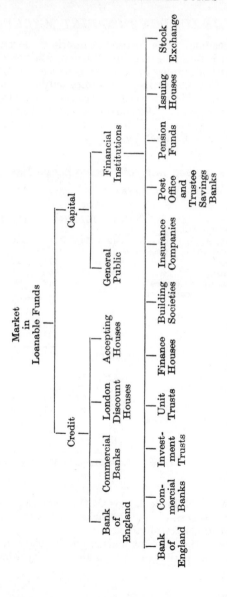

Structure of the market in loanable funds

THE LONDON DISCOUNT MARKET

3. Composition. The market comprises eleven discount houses which form the London Discount Market Association together with a number of other firms which are not members and whose discounting operations form only a portion of their total business. The three principal companies are the National Discount Company, Alexanders and the Union Discount Company of London. There is no common market-place, contact being maintained by telephone or in person.

4. Assets and borrowing of discount houses 1966–71.

TABLE X. DISCOUNT HOUSES' BALANCE SHEET, YEAR END

(£ *million*)

	1966	1967	1968	1969	1970	1971
Assets						
U.K. Government stocks	542	544	306	256	160	430
U.K. Government Treasury bills	424	548	471	212	876	320
Other sterling bills	404	437	560	561	697	505
Local authority securities	101	115	148	180	189	365
Sterling certificates of deposit	—	—	56	79	268	374
Dollar certificates of deposit	—	14	39	20	39	78
Other	95	89	83	88	123	218
Total	£1,565	£1,747	£1,663	£1,398	£2,352	£2,290
Borrowed Funds						
Bank of England	82	116	—	—	—	5
London clearing banks	978	1,076	1,132	974	1,407	996
Scottish banks	94	102	100	62	108	88
Other deposit banks	11	21	15	9	29	47
Accepting houses, overseas and other banks	201	218	204	166	510	760
Other sources	119	130	121	99	205	278
Total	£1,484	£1,662	£1,573	£1,311	£2,259	£2,174

(*Source: B.E.Q.B.*)

Examination of Table X reveals the relative importance of the various assets in which the market deals and of the sources from which funds are obtained.

The work of the discount market and its place in the financial system may perhaps be best understood by a brief examination of its origins and development.   Eight phases can be distinguished.

5. Phase I. Unitary banking system of the early nineteenth century.

The early banking system comprised a large number of banks, often with only one office. At this time much inland trade was financed by bills of exchange. This practice gave rise to the "running broker" who found "good" bills for banks which had surplus funds to employ, *e.g.* banks in agricultural areas which at certain times of the year had few demands for loans. In the expanding industrial areas, on the other hand, the demand for loans exceeded the supply of funds. The running broker therefore served an equalising function, collecting bills from "industrial" banks for resale to "agricultural" banks. For this service he took his commission.

6. Phase II. Growth of bill-dealers after 1820.

Certain influential brokers, *e.g.* Overend, Gurney and Co., became so well established that they were able to borrow from the banks on their own account and therefore finance their own bill portfolios. In 1829 the Bank of England itself agreed to establish discount accounts, *i.e.* the bill-dealer acquired the right in certain circumstances to rediscount bills.

These developments were agreeable to the commercial banks. A financial crisis in 1825 had seen them hard pressed and many had been compelled to borrow from the Bank of England. They therefore resolved to increase the level of their reserves. To have increased cash ratios would have diminished profits since cash of course yields no interest. They were therefore only too pleased to lend funds to established bill-dealers against the security of first-class bills and against the guarantee to repay at "call or short notice." This guarantee was underwritten by the Bank of England's willingness to act as lender of last resort to the bill-dealers.

Already at this stage can be observed the distinctive feature of the London Discount Market. It serves as a specialised financial intermediary.

(*a*) To begin with it stood between borrowing banks and lending banks.

(*b*) It then developed as an intermediary between banks and ultimate borrowers.

(c) Finally, it stood between the commercial banks and the Bank of England. The former acquired a new category of highly liquid assets. They could always make good their cash ratios by recalling loans from the Discount Market and without having themselves to go directly to the Bank of England.

7. Phase III. International business 1870–1914.

Bank amalgamations in the second half of the nineteenth century brought about the substitution of a branch banking system for the unitary system. The new large banks were able to balance internally the cash surpluses of one area against the shortages of another. Moreover, with the development of the cheque and the overdraft, business in inland bills declined.

The Discount Market therefore turned its attention elsewhere and during this period a large business in foreign trade bills was created. These bills now provided the Market's stock-in-trade until 1914.

8. Phase IV. Treasury bills 1914–18.

The decline in international trade brought an almost total disappearance of commercial bills. It seemed that the discount market must now wither away. The Government, however, began for the first time to increase the level of the floating debt using the instrument of the Treasury bill which now became the Market's stock-in-trade.

Dealings in Treasury bills continued after the war and in the late 1920s were supplemented by a revival of commercial paper. With the slump of 1929–31, commercial bills once more declined.

9. Phase V. Development of business in short bonds in the 1930s.

The Market's existence was once more threatened during the trade depression of the 1930s. Firstly, the supply of commercial bills was much depleted. Secondly, a glut of loan funds sought outlets with a consequent intensification of competition between lenders and the forcing down of interest rates. The discount houses found themselves competing for the limited supply of bills not only with an increasing number of outside lenders but also with the commercial banks from whom they borrowed their money at call. The ludicrous situation arose from time to time that when the "money rate" charged by the banks to the discount houses stood at 1 per cent, discount rates had fallen as low as ⅛ per cent. In these circumstances a number of houses were forced out of business.

Since it was believed that the discount houses still had a useful function to perform, a salvage operation was undertaken. In 1934 the commercial banks agreed:

(a) To accept officially for the first time the security of bonds against which money would be lent.

(b) Not to buy bills at less than their own money rate.

(c) Not to compete at the weekly tender for the supply of Treasury bills.

(d) to buy only Treasury bills from the Market and when they were at least a week old.

These fundamental principles still apply.

The result of this limitation of competition was the edging up of Treasury bill rate to a point marginally above money rate. There was now a strong incentive (because of points (c) and (d) above) to increase the volume of resale business to the banks and there once again developed intensive competition at the weekly tenders from lenders of all kinds. It seemed likely that Treasury bill rate would once more be forced below money rate. In another attempt to limit competition the discount houses therefore formulated the "syndicated tender system." The price at which they tendered was agreed and each was allotted a quota in proportion to its capital resources and beyond which it must not bid. This agreement was abandoned in September 1971 (see VII, 55).

Through these devices the Market was able to continue to deal in bills even though this business was only just profitable. Its survival, however, was due primarily to its having ventured into the more profitable short bond business, this having been made possible by the banks, willingness to accept bonds as collateral security.

10. Phase VI. Expansion of short bond business 19‿9–45. During the war the Market was officially encouraged to expand its business in short bonds. The Treasury was attempting to finance the war cheaply with short-dated stock. It was appreciated that after the war investors would liquidate their holdings in favour of investment in industry. The gilt-edged market would therefore come under considerable strain. The Discount Market could therefore help cushion the shock by absorbing short maturities as they came along and thus ease the problem of reconversion finance.

11. Phase VII. Renewed profitability of Treasury bills in 1951. In 1951, after an interval of twenty years, an active monetary policy was revived. This implied a moving Bank Rate and money rates which fluctuated through a fairly wide range. Since bill discounting was consequently riskier there was now an unwillingness to discount except at rates substantially higher than money rate. Thus for the first time in twenty years dealing in bills became really profitable. Outside lenders were now drawn to the Market with the result that the discount houses began to hold smaller bill portfolios and still more bonds. This is not to say that their turnover of bills has not been good but that bills have been held for shorter periods.

12. Phase VIII. Revival of commercial bills and the development of other assets in the 1960s. In pursuit of its monetary policy the Treasury has been concerned in the 1950s and 1960s to reduce the liquidity of the banking system by curtailing the supply of Treasury bills and, where possible, of short bonds. However, there was in the 1960s a strong revival of dealing in commercial bills. Moreover, the Market has developed fresh interests, among them an increasingly brisk business in local authority securities.

13. Appraisal of the work of the London Discount Market. From the preceding account it can be observed that the Market has today six main functions:

(a) *An equalising function.* It provides a highly efficient market in short-term loans which has enabled the banks to work to low cash ratios. Their liquid assets can be quickly mobilised as the need arises. In this respect the Market still performs an equalising function between those banks with surpluses and those with shortages. Banks which are short, call in money from the Market which will now probably be able to increase its borrowing from banks with surplus cash.

(b) *Cash and credit intermediary.*   The Market is a channel for the provision of central bank cash and credit.

(i) *Cash.*   Fresh cash may be injected into the economy when the Bank chooses to purchase bills on the Market. (Today the Bank may accomplish the same purpose by buying bills direct from the commercial banks.)

(ii) *Credit.*   It is only through the Market that Bank of England credit can be provided at last resort.   When the desire to increase the cash supply originates not at the Bank but elsewhere in the economy the tightness of money will ultimately force the discount houses to borrow from the Bank of England.

(c) *An instrument for Government short-term finance.*   The irregular and massive cash flows between the private sector and the Exchequer can be smoothed out by the judicious use of the Treasury bill.

(d) *The short bond market.*   In this sphere the Market has two functions:

(i) *A shock-absorber.*   To a limited degree the Market serves to cushion the effect upon capital values of quantities of bonds suddenly being offered for sale.   However, the discount houses would be unable to absorb the impact of large-scale sales of bonds without resorting to the Bank of England.   This function is therefore of less importance than its role as:

(ii) *A channel for maturing bonds.*   A considerable quantity of bonds approaching maturity are funnelled into the Discount Market.   When the Treasury is carrying out refinancing operations it therefore knows where it can find new maturities at times convenient to itself.

(e) *Commercial bills.*   The Market has retained its original role as a source of trade finance and it has been observed that during the 1960s commercial bill business has expanded.

(f) *Local authority securities.*   It has also been noted that the Market has developed a substantial interest as an intermediary for local authority finance.

14. The discount market and the new arrangements for credit control.   It has already been observed that after the 1971 reappraisal of monetary policy the Bank concluded that it wished to preserve its basic mode of operation in the money market (*see* VII, **55**). Thus the Bank asked the market to agree to continue to apply each week for a quantity of Treasury bills sufficient to cover the amount offered for sale, *i.e.* to continue to underwrite the tender. For the Bank's part it would continue to confine "last resort" lending facilities to the market.

However, the authorities needed to ensure that they would have adequate influence over credit extended through the discount market. Moreover, the Bank had a special eye to the fact that the new reserve ratio requirements permitted the banks to treat money at call as a reserve asset without limitation. With this in view two new restrictions were imposed upon the market.

(*a*) *Restriction of acceptable collateral.* The Bank now insists that when it extends "last resort" facilities, part of the collateral security up to an agreed minimum proportion shall be in the form of Treasury bills.

(*b*) *Restriction upon market assets.* The market is now obliged to hold a minimum of 50 per cent of its borrowed funds in public-sector debt.

Since the authorities themselves have ultimate control over the availability of public securities it puts them in a position to influence credit creation not only by the market itself but also by the banks since the expansion of the reserve asset "money at call" can be restrained.

15. Definition of the public-sector debt ratio. The 50 per cent minimum is observed by the members of the London Discount Market Association plus the three discount brokers and the money trading departments of six named banks traditionally concerned with discounting. The ratio is one of public-sector debt to borrowed funds defined as follows:

(*a*) *Borrowed funds.* Total sterling borrowing (other than capital) less sterling lending to other discount houses, the three brokers and the six banks together with net liabilities in non-sterling currencies.

(*b*) *Public-sector debt.* This includes:

(*i*) U.K. Treasury bills.

(*ii*) Local authority bills eligible for rediscount at the Bank of England.

(*iii*) Public sector bills guaranteed by H.M. Government.

(*iv*) Company tax reserve certificates.

(*v*) British Government stocks and stocks of nationalised industries guaranteed by H.M. Government *with not more than five years to final maturity.*

(*vi*) Local authority stocks *with not more than five years to final maturity.*

The actual public-sector lending ratios in October 1971 were as follows:

Discount houses	58.8%
Discount brokers	61.1%
Money trading banks	86.9%

THE ACCEPTING HOUSES

16. The acceptance. The acceptance credit is the basic business of the merchant banks or accepting houses. A bill of exchange is drawn by the supplier or buyer who will then receive spot cash immediately the bill has been "'accepted'' or guaranteed by a bank. The bill can then be discounted on the London Discount Market. In this way credit, normally for ninety days, is provided for the finance of trade transactions.

17. Origin and development. The banking aspects of the merchant banks' business originated as an interest subsidiary to their normal trading activities. Merchants tended to specialise in trade in particular goods with particular parts of the world. They therefore developed an exceptional knowledge of the credit-worthiness of the firms with which they traded. This intimate knowledge enabled them on occasion to accept bills on behalf of firms which were little known outside their own countries. For this service they charged a small commission. As international trade expanded during the nineteenth century they developed their banking activities and finally abandoned their role as merchants. Moreover, since London was developing as the world's financial and commercial centre, merchant bankers from Europe were led to settle there. In this period some of the great names in merchant banking appeared, *e.g.* Rothschild, Baring, Schroder, Lazard, Kleinwort.

It soon became customary for overseas merchants to open "acceptance credits" to an agreed limit with a London accepting house. Other merchants could then draw bills upon that house. Having been accepted these bills became "bank bills," readily discountable on the discount market since they were recognised as elegible security by the Bank of England. The fact that such instruments therefore enjoy the highest degree of liquidity gives to the accepting houses their main significance in the British banking system.

18. Extension of banking functions. In this century the merchant banks have undertaken some of the functions of the commercial banks by accepting deposits and making loans. The latter have in turn extended their interests by undertaking acceptance business.

19. The "euro-markets." In recent years there has developed a strong market in international deposits. The interest of the British accepting houses and exchange banks has made London the principal European centre.

Overseas banks and commercial institutions with large sums available for short-term lending make deposits in London with the accepting houses or exchange banks in a wide variety of currencies, *e.g.* dollars, pounds, Swiss francs, gilders, etc. In this way an international market in loanable funds has developed known variously as the "euro-dollar, euro-sterling, euro-franc markets," etc.

The accepting house or exchange bank lends these funds either in the currency in which they were deposited or in another currency, forward exchange cover having been obtained.

20. The foreign exchange market. Closely associated with their work in the euro-markets is the interest held by the accepting houses in the foreign exchange market which comprises more than 120 authorised dealers. Two of the houses with strong foreign exchange departments specialise in supplying foreign currency notes to other banks and travel agents.

21. The London Gold Market. A considerable part of world dealings in gold takes place on the London Gold Market. This is made up of two accepting houses, a firm of brokers owned by an accepting house and two independent brokers.

22. Medium-term export finance. It has been observed that in the increasingly competitive circumstances of international trade credit terms are often decisive (*see* VI, **16**). Together with the commercial banks, the accepting houses assist by arranging medium-term finance. The usual method is to provide funds by discounting the buyer's acceptances which mature at intervals over the period of the credit. The accepting houses may themselves discount some bills but where large sums are involved will make arrangements for them to be discounted by the commercial banks.

23. Long-term finance. Some accepting houses may also take an interest in the capital market. Like the issuing houses they may take part in raising long-term loans for overseas governments and institutions and in the issuing of shares and debentures on behalf of British companies.

24. Combined balance sheet of the accepting houses (selected items) December 1966 and October 1971.

TABLE XI. ACCEPTING HOUSES' BALANCE SHEET, YEAR END

(*£ million*)

Current and deposit accounts

Liabilities	1966	1971	Assets	1966	1971
U.K. banks	227	855	Coin, notes and Bank balances	1	1
Other U.K. residents	474	1,127	Balances with other U.K. banks	250	512
Overseas residents	434	1,355	Money at call and short notice	72	180
			Local authority loans	186	430
			Sterling bills discounted	33	34
			U.K. Government stocks	75	110
			Advances	529	1,751
			Other assets	136	342
			Acceptances	271	334
Total	£1,135	£3,337	Total	£1,553	£3,694

(*Source: B.E.Q.B.*)

Examination of the assets shown in Table XI reveals the relative importance of the different classes of business undertaken by the accepting houses and the rapid rate at which certain items expanded in the late 1960s. On the liabilities side the expansion of the deposits of other U.K. residents must be considered significant to the domestic money supply (*see* VI, **37, 38**).

THE CAPITAL MARKET AND THE GENERAL PUBLIC

25. Savings. The source of most capital is the savings of individuals and business firms. More than half of this total derives from the undistributed profits of limited liability companies and is employed for their own expansion or renewal.

26. Investment institutions. The individual may employ savings through the media of a large number of institutions. He may purchase new issues of shares, debentures or Government stock through a bank, a stockbroker or on occasion an issuing house. His savings may also find their way on to the capital market through his savings account, life assurance policy, superannuation contributions or deposits with a building society or finance house. It is with the part played by these institutions in the provision of capital that we are now concerned.

INVESTMENT TRUSTS

27. Definition. These limited liability companies which specialise in the investment of funds raised through shares or debentures are not trusts in the legal sense. They are not governed by trust deeds which lay down the terms for the management of trust funds. There are currently some 300 investment trusts with assets amounting to £4,519 million at the end of 1971. Of this total overseas investments amounted to £1,505 million.

28. Mode of operation. Expansion takes place either by ploughing back a portion of profits or by issuing new shares. In determining the distribution of their assets the investment trusts will take into the balance prospective capital values and yields. Post-war this has resulted in a heavy concentration upon ordinary shares since the real values of fixed-interest securities have been steadily eroded by inflation.

UNIT TRUSTS

29. Definition. They differ from investment trusts in that they require Board of Trade authorisation, function under trust deeds and are supervised by trustees. At the end of 1971 their total assets amounted to £1,322 million of which £138 million was invested overseas.

30. Mode of operation. Unit trusts, unlike investment trusts, are "open-ended" in that expansion is not limited by the need to make a new share issue. In place of share capital units are sold which give the owner the right to a part of the benefits which derive from the trust's assets. The market value of units reflects the market value of these assets. Units can always be sold to or bought from the trust managers. As more are bought so the managers are able to make further investments and the trust expands.

FINANCE HOUSES

31. Definition. The finance houses are significant to the capital market in providing a major source of "medium-term loans," *i.e.* from six months to five years. There are well over 1,000 companies engaged in this business but the bulk of transactions is concentrated in about twenty major companies who are members of the Finance Houses Association and a number of smaller companies who are members of the Industrial Bankers Association. The majority of these companies are a subsidiary of the commercial banks.

NOTE: The term "industrial banker" has no special significance. Their business is similar to that of the finance houses.

32. Assets. By far the greater part of the business undertaken by these companies is in the form of hire-purchase finance. The purchaser makes a down-payment followed by instalments over an agreed period of time. The instalments include an element of interest.

The period of repayment varies with the type of product although it should be noted that the only items financed are of a durable or semi-durable nature. The object here is to give the finance house some degree of security. More than half of hire-purchase business is in private and commercial vehicles for periods ranging up to three years. A further quarter is in furniture and much of the remainder is in radios, television and domestic equipment normally over periods shorter than three years. Of relatively minor importance is the hire-purchase credit employed for the purchase of industrial and farm equipment where repayment may be made over periods up to five years.

Apart from direct transactions with the purchaser the finance houses make "block discounts" for retailers. In this case the retailer obtains an advance against the security of hire-purchase paper which he repays as he receives the instalments of the purchaser.

Other assets are advances and loans to commercial and industrial companies. Retailers' stocks of vehicles are frequently financed in this way.

Until September 1971 the finance houses observed no fixed liquidity rules but had an eye to the monthly inflow of funds in relation to quick liabilities. On the other hand the Industrial Bankers Association imposed the rule on its members that they should hold liquid assets in the form of cash and Treasury bills at the ratio of 10 per cent of deposit liabilities. The introduction of the new reserve assets requirement in 1971 applied a minimum reserve ratio of 10 per cent to *all* finance houses.

33. Liabilities. The finance houses' reliance on funds from the joint-stock banks has been severely curtailed by recurrent post-war restrictions on bank advances. Restrictions upon capital issues have curbed expansion based upon increased share capital. The principal source of funds has therefore been deposits. Industrial and commercial concerns are the chief depositors of the members of the Finance Houses Association while the smaller companies of the Industrial Bankers Association rely primarily on the deposits of the general public.

Most deposits are at three or six months' notice and the rate of interest which varies with the period of notice ranges upward from Bank Rate. It is therefore well in excess of the deposit rate paid by the clearing banks.

34. Hire-purchase controls. The great expansion of this form of credit has led the Government to introduce hire-purchase controls as part of their efforts to regulate demand. These controls take the form of specified minimum down-payments and maximum repayment periods.

It is clear that these regulations have a powerful impact upon the sales of consumer durables This is especially true of motor vehicles. Therefore, while a dampening of consumer demand may be achieved there will also be discriminatory effects between consumer purchases. Moreover, it is questionable whether in the long run there is much restriction of total demand. Expenditure upon down-payments and instalments may simply be transferred to other products.

BUILDING SOCIETIES

35. Definition. There are rather more than 600 societies registered as members of the Building Societies Association. This does not include the Halifax Building Society which is the biggest, holding 15 per cent of total building-society assets, but which is no longer a member.

The societies are mutual or non-profit-making corporate bodies whose historical purpose has been the promotion of thrift and home-ownership.

36. Liabilities. Liabilities are made up almost entirely of shares and deposits. A "share" in this context has a different meaning to its ordinary usage. It is not marketable but withdrawable on terms which do not differ greatly from those governing deposits. Theoretically, shares require longer notice of withdrawal than deposits and yield on average a $\frac{1}{2}$ per cent higher rate of interest. In practice, both shares and deposits may well be repaid on demand. It is therefore not surprising that in recent years there has been an increasing preference for shares which now represent about 90 per cent of total liabilities.

There are more than 4 million investors in the movement

and the average holding is relatively small. This feature is encouraged by the societies who dislike the volatility of large holdings in an enterprise where semi-permanent investment is desirable.

37. Assets. Mortgages, chiefly on private houses, account for more than 80 per cent of total assets. These loans are limited statutorily to first mortgages on freehold or leasehold estate in the U.K. and are repaid in regular instalments over periods ranging normally from ten to twenty-five years. There is therefore a regular annual turnover of a substantial fraction of total assets as repayments are made and new mortgages advanced.

As a liquidity reserve against the contingency of withdrawals, the societies hold trustee securities and cash, chiefly in bank balances. A condition of membership of the Building Societies Association is that this reserve should not fall below $7\frac{1}{2}$ per cent of total assets. In practice the societies maintain a substantially higher ratio.

38. Economic significance. The operations of the building societies are significant to the rate of investment since their interest rate policy will have a direct bearing upon the level of activity in a major area of the economy, the building industry.

House-building is highly dependent upon the availability of building-society finance which in turn depends upon the adequate influx of funds from the public. The level of deposits will be largely determined by the rate of interest offered by the societies in comparison with rates obtainable elsewhere. In general, the societies favour stable interest rates so that if other rates are rising and building-society rates remain unchanged there is likely to be a shortage of funds and depression in the building industry.

INSURANCE COMPANIES

39. The work of the insurance companies. There are about 500 companies in the U.K. engaged in insurance business of which about half are members of the British Insurance Association. Their activities fall into two groups, "life" and "general," the latter including fire, accident and marine insurance.

The distinction is significant to the supply of capital since life assurance gives rise to long-term contracts, the accumulation of very large funds and their employment in long-term investments. On the other hand, general insurance is short term in character and involves holding contingency reserves in assets which can be quickly realised without capital loss in order that claims can be met.

In "general" insurance, overseas business is twice the volume of domestic business and involves holding substantial assets overseas. This aspect of insurance work makes a worthwhile contribution to Britain's invisible exports.

40. Distribution of assets. Table XII gives an approximation of the normal distribution of assets of members of the British Insurance Association in respect of their domestic business.

TABLE XII. DISTRIBUTION OF DOMESTIC INSURANCE ASSETS OF INSURANCE COMPANIES

	Life funds % *of total*	*General funds* % *of total*
Assets		
Mortgages	14	6
British Government securities	28	37
Commonwealth Government stocks	2	2
Foreign Government stocks	1	1
Debentures and loan stock	14	13
Preference stocks and shares	7	6
Ordinary stocks and shares	17	19
Real property and ground rents	10	7
Other investments	7	9
Total	100	100

NATIONAL SAVINGS AND TRUSTEE SAVINGS BANKS

41. National Savings Bank. Established in 1861 as the Post Office Savings Bank, the National Savings Bank has grown to be one of the largest organisations of its kind in the world and handles well over 100 million transactions annually. Deposits up to a maximum of £10,000 and withdrawals up to £10 on demand may be made at some 21,000 post offices.

Interest is paid at the statutory rate of $3\frac{1}{2}$ per cent and the first £21 interest is annually exempt from income tax. Deposits are handed over to the National Debt Commissioner for investment in Government stock.

42. Trustee Savings Banks. These are local banks and are to be found in the majority of towns and cities in the U.K. They have in total over 9 million active accounts. The banks are linked through the Trustee Savings Banks Association which has certain co-ordinating functions. They are inspected by a statutory body, the Trustee Savings Banks Inspection Committee, which submits an annual report to Parliament. The banks maintain two departments, "Ordinary" and "Special Investment." Like Post Office savings, Ordinary Department deposits have a ceiling of £10,000 and yield $3\frac{1}{2}$ per cent interest with income-tax relief on the first £15. In the Special Investment Department, deposits have a ceiling of £10,000 and yield a rather higher rate of interest. In 1965 the Trustee Savings Banks were given the power to provide current accounts with cheque facilities.

Ordinary Department deposits are invested in the same way as National Savings. Special Investment Department deposits are invested in Government-guaranteed and local authority stocks and local authority mortgages.

SUPERANNUATION AND PENSION FUNDS

43. A growth sector. The superannuation and pension funds of public corporations, local authorities and industrial and commercial companies represent in the post-war period one of the fastest-growing sectors of the U.K.'s financial organisation. Possibly one-quarter of the inflowing funds are placed with life assurance offices, the remainder being self-administered. Some funds have full-time investment managers. Others rely on consultants, particularly merchant bankers. They play a significant part in the resources available to the capital market.

44. Distribution of assets. Table XIII gives an approximation of the normal distribution of assets. Earlier in the century the trust deeds governing these funds usually limited investment to trustee securities. Inflationary pressures which bring about demands for higher pensions have led them increasingly to look for high-yielding but safe long-term investments, *i.e.* there has been a continuing movement into equities.

TABLE XIII. DISTRIBUTION OF ASSETS OF SUPERANNUATION AND PENSION FUNDS

Assets	% of total
British Government securities	34
Overseas Government securities	3
Local authority securities	6
Company debentures	12
Preference shares	4
Ordinary shares	21
Mortgages	2
Real estate	3
Cash and other assets	15
Total	100

ISSUING HOUSES

45. Functions. The issuing houses are a group of merchant banks and other financial institutions who serve as intermediaries in the provision of industrial and commercial capital. They may also engage in other activities as accepting houses, investment banks or managers of investment trusts. Some sixty companies are members of the Issuing Houses Association.

Essentially, they are concerned with raising new capital from the general public for the formation of new public companies, the expansion of existing ones or the conversion of private companies. They advise their clients on the best terms for a new issue and make themselves responsible for raising the whole amount. Although they have large resources they are unlikely themselves to take up more than a small portion of any new issue. Their function is to underwrite the issue guranteeing to purchase at a discount any shares not taken up by the public. As part of this function they will subcontract to institutional investors such as the insurance companies.

The trend towards large-scale business units achieved through mergers and take-overs has meant increased business for the issuing houses. Because of their specialised technical knowledge they can give expert advice on the methods and terms of amalgamation.

THE STOCK EXCHANGE

46. Organisation and function. The London Stock Exchange (together with a number of provincial stock exchanges of much less importance) provides a highly organised market in both Government and company securities. As the description suggests, it serves the primary purpose of trading in existing stock although to a limited extent new capital may be raised by private placing through the Exchange.

Stockbrokers buy and sell securities on behalf of customers, dealing frequently with jobbers. Jobbers buy and sell on their own behalf and are always ready to quote a price for the securities in which they specialise. A profit is taken between buying and selling prices.

47. Economic significance. The Stock Exchange is important in giving an element of liquidity to long-dated and fixed investment. The presence of buyers and sellers enables a holder to encash his investment at any time or a saver to find a profitable outlet for his savings.

48. Conclusion. From this examination of the markets in credit and capital it is clear that the would-be borrower has many alternatives to the commercial banks in his quest for loanable funds. It therefore follows that the authorities must take account of them when pressing their monetary policy.

PROGRESS TEST 8

1. Distinguish between the markets in credit and capital. **(1, 2)**

2. Outline the main classes of business in which the London Discount Market engages. **(4)**

3. Why may adaptability be claimed as a major characteristic of the London Discount Market? **(5–12)**

4. In what sense does the London Discount Market occupy a central position in the monetary system. **(13)**

5. Describe the work of the accepting houses. **(16–23)**

6. Describe the nature of the "euro-markets." **(19)**

7. Distinguish between investment trusts and unit trusts. **(27, 29)**

8. Compare the modes of operation of investment and unit trusts. **(28, 30)**

9. Assess the relative importance of the various assets of the finance houses. **(32)**

10. From what sources do the finance houses obtain funds? **(33)**

11. How important is building society activity to the economy as a whole? **(38)**

12. How do insurance companies deploy their investment funds? **(40)**

13. To what extent are the National Savings and Trustee Savings Banks a useful source of capital for investment in the private sector? **(41, 42)**

14. What part do superannuation and pension funds play in the capital market? **(43, 44)**

15. Describe the operations of the issuing houses. **(43)**

16. What is the economic significance of the Stock Exchange? **(47)**

CHAPTER IX

MONETARY POLICY, 1951–1971

BACKGROUND TO THE REVIVAL OF MONETARY POLICY

1. Loss of confidence in monetary policy, 1931. In the depth of the depression of 1931 a flexible monetary policy (*i.e.* one based upon a moving Bank Rate) was abandoned in favour of cheap money. During the following twenty years Bank Rate was held at 2 per cent save for a short period in 1939 when it stood at 4 per cent and then 3 per cent. It was argued that a falling price level which increased the real value of money equally increased the burden of servicing the National Debt (*see* IV, 5–8). It followed that there was a greater likelihood of revived investment if the businessman could borrow cheaply. In the event, it was not until 1938 that the economy began to accelerate.

2. Cheap war-finance, 1939–45. During the war it was considered desirable to continue a cheap money policy in order to minimise the cost of the vast increase in Government borrowing. In this period the National Debt grew from £7,000 million to £24,000 million. Much of the new borrowing was short term, either against Treasury Deposit Receipt or from the banks on short-dated bonds. This method was consistent with keeping interest rates low but was potentially inflationary. It was recognised that after the war there would be a strong tendency for the general public to seek to encash these liquid assets in order to increase both consumption and investment expenditure. This excessive liquidity in the economy was to remain a problem throughout the 1950s.

3. Dalton's low interest rate policy, 1945–47. Post-war, the British Government was committed to a policy of full employment and rapid reconstruction. As Chancellor of the Exchequer, Hugh Dalton forced interest rates still lower in the belief that this action was consistent with these objectives. Despite the retention of wartime controls on both home markets and imports this policy generated powerful inflationary pressures and a balance of payments crisis in 1947.   Dalton was replaced at the Treasury by Sir Stafford Cripps and from 1948 onwards an active fiscal policy was deemed to be the principal instrument of economic management.

4. Moving interest rates after 1951.   Even with severe taxation inflation continued with a resulting devaluation in 1949.   Renewed pressure on the balance of payments induced fresh economic thinking and in 1951 a flexible monetary policy was tentatively reactivated as an instrument of economic management.   Somewhat cautiously Bank Rate was raised from 2 to $2\frac{1}{2}$ per cent.   Thereafter, the economy was to be controlled through the "package deal," a combination of fiscal, monetary and physical measures.

5. Five Bank Rate cycles, 1951–71.   In the period 1951–71 there can be discerned four complete cycles in which Bank Rate rose and then fell.   It will be observed that in cycles II, III, IV and V Bank Rate reached one peak and fell only to rise again to a second peak.   The fifth cycle is still incomplete.

(a) Cycle I. November 1951–December 1954.
(b) Cycle II. January 1955–December 1959.
(c) Cycle III. January 1960–January 1964.
(d) Cycle IV. February 1964–September 1967.
(e) Cycle V. October 1967–

Within these periods the monetary impact of variations in Bank Rate was reinforced by Treasury directives, Special deposits and restrictions upon consumer credit.

CYCLE I. NOVEMBER 1951–DECEMBER 1954

6. Chronicle of events.

November 1951. Bank Rate rises from 2 to $2\frac{1}{2}$ per cent. Banks requested to restrict lending to those activities in the national interest.

February 1952. Consumer loan terms imposed for the first time on four groups of goods: cars and motor cycles;

furniture; cookers and water-heaters; other durables.   Minimum down-payment and maximum repayment periods specified.

March 1952.   Bank Rate rose from 2½ to 4 per cent.   Further Treasury directive.

September 1953.   Bank Rate fell from 4½ to 3½ per cent.

May 1954.   Bank Rate fell from 3½ to 3 per cent.

July 1954.   All consumer credit restrictions removed.

7. Reasons for reactivating monetary policy.   There were a number of developments in the period 1945–51 which led to the reactivation of monetary policy:

(*a*) *The Government was committed to full employment but danger of recession did not arise.*   Reconstruction needs were more far-reaching than had first been anticipated and the pressure of demand was sustained.   The labour force was in fact over-extended.

(*b*) *Rises in food prices, particularly imports, resulted from world scarcities, devaluation and the Korean War.*   In a tight labour market it was impossible to resist the consequent demands for higher wages.   In the absence of any monetary barriers these higher costs were simply handed on in higher prices.

(*c*) *The abnormal liquidity of the general public and the banking system remained unabsorbed.*   The maturing financial assets accumulated during the war were now expressing themselves in two ways:

(*i*) A greater capacity by the banks to make advances since their liquidity ratios were extraordinarily high.

(*ii*) A greater capacity by the consumer and the investor to spend since they now had cash.

This liquidity was increased by the growth of financial institutions, particularly the building societies and the hire-purchase companies.

(*d*) *The continuing weakness of sterling abroad* added to the belief that the time was ripe to reinforce fiscal policy as an instrument of economic mangement, particularly since direct phsyical controls had fallen into disrepute.

8. Obstacles to the new monetary policy.   In reactivating monetary policy the authorities were from the outset inhibited in the use of the traditional instruments of control by their responsibilities in respect of National Debt management.

(a) *Excessive liquidity of the banking system.* One of the very reasons which made the reintroduction of an active monetary policy desirable was itself an obstacle. During the war, in the absence of opportunities for lending to the private sector, the banks had accumulated a large volume of Government short-term paper. A part of this was made up of Treasury Deposit Receipts, a form of compulsory wartime lending to Government. The result was a liquidity ratio in 1951 of 39 per cent. This position put the banking system out of reach of normal restrictive measures.

(b) *Continued Government borrowing.* After 1945, Government was committed to a vast social programme and to the reconstruction of industries which had been nationalised. The accompanying capital expenditure could not be met solely from current taxation. Therefore, for the first time in peace Government became a regular net borrower. Consequently, in pursuing monetary policy the authorities were impeded by the difficulties of refinancing wartime issues at the same time as they found it necessary to sell fresh debt.

9. Action taken. In view of the difficulties action was taken in a number of ways which differed from the traditional methods.

(a) *Bank Rate.* In November 1951 Bank Rate was hesitatingly raised from 2 to $2\frac{1}{2}$ per cent. However, a special Treasury bill rediscount rate was introduced at $\frac{1}{2}$ per cent below Bank Rate. This meant that the discount houses would still be able to satisfy their marginal borrowing requirements at the Bank at 2 per cent. Nevertheless, the Bank let it be known that it would no longer relieve money shortage in the market by purchases through the special buyer at market rates. If the discount houses were short of money they were once more under the traditional risk of having to borrow at a penal rate from the Bank.

(b) *Capital issues.* More restrictive instructions were given to the Capital Issues Committee in respect of applications to make new share issues.

(c) *Treasury directive.* The banks were requested to

confine their lending to those activities in the national interest.

(d) *Serial Funding Stocks.* An attempt was made to reduce abnormal post-war liquidity, particularly of the banks, through a "forced funding" operation. Serial Funding Stocks to the value of £1,000 million and yielding $1\frac{3}{4}$ per cent were offered in exchange for Treasury bills. In effect the banks were compelled to accept £500 million, thus converting liquid assets of this value to investments. Their liquidity ratios were immediately reduced from 39 to 32 per cent.

10. Development of the interest rate weapon. By 1952 the balance of payments had improved but the reserves were insufficiently strong to take risks. In view of the fact that international interest rates were rising and could potentially attract funds out of sterling the decision was taken to raise Bank Rate from $2\frac{1}{2}$ to 4 per cent. It was also felt that this rise would relieve inflationary pressures in investment in fixed capital and stocks. By 1953 the balance of payments situation was sufficiently healthy to permit a measure of reflation and, after a concessionary Budget, Bank Rate was reduced in the September from 4 to $3\frac{1}{2}$ per cent. Simultaneously, the special rediscount rate for Treasury bills (previously $\frac{1}{2}$ per cent below Bank Rate) was merged with Bank Rate. In 1954 the external position continued to be sound and therefore in the hope of stimulating a more rapid rate of growth Bank Rate was reduced in May from $3\frac{1}{2}$ to 3 per cent.

11. The "package deal." During this first Bank Rate cycle it was clear that the monetary weapon had been restored to favour. However, from the 1952 Budget onwards it was seen as part of a "package deal" of measures which were primarily fiscal but which also included direct controls.

CYCLE II. JANUARY 1955–DECEMBER 1959

12. Chronicle of events.

January 1955.　Bank Rate rises from 3 to $3\frac{1}{2}$ per cent.
February 1955.　Reimposition of hire-purchase restrictions.
February 1955.　Bank Rate rises from $3\frac{1}{2}$ to $4\frac{1}{2}$ per cent.

July 1955.   Banks requested to make "a positive and signi-
ficant reduction in bank advances." Interpreted as
meaning 10 per cent.   Hire-purchase restrictions tightened.
February 1956.   Bank Rate rises from 4½ to 5½ per cent.
Hire-purchase restrictions made still more severe.
February 1957.   Bank Rate falls from 5½ to 5 per cent.
September 1957.   Bank Rate rises from 5 to 7 per cent.
Treasury directive that "average level of advances for the
next twelve months be held at the average level for the last
twelve months."
March 1958.   Bank Rate falls from 7 to 6 per cent.
May–November 1958.   Bank Rate falls from 6 to 4 per cent.
July 1958.   All Treasury directives withdrawn.
October 1958.   All hire-purchase restrictions removed.

13. Deterioration of gold and dollar reserves 1954–55.   The
Radcliffe Committee suggested that in 1954 the authorities
went too far in stimulating demand and were slow to recognise
the signs of inflation.   In the event the removal of controls
brought an investment boom, a current account deficit and a
deterioration in gold and dollar reserves.   Only in January
1955 was Bank Rate raised from 3 to 3½ per cent.   This
measure was indecisive and in the following month Bank Rate
was again raised to 4½ per cent and hire-purchase controls were
reimposed with the object of reducing consumption and
investment demand and easing the strain on the reserves.

14. Contrasting budgetary and monetary measures.   Such
was the confidence that the authorities placed in the newly
developed monetary weapon that in 1955 the Chancellor felt
able to deliver an expansionary Budget.   Any error in the
direction of inflation was to be corrected by "the resources of a
flexible monetary policy."

15. Reduction of the banks' liquidity.   Early in 1955 an
Exchequer surplus and sterling receipts by the Exchange
Equalisation Account made possible the reduction of outstanding Treasury bills to the value of £373 million.   Of these
the banks held £350 million and their liquid assets were
correspondingly reduced.   Liquidity ratios stood at 30 per
cent and it appeared that traditional monetary measures could
now be made wholly effective.

16. An over-estimate of the effectiveness of monetary measures. Despite the higher Bank Rate of $4\frac{1}{2}$ per cent and the reduced liquidity of banks the level of demand continued to rise excessively and the balance of trade remained adverse. The accompanying expansion of bank advances was financed by the sale of investments, a switch that the banks were able to accomplish easily since they were well supplied with short-dated Government stock.

By the end of July the Chancellor felt compelled to make a direct request to the banks for a "positive and significant reduction in their advances over the next few months." He also announced a tightening of hire-purchase restrictions and a reduction in the rate of public investment. It appeared that a flexible monetary policy was not achieving the desired effect.

The balance of payments continued to be heavily adverse and in October a supplementary Budget was announced in which both purchase tax and profits tax were raised.

17. Continued expansion of bank advances. Although at the beginning of 1956 the external position had improved the authorities considered the level of domestic demand to be excessive. In February, Bank Rate was raised from $4\frac{1}{2}$ to $5\frac{1}{2}$ per cent and hire-purchase restrictions were stiffened. Investment allowances were withdrawn and the Capital Issues Committee and the banks were requested to maintain stringency in dealing with applications to borrow. The request to the banks was reinforced in the Budget speech when the Chancellor declared the need to curtail bank deposits by debt-funding operations.

Despite these measures, bank advances continued to rise throughout the first half of 1956 until the Chancellor took the unprecedented step of summoning the representatives of the banks to a meeting at which he asked that "the contraction of credit should be resolutely pursued."

The external position improved in the second half of 1956 and interest rates were permitted to decline. In February 1957, Bank Rate was reduced from $5\frac{1}{2}$ to 5 per cent "as an adjustment to technical conditions". It was emphasised that this was not to be interpreted as a relaxation of monetary discipline.

18. Sterling crisis, 1957. In the first half of 1957 the economy began to expand again, bank advances rose rapidly and there were fears of a further inflationary spiral. The resulting loss of foreign confidence in Britain's ability to adhere to a $2·80 parity coupled with rumours of a revaluation of the German mark brought a flight from sterling. Although there was a substantial surplus in the balance of payments on current account this outflow of short-term capital produced a heavy deficit on capital account. The exchange rate was forced to the lower limit of $2·78.

In September Bank Rate was raised by 2 to 7 per cent and the banks were required to hold the level of their advances for the following twelve months at the average level for the preceding twelve months.

19. An expansionary monetary policy. In 1958, with the balance of payments on current account strongly in surplus and unemployment figures rising, there seemed good grounds for reflationary monetary measures. In March Bank Rate was reduced to 6 per cent and between May and November, by stages, to 4 per cent. In July all restrictions upon bank lending were lifted and in October all hire-purchase controls were removed. In July, capital issues controls were eased and, in February 1959, removed in respect of domestic share issues.

There were no further reductions in Bank Rate during 1959 although heavy purchases by the authorities of gilt-edged securities brought a decline in rates on short- and long-term Government debt, *i.e.* monetary policy continued to be expansionary.

20. The results of an expansionary policy. Between 1958 and 1959 the price level remained relatively stable while output increased and unemployment declined. However, the balance of payments became gradually less favourable and by the last quarter of 1959 showed a small deficit. The authorities now began to evince some concern.

CYCLE III. JANUARY 1960–JANUARY 1964

21. Chronicle of events.

January 1960. Bank Rate rises from 4 to 5 per cent.

April 1960. No Treasury directive but "official concern" made known. Special deposits of 1 per cent called for the first time. Hire-purchase restrictions reimposed.

June 1960. Bank Rate rises from 5 to 6 per cent. Further call for special deposits of 1 per cent.

November 1960. Bank Rate falls from 6 to 5½ per cent.

December 1960. Bank Rate falls from 5½ to 5 per cent.

January 1961. Hire-purchase controls relaxed.

July 1961. Bank Rate rises from 5 to 7 per cent. Further call for special deposits of 1 per cent. Indication to banks that the authorities wished this call to have an impact on advances and not investments as had previously been the case.

October 1961. Bank Rate falls from 7 to 6½ per cent.

November 1961–*January* 1963. Bank Rate falls by stages from 6 to 4 per cent.

May, September, December 1962. All Special deposits gradually released.

May 1962. Informal advice to the banks that the authorities no longer concerned.

June 1962. Hire-purchase controls relaxed.

22. Development of a sterling crisis, 1960. In the first half of 1960 the balance of payments showed a marked deficit on both current and capital account. Paradoxically, foreign currency reserves increased. The explanation lay in the attraction of short-term foreign funds by the higher interest rates which resulted from the rise in Bank Rate from 4 to 5 per cent in January and from 5 to 6 per cent in June. The April Budget was on the whole expansionary but additional monetary restrictions were imposed with two calls for Special deposits and the revival of hire-purchase controls.

During this period the rate of growth declined without any improvement in the balance of payments. In the second half of the year the position worsened but foreign funds continued to flow into London with the result that the reserves in fact increased. Since these funds could be withdrawn with equal rapidity and with potentially calamitous results for the exchange rate, the authorities were moved to reduce Bank Rate in two stages from 6 to 5 per cent. Despite their anxiety that these reductions should not be interpreted as any relaxation of domestic credit policy, a course unwarranted by the balance of payments situation, hire-purchase controls were relaxed in January 1961.

23. Sterling crisis, 1961. Foreign funds began to leave London in February 1961, in anticipation of revaluations of the German mark and the Dutch guilder. Overseas central bank assistance staved off the immediate threat but the reserves continued to decline even though the underlying balance of payments position was beginning to improve. When the crisis reached its peak in July, a number of severe restrictive measures were imposed by the Chancellor, Selwyn Lloyd.

(a) *Bank Rate* was raised from 2 to 7 per cent.

(b) *Special deposits.* A call was made for a further 1 per cent.

(c) *Estimated Government expenditure* for the year 1962–63 was cut back.

(d) *Purchase tax and customs and excise surcharges of 10 per cent* were imposed for the first time.

(e) *Embryonic incomes policy.* The Chancellor called for "a pause in the growth of wages, salaries and dividends."

(f) *Drawing rights* at the International Monetary Fund were exercised to the value of $2,000 million.

24. Recovery. In the second half of 1961 the balance of payments showed some improvement. Since the end of 1960, the trend in imports and growth had been downwards while the unemployment figures rose steadily. These trends were accelerated by the July measures and by October the authorities felt able to reduce Bank Rate from 7 to $6\frac{1}{2}$ per cent.

Although in 1962, industrial production began to expand unemployment figures remained abnormally high. Consequently, between November 1961 and January 1963 the economy was given further stimulus with reductions in Bank Rate by four stages to 4 per cent. Between May and December 1962 all special deposits were released and in June 1962 hire-purchase controls were relaxed. Despite these measures there was still slack in the economy and relatively high unemployment figures.

An expansionary Budget in 1963 to supplement the earlier measures finally shifted the economy into top gear. There was a rapid increase in activity and employment but by the end of the year the balance of payments had run into deficit and the reserves recorded a loss of £53 million.

CYCLE IV. FEBRUARY 1964–SEPTEMBER 1967

25. Chronicle of events.

February 1964.   Bank Rate rises from 4 to 5 per cent.

November 1964.   Bank Rate rises from 5 to 7 per cent.

December 1964.   Directive to the banks to confine advances to exports, manufacturing, agriculture, house-buying and house-building.

April 1965.   Call for special deposits of 1 per cent from the banks with the request that the impact should be on advances and not investments.

May 1965.   Directive to the banks to restrict advances, acceptances and commercial bills to a 5 per cent increase over the twelve-month period to March 1966.   This was the first occasion on which a request had been made in respect of acceptances and commercial bills.   A request was also made to the Accepting Houses Committee, the London Discount Market Association and the major operators in the capital market to exercise similar restraint.

June 1965.   Bank Rate falls from 7 to 6 per cent.   Hire-purchase down-payments increased.

February 1966.   Hire-purchase repayment periods decreased.

July 1966.   Bank Rate rises from 6 to 7 per cent.   A Special deposit call for a further 1 per cent bringing the total to 2 per cent.   Hire-purchase controls made more restrictive. The Treasury directive of May 1965 reaffirmed.   Advances restricted to 105 per cent March 1965 level until at least March 1967.   A reminder also of the December 1964 loan priorities.

January 1967.   Bank Rate falls from 7 to $6\frac{1}{2}$ per cent.

March 1967.   Bank Rate falls from $6\frac{1}{2}$ to 6 per cent.

May 1967.   Bank Rate falls from 6 to $5\frac{1}{2}$ per cent.

June–August 1967.   Hire-purchase controls relaxed.

26. Development of a sterling crisis, 1964.   In view of continued weakness in the balance of payments it seemed likely that the authorities had over-accentuated their reflationary measures in 1963.   In February, Bank Rate was raised from 4 to 5 per cent.   There then followed a Budget which in the circumstances was of questionable wisdom.   A small surplus was planned on current account together with a

large net borrowing requirement which could only add to the
pressure of aggregate demand.

The results were:

(a) *Continued expansion* but at a rather slower rate than
in the previous year.

(b) *Some rise in interest rates* but substantially checked by
large purchases of gilt-edged securities by the authorities.

(c) *An increase in the rate of wage and price inflation.*

(d) *An increase in the rate of growth of bank advances and
deposits.*

(e) *A sharp and continued deterioration in the balance of
payments.*

27. Sterling crisis, 1964.   The seriousness of the situation
was at first disguised in the reserves by a continued flow of
foreign funds into London.   The flow was reversed in the
third quarter when the extent of the balance of payments
deficits was appreciated by sterling-holders.   This loss of
confidence was accentuated when after the general election a
magnified version of the legacy which the new Government had
inherited was much publicised.   An imports surcharge in
October and a disinflationary supplementary Budget in
November did nothing to restore foreign confidence.   After
some delay, in late November these measures were reinforced
by a rise in Bank Rate from 5 to 7 per cent.   Sterling-holders
were still not reassured and the exchange rate was under
extreme pressure as funds continued to flow out of London.
The crisis was surmounted only when the authorities quickly
negotiated credit facilities worth $3,000 million with overseas
central banks.   Although the worst was over sterling remained
in some difficulty for the next few months.

28. "Stop" or "go," 1965–67.   During the following two
years there appears to have been a considerable degree of
indecisiveness in determining economic policy objectives.   On
the one hand a substantial body of opinion centred upon the
new Department of Economic Affairs favoured an expansionary
approach even at the risk of further inflation and devaluation.
On the other hand, traditional opinion centred on the Treasury
gave priority to the preservation of the exchange rate even
though this might necessitate severe disinflationary measures.

In the event the economy in this period suffered the disadvantages of both approaches without enjoying any of the benefits.

29. Expansion during 1966. By April 1965 there was little evidence that the measures of the previous November were relieving the pressures within the economy. Prices, wages and production were all rising while unemployment remained low. Nevertheless, the balance of payments had improved. Although an attempt was made to curb bank lending by a call for special deposits, fiscal policy moved in the opposite direction since the net effect of the April Budget could only be expansionary. While planning for an increased Budget surplus on current account, once public capital requirements had been allowed there remained a substantial net borrowing requirement. At the same time exchange control restrictions were made more severe in respect of private overseas investment.

In May, concerned about the rapid expansion of credit, the Treasury issued an extensive directive to the banks and various financial institutions (*see* **25** above). Apparently confident that this measure was sufficient to control the supply of credit in June the authorities lowered Bank Rate from 7 to 6 per cent.

The year closed with the G.N.P. increasing by some 3 per cent, unemployment remaining low at 1·5 per cent and wages and prices continuing their rapid upward spiral by 8 per cent and 5 per cent respectively. What is notable is that in a period of severe credit restraint the money supply nevertheless increased by 6·5 per cent. The balance of payments could scarcely fail to improve upon the disastrous 1964 figure of —£776 million but remained insupportably high at —£342 million. It seemed clear that economic policy would have to be more restrictive if the exchange rate was to be sustained.

30. The economy slows down in 1966. In February, hire-purchase restrictions were intensified. A May Budget increased the level of taxation by some £386 million and a still larger surplus on current account was planned. Nevertheless, the Exchequer had a net borrowing requirement of £287 million whose ultimate effect could only be inflationary.

By July the authorities were clearly anxious about the pressure of demand in the economy and the balance of payments position. There was little foreign confidence in sterling

and heavy selling resulted, accentuated by the attraction of
rising interest rates overseas. In these circumstances Bank
Rate was raised from 6 to 7 per cent and a further call was
made for special deposits. A Treasury directive was issued
and hire-purchase controls stiffened (*see* **25** above). Simultaneously, "the regulator" was used and a standstill imposed
upon prices and incomes for a period of six months to be
followed by a six-month period of severe restraint.

By the end of the year the economy had responded to these
measures. Production was static and the inflation of wages
and prices had slowed to $3\frac{1}{2}$ per cent and $2\frac{1}{2}$ per cent respectively. On the other hand the money supply continued to
grow at about $6\frac{1}{2}$ per cent, the same rate as in the previous
year. The balance of payments deficit was reduced to
£175 million, a substantial surplus having been achieved in
the final quarter.

31. Development of a sterling crisis, 1967.   With unemploy-
ment now standing at about 2 per cent, foreign funds returning
to London and the anticipation of a balance of payments
surplus by the end of the year, it was felt that there was room
for some stimulus to the economy. Between January and
May Bank Rate was reduced from 7 to $5\frac{1}{2}$ per cent.

The Budget was essentially neutral with the estimated
surplus on current account somewhat reduced on the previous
year's figure. However, the capital account showed a marked
upward surge to £1,580 million. This left the Exchequer with
an estimated net borrowing requirement of £943 million. Once
again it was inevitable that this expenditure would ultimately
prove both expansionary and inflationary.

The trade figures for the first two quarters of the year
proved in the event to be disappointing and heavy selling of
sterling resulted. Nevertheless, the authorities found the
continuing unemployment figure of 2 per cent sufficiently high
to justify further stimulus to the economy. In June and
August there was therefore a relaxation of hire-purchase
controls which led to further heavy sales of sterling. When the
deficit in the balance of payments for the third quarter became
known the pressure on the exchange rate increased. The
position was exacerbated by speculation on the prospect of a
devaluation and by the attraction of rising overseas interest
rates.

CYCLE V. OCTOBER 1967–

32. Chronicle of events.

October 1967.   Bank Rate rises from 5½ to 6 per cent.
9th November 1967.   Bank Rate rises from 6 to 6½ per cent.
18th November 1967.   Devaluation.
18th November 1967.   Bank Rate rises from 6½ to 8 per cent.
All financial institutions requested to limit private-sector loans to current level. New loan priorities announced. All hire-purchase terms more restrictive.
March 1968.   Bank Rate falls from 8 to 7½ per cent.
September 1968.   Bank Rate falls from 7½ to 7 per cent.
February 1969.   Bank Rate rises from 7 to 8 per cent.
March 1970.   Bank Rate falls from 8 to 7½ per cent.
April 1970.   Bank Rate falls from 7½ to 7 per cent.
April 1971 Bank Rate falls from 7 to 6 per cent.
July 1971.   Hire-purchase restrictions removed.
September 1971.   Bank Rate falls from 6 to 5 per cent.

33. Sterling crisis and devaluation, 1967. The authorities responded to the new crisis by raising Bank Rate from 5½ to 6 per cent in October and in early November to 6½ per cent. It was quite clear, however, that radical measures would have to be taken if the balance of payments were to be rectified and the prospect that these measures might include devaluation hastened the flight from sterling. In these circumstances the reserves were insufficient to hold the exchange rate and on 18th November the pound was devalued to a new parity of $2·40.

34. Measures which accompanied devaluation. It was apparent that in order to enlist the support of the I.M.F. and foreign central banks severe restrictions would have to be imposed upon the domestic economy:

    (*a*) *Bank Rate* was raised from 6½ to 8 per cent.

    (*b*) *Treasury directive* to all financial institutions to hold private-sector lending (with the exception of export finance) to current levels.

    (*c*) *Hire-purchase controls* were made more restrictive.

    (*d*) *Taxation and public expenditure.* Future tax increases and cuts in public expenditure were announced.

Against this background credits worth about $3,000 million were negotiated with the I.M.F. and foreign central banks.

35. Post-devaluation strategy. The objective was a large and continuing balance of payments surplus to be achieved by diverting additional resources to exports and import saving. Measures were therefore necessary to make room in the economy for additional private investment in these activities. Consumer demand, both public and private, had to be curtailed

In January, the Prime Minister announced cuts in public expenditure over the following two years. This was followed by a severely deflationary March Budget intended to curb consumer spending. Two days later, ever anxious about the record level of interest rates, the authorities felt able to reduce Bank Rate from 8 to $7\frac{1}{2}$ per cent.

36. The results. Perhaps due to rising world demand rather than the more competitive position deriving from devaluation exports expanded strongly in the second half of 1968. However, post-devaluation strategy was frustrated on two important counts.

(a) *Consumer spending increased* instead of declining.

(b) *Imports rose* instead of falling, the rise at least in part being explained by the growth in consumption expenditure.

Prior to the Budget consumer demand had risen in consequence of the warning of stringent tax increases. After the Budget it fell only to rise again towards the end of the year as the rate of personal savings fell.

The overall result was that devaluation was taking longer to produce real benefits than had been anticipated. Sterling was periodically pressed towards the lower exchange limit of $2·38, a pressure which was increased by the unsettled state of world foreign exchange markets, *e.g.* speculation on the possibility of a devaluation of the U.S. dollar, the French franc and revaluation of the German mark. Further measures had now to be taken to strengthen the pound.

37. Credit restriction. On 2nd November, hire-purchase controls were tightened. On 22nd November an import deposit scheme was established and a strong directive issued to the banks (*see* **32** above). These moves represented the most determined attempts yet made to use the regulator.

(*a*) *The import deposit scheme.* A deposit of 50 per cent of the value of the goods was to be made with H.M. Customs and would be repaid 180 days later. This scheme was intended to restrict credit in two ways:

(*i*) *Interest charges* on deposit finance would deter borrowing and hence imports.

(*ii*) *Liquidity of the banks* would be reduced as cash was drawn off for deposits.

The results were not as effective as had been hoped since importers proved willing to pay rates as high as 15 and 16 per cent for loans outside the banks. Moreover, there was a tendency for finance to be provided from foreign sources.

(*b*) *The Treasury directive.* The banks had extreme difficulty in attempting to meet the Treasury's request and at the same time honour their commitments to their customers. Advances to domestic private borrowers in fact increased by £425 million while total bank deposits rose by $7\frac{1}{2}$ per cent during the year ending March 1969.

In view of the banks' lack of success in giving effect to the Treasury request and since by now the cost of bank borrowing was far exceeded by that of other forms of finance, Bank Rate was again raised to 8 per cent on 27th February 1969.

38. Improved balance of payments, 1969–70. During 1969 the restrictive measures of the previous two years began to yield results. By the third quarter there was a seasonally adjusted surplus on current and long-term capital account of £200 million, a substantial improvement on the preceding year.

However, throughout the year the authorities saw no reason to relax their grip on domestic demand. In the Budget, the Chancellor proposed to raise an additional £270 million of net additional revenue. Central Government's net balance which had moved into a surplus of £273 million in 1968–69 (the first surplus since 1962–63), was planned to increase to £800 million in 1969–70, *i.e.* instead of being a net borrower Government had become a net repayer of debt.

The banks, however, continued to experience difficulty in

reducing their lending to the ceiling requested in November 1968.   As an "incentive," the interest payable on special deposits was halved in June, to be restored to normal only when compliance with the ceiling had been achieved.   Despite these urgings, by October bank lending was still some $2\frac{1}{2}$ per cent above the required level.

In the early months of 1970, sterling continued to gain strength and as an indication of their confidence the authorities reduced Bank Rate from 8 to $7\frac{1}{2}$ per cent on 5th March.   This reduction was not to be interpreted as any relaxation in domestic credit policy.   Nevertheless the following month Bank Rate fell a further $\frac{1}{2}$ per cent.

39. Easier monetary conditions, 1970–71.   During 1970 mounting wage claims gave rise to inflationary pressures which caused concern that the strong surplus in the current balance of payments might be quickly eroded.   At the same time the economy was increasingly experiencing the new phenomenon of rising prices accompanied by rising unemployment.   The incoming Government of 1970 made it clear that the control of inflation was a priority but one to be dealt with by resistance to individual wage claims rather than by any attempt to restrict demand.   There was no immediate response to this policy and in the twelve-month period from June 1970 there was a 10 per cent inflation.   The last half of 1971 finally saw a reduction in the rate of inflation to about $2\frac{1}{2}$ per cent for the half year.

Meanwhile unemployment was approaching record post-war levels and mild reflationary measures were adopted in April 1971 in the form of tax concessions and a fall in Bank Rate from 7 to 6 per cent.

These measures were strengthened in July through the use of the purchase-tax regulator and the removal of hire-purchase restrictions.   Further action was taken in September with a reduction of Bank Rate from 6 to 5 per cent followed by the announcement of increases in public expenditure.   By the year end the upward trend in unemployment had still to respond to this stimulus.

SUMMARY AND APPRAISAL OF THE OPERATION OF MONETARY POLICY IN THE 1960s

40. The approach to monetary policy. The 1960s have witnessed spectacular developments in financial institutions and markets both domestic and international. Of necessity therefore the methods of monetary policy were considerably broadened. In the main the approach has been that of the Radcliffe Committee in that the authorities attempted to pay attention to the liquidity position of all sectors of the economy and not simply to one variable, the quantity of money, important as that might be. However, by 1971 the money supply had been reinvested with a significance denied to it by the Radcliffe Committee.

41. Increased emphasis upon the monetary instrument. Conflict has continued between the major policy objectives of an increased growth rate, a stable balance of payments and a high level of employment. In the early part of the period stability in the balance of payments was sought through an accelerated growth rate. Monetary policy was then seen in a subsidiary role, supporting a general "package" of measures. As the conflict between the balance of payments and economic growth loomed larger ever-more reliance had to be placed upon stringent and sustained monetary measures since fiscal and incomes policies appeared to have reached the limits of their effectiveness.

42. International developments, 1958–69. Two major developments after 1958 had great significance for U.K. monetary policy. Firstly, in 1958 the principal European currencies became fully convertible, a factor which led to large and rapid short-term capital movements. Secondly, from a position in the 1950s in which the world suffered from a continuing dollar shortage in 1959 the U.S. balance of payments moved into deficit where it has remained. There has therefore been a dollar surplus.

Two important consequences may be singled out:

(a) *Need for harmony in international interest rates.* It has become increasingly necessary for international interest rates to move broadly in line in order to avoid excessive and unstabilising "hot money" flows.

(b) *Growth of the euro-dollar market.* In 1959, this market barely existed. By the end of 1969 it had grown to some $40 billion. Since the bulk of transactions are centred on London there has been a great impact upon financial institutions and financial markets.

43. The Exchequer borrowing requirement. From a position of approximate balance in 1958–59 the overall deficit of Central Government grew to £1,335 million in 1967–68. The problem of financing this deficit had severe repercussions for monetary policy. In the main, the private sector proved reluctant to lend to Government since fixed interest securities were unattractive in a period of inflation. The borrowing requirement was therefore largely financed by the sterling proceeds which resulted from running down the gold and foreign currency reserves and from overseas borrowing as well as by the increase in the issue of notes and coins which accompanied the expansion of bank deposits. The consequences were inevitably inflationary.

A good deal of effort has been directed to holding expenditure on course and to ensuring that any Government borrowing is financed "legitimately." These efforts met with success. In 1968–69, Government moved into a surplus of £273 million.

44. Monetary significance of developments in financial institutions. At the close of the 1950s the deposit banks accounted for 85 per cent of the total sterling deposits of the U.K. banking sector. By the end of 1968, although their deposits of the accepting houses, overseas banks and other total fell to 75 per cent. At the same time the sterling deposits of the accepting houses, overseas banks and other banks grew from £1,000 million to £3,000 million.

In the same period there was a massive increase in foreign currency deposits associated with the London euro-markets from a few hundred million pounds in 1959 to £16,000 million at the end of 1969. This was accompanied by a 50 per cent increase in the total number of banks in London. The deposit banks were unable to participate to any great extent in this business since their liquidity requirements made it difficult to employ these funds profitably. The result has been that their share of total sterling and foreign currency deposits fell to 50 per cent.

There are a number of implications in these developments:

(a) *Restriction of bank credit.* It would have been increasingly ineffective to attempt to limit total bank credit by imposing restrictions on the deposit banks alone.

(b) *Difficulty of restricting other bank lending.* The balance-sheets of the other banks differ from those of each other and from those of the deposit banks so fundamentally that control over their lending through balance-sheet ratios is made extremely difficult.

(c) *Problems of switching in and out of sterling.* In the case of these other banks the possibility of rapid switches in and out of sterling raises problems for interest rate policy, exchange control and the balance of payments.

In view of the changing financial environment there have been of necessity developments in the application of monetary controls.

45. Developments in the technique of monetary policy. Broadly, the authorities have continued a policy of influencing the cost or availability of credit to the various sectors of the economy. The developments lay in the application of more direct and specific controls and the inclusion within these controls of a widening range of banking and financial institutions. Dissatisfaction with the results of these controls led in 1971 to a reversion to more traditional methods.

Two specific financial sectors which were especially subject to the effects of monetary policy were:

(a) *Hire-purchase finance.* Controls were actively employed during the 1950s but for only short periods. In the 1960s their use was prolonged and stringent.

(b) *Building-society finance.* Due to the stickiness with which building-society interest rates have followed the general upward movement in interest rates there was a reduction in funds available for house-building loans with a consequent effect upon the building industry.

Beyond these specific effects monetary policy has been directed largely to limiting lending by the banking system. In this respect it became apparent that the authorities were having little success in exercising control through open market operations designed to influence liquidity ratios. In the first place, liquidity ratios have remained high even after the introduction of the special deposit scheme in 1960. In the second place open market operations designed to reduce this liquidity were inhibited by the authorities' desire for a pattern of interest rates at a "reasonable" level. More recently there has been a greater willingness to see upward pressure on interest rates take effect and this has given greater latitude for a more flexible approach to debt management.

It was therefore necessary throughout the greater part of the period to place ever-greater reliance upon the Treasury directive. These requests were both quantitative and qualitative in character, *i.e.* loan ceilings have been imposed and priorities established. It was also necessary to extend the coverage of these requests to banks other than the clearing banks and to other financial institutions.

46. Control over the lending of other banks and financial institutions. A cash deposits scheme analogous to the special deposits of the clearing banks was devised for use in periods when moderate rather than severe restraint is desired. It provided for the other banks to make cash deposits with the Bank of England calculated as a percentage of certain of their sterling deposit liabilities. Interest was to be payable at a rate linked to Treasury bill rate.

This scheme was never implemented since conditions called for severe lending restraint, and tight control was exercised through loan ceilings.

There were also difficulties in controlling the lending of institutions outside the banking sector, particularly the finance houses. Hire-purchase controls affected some but not all of their lending activities and therefore it was felt necessary in 1965 to extend requests for loan ceilings to the members of the Finance Houses Association and to the larger non-members.

47. Objections to control by loan ceilings. The short-comings of this method of credit restraint may be listed as follows:

(a) *Directional effects.* The impact of credit restraint is likely to be quite arbitrary, *e.g.* it is probable that large customers will fare better than small businesses even though the latter may be perfectly sound and credit-worthy.

(*b*) *An arbitrary base date.* The selection of a base date against which to establish ceilings is purely arbitrary.

(*c*) *Limitation of competition.* Competition between controlled institutions is inevitably restricted.

(*d*) *Arbitrary decision as to which institutions should be controlled.* Check traders, small finance houses and an increasing number of new merchant banks charging extraordinarily high interest rates (seven in the period June 1968–March 1970) either fell outside the scope of Treasury requests or seemed to ignore them. A period in which money was scarce and the established institutions controlled gave considerable impetus to the growth of sources of credit which sought to avoid co-operation with the authorities' desire for restraint.

48. Effectiveness of monetary policy in the 1960s. It is extremely difficult to assess the extent to which monetary measures alone have accounted for economic trends. In the first place they have invariably formed a part of a complete package of measures and their effects cannot be assessed in isolation. In the second place it is apparent that "business expectations," an independent variable which cannot be predicted, play a great part in either negating or reinforcing policy measures.

However, certain conclusions may be drawn:

(*a*) *Hire-purchase controls* would seem always to produce a marked change in expenditure on the goods affected, *e.g.* in 1966 expenditure on consumer durables declined from £492 million in the second quarter to £404 million in the fourth quarter following the tightening of controls in February and July of that year.

(*b*) *Building loans.* The rate of house-building has also been sensitive to the availability of mortgage finance, *e.g.* in 1965 when such finance was very difficult to find only 48,000 houses were started for private owners in the last quarter of the year compared with 64,000 in the last quarter of the previous year.

(*c*) *Rate of business investment.* There is some broad

support for the view that the rate of investment is affected by the availability and cost of funds but despite intensive research the evidence is imprecise and inconclusive. Moreover, the time-lag between the implementation of policy and discernible results tends to be both long and variable.

(*d*) *Rate of consumption.* The evidence is even more inconclusive although there are some grounds for believing that a really stringent control of bank lending has some impact on consumption expenditure.

49. Conclusion. In conclusion it may be said that the authorities, while attaching considerably more importance to a positive monetary policy than they did ten years ago, do not envisage a time when they will rely upon it as the primary instrument for short-term stabilisation of the economy. Fiscal and monetary policies must work in close harmony. Over-reliance upon one to the neglect of the other will produce results which are either ineffective or damaging. Excessive reliance upon the fiscal weapon as an instrument of disinflation may have dangerous effects upon incentives or the provision of public services. Excessive reliance upon the monetary weapon at a time when there is a large public-sector deficit implies credit restraints so severe that the effects for the whole economy would be entirely unpredictable.

PROGRESS TEST 9

1. Why were interest rates depressed in the period 1931–47? **(1–3)**

2. What is a "package deal"? **(4, 11)**

3. Account for the reactivation of monetary policy in 1951. **(7)**

4. In 1951, what especial difficulties confronted the new monetary policy? **(8)**

5. Account for the 1957 sterling crisis. **(18)**

6. Describe the series of events which led to the 1961 sterling crisis. **(21–23)**

7. What were the manifestations of the 1964 sterling crisis? **(26)**

8. Why might the period 1965–67 be described as one of neither "stop" nor "go"? **(28)**

9. What measures were employed to support the 1967 devaluation? **(34)**

10. What were the results of devaluation? **(36)**

PART THREE

INTERNATIONAL TRADE AND PAYMENTS

CHAPTER X

THE LIBERALISATION OF WORLD TRADE

THE THEORETICAL CASE FOR FREE TRADE

1. The theory of comparative costs. The gains to be derived from international trade are explained by the theory of comparative costs. This theory is best developed in stages, the first of which is the proposition that the immediate cause of international trade lies in absolute differences between domestic and foreign prices.

2. Absolute differences in international prices. Given a rate of exchange between the currencies of two countries it is possible to make direct price comparisons. When price differences exceed transportation costs between these countries it is clearly profitable for them to engage in trade. However, this is not the end of the argument, for we must now discover the reason for these price differences.

3. Absolute differences in international costs. International price differences imply absolute international differences in production costs since long-run prices, whatever the degree of competition or monopoly, must at least cover long-run costs.

So far the theory seems to make the obvious suggestion that trade between two countries will be profitable when each specialises in the production of those goods for which it has the lowest costs of production. This is not the whole story, however, for trade may still take place in two commodities between two countries and to their mutual benefit even when one country has an absolute advantage in the production of both goods provided that each country has dissimilar cost ratios. This proposition is the core of the theory of comparative cost.

4. Dissimilar cost ratios. The principle may be illustrated by two simple arithmetical examples. Assume in each case trade between two countries only, the U.S.A. and the U.K., and in only two goods, wheat and textiles.

EXAMPLE 1. *The U.S.A. having lower production costs in wheat, the U.K. in textiles.*

Let us assume that in the U.S.A. 10 units of resources (land, labour and capital) will produce either 10 bushels of wheat or 5 yards of cloth and that in the U.K. 10 units of resources will produce either 10 yards of cloth or 5 bushels of wheat. While in this example neither country has an absolute advantage in the production of both goods each has a comparative advantage in the production of one.

If we further assume that the U.S.A. has 300 resource units and the U.K. 200 and that each divides its production evenly between wheat and textiles, total output will be as follows:

TABLE XIV. EXAMPLE OF PRODUCTION FIGURES BEFORE TRADE

	Resource units	Yards of cloth	Bushels of wheat
U.S.A.	300	75	150
U.K.	200	100	50
Total	500	175	200

Let each country now specialise completely in that commodity in which it enjoys a comparative advantage and the result will be as follows:

TABLE XV. PRODUCTION FIGURES AFTER SPECIALISATION

	Resource units	Yards of cloth	Bushels of wheat
U.S.A.	300	—	300
U.K.	200	200	—
Total	500	200	300

As a result of specialisation, the total output of the two countries has been maximised and trade will take place to their mutual advantage at any exchange rate within the limits determined by their respective cost ratios, *i.e.* 5 yards of cloth : 10 bushels of wheat and 5 bushels of wheat : 10 yards of

cloth. At the limits trade may still take place although all the
benefit will be enjoyed by one or the other country.

EXAMPLE 2. *The U.S.A. having lower production costs in both
wheat and textiles.*

More significantly trade may still be mutually advantageous
even though the U.S.A. has an absolute advantage in the
production of both wheat and textiles.

Let us now assume that in the U.S.A. 10 units of resources
will produce 10 bushels of wheat or 9 yards of cloth and that in
the U.K. the same quantity of resources will yield only 4
bushels of wheat or 8 yards of cloth. Again assuming the
U.S.A. to have 300 resource units and the U.K. 200, each
dividing their resources equally between the two goods, the
result will be as follows:

TABLE XVI. PRODUCTION FIGURES BEFORE TRADE, ONE COUNTRY
HAVING AN ABSOLUTE ADVANTAGE

	Resource units	Yards of cloth	Bushels of wheat
U.S.A.	300	135	150
U.K.	200	80	40
Total	500	215	190

If there is now complete specialisation in the products for
which each has a comparative advantage the result will be:

TABLE XVII. PRODUCTION FIGURES AFTER TRADE, EACH COUNTRY
HAVING A COMPARATIVE ADVANTAGE

	Resource units	Yards of cloth	Bushels of wheat
U.S.A.	300	—	300
U.K.	200	160	—
Total	500	160	300

The effect of complete specialisation has been a substantial
increase in total wheat production but a fall in the production
of cloth. The U.K. even when devoting all its resources to this
activity is unable to achieve the previous figures. For this
reason specialisation in the U.S.A. will not be complete and
resources will still be directed to cloth production:

TABLE XVIII. PRODUCTION FIGURES INCREASED EVEN WITH IN-
COMPLETE SPECIALISATION

	Resource units	Yards of cloth	Bushels of wheat
U.S.A.	300	81	210
U.K.	200	160	—
Total	500	241	210

Let us assume that 30 per cent of her resources are so used. In this position total output of both cloth and wheat has been increased as a result of specialisation. Again, at any exchange rate within the limits set by their respective cost ratios each is able to enjoy a higher consumption of both cloth and wheat.

5. Significance of comparative costs. From the foregoing discussion it will be seen that it is differences in "comparative" not "absolute" costs which provide the basis for international trade and that impediments to such trade serve to restrict the growth of total output and rising world living standards.

However, the benefits of increased world output will not be evenly distributed between countries but will depend upon "the terms of trade."

6. The terms of trade. The terms of trade between two countries are dictated by the elasticity of each country's demand for imports relative to the elasticity of the supply of the other country's exports.

In Table XV above if U.S. demand for textiles is relatively stronger than the U.K. demand for wheat then the terms of trade will move in favour of the U.K. A world price for wheat will be established at an exchange ratio approximating to 10 bushels of wheat: 5 yards of cloth. If the terms of trade move against the U.K. the world price of textiles is falling and the new exchange ratio will be closer to 5 bushels of wheat : 10 yards of cloth.

In the inter-war period the terms of trade moved against the primary producing countries in favour of the manufacturing countries since the world price of raw materials and foodstuffs fell more steeply than the world price of manufactures. To this extent the hardships of industrial depression were somewhat mitigated. After 1945 the sharp upturn in the demand of the manufacturing countries for raw materials moved the terms of trade in favour of the primary producers, until 1955. Thereafter, the movement was again generally in favour of the industrial countries.

THE EMPIRICAL ARGUMENT FOR FREE TRADE

7. Great Britain and the free traders. At the close of the Napoleonic Wars British commerce lay strangled by a complex web of import and export duties. Almost every item which entered into trade was subject to taxes upon which Government depended for the greater part of its revenue.

On the other hand British industry had no rival anywhere else in the world and felt in no need of protective customs duties. Rapid industrialisation had built up enormous production potential which required the safety-valve of wider overseas markets. It was argued that lower import duties would reduce the price of food and raw materials. The result would be lower wage and production costs. Moreover, if Britain led the way in lowering duties the foreigner might be induced to follow.

The consequence of these pressures was the great British free trade movement beginning in the 1820s when Huskisson initiated a reduction of duties. The process was continued by Peel and completed by Gladstone. By the 1860s all protective duties had been abolished. There remained only a few "countervailing customs duties" (*i.e.* duties on imports which correspond to internal excise duties).

8. The results of free trade. The full effects of free trading policies can be observed in the extremely rapid expansion of British overseas trade in the years 1850–70. (It should, however, be noted that there also existed other favourable circumstances.)

APPROXIMATE VALUE OF EXPORTS

(£ million)

1850	1854	1860	1870
71	97	135	250

Moreover, as had been hoped, other European nations began to emulate Britain's example in reducing tariffs (*e.g.* Holland, Portugal, Switzerland, Germany, Austria and most notably France as a result of the Cobden Commercial Treaty, 1860).

The last quarter of the century, although a period of depression and falling prices, saw a continued expansion in the volume of British exports.

9. Reaction to free trade. Until 1870 the strength of her industry enabled Britain to enjoy a virtual monopoly of exported manufactures throughout the world. Thereafter, her competitors began to gather strength, their developing industry increasingly sheltered by rising tariffs. In 1880 Germany raised duties and was shortly followed by France. In 1890 the effects of the McKinley Tariff in the U.S.A. were especially severe for U.K. exports. The Dingley Tariff of 1897 finally committed the U.S.A. to a policy of protection and in 1902 Germany followed suit.

At this stage it may be argued that protection was invaluable to the newly developing industrial countries since it assisted them to narrow Britain's lead and, in some industries, to overhaul her. In any event the total volume of world trade continued to expand and by 1914 there had developed an intricate pattern of international specialisation.

10. Economic nationalism, 1920–39. After a short-lived boom the world economy sank into depression. Four years of war had disrupted the pattern of international trade. Old customers had turned to alternative suppliers or had developed domestic sources. Throughout the industrial world unemployment figures rose and international payments were unbalanced. In the prevailing climate of political and economic uncertainty nations everywhere sought self-sufficiency. Reverting to an earlier ideal they believed that only in economic independence could national security be achieved. This thinking made itself manifest in high protective tariffs which aimed hopefully to conserve the domestic market for domestic industry, thus guaranteeing some measure of employment.

11. The consequences for international trade. Attempts by one country to penalise the exports of another could only lead to retaliatory action, to the detriment of both. The volume of world trade therefore shrank. The decline was accelerated by the practice, adopted increasingly after the 1929–31 slump, of bilateral trading agreements which replaced the normal multilateral basis of world trade and payments. (Bilateral trade requires each country to balance its payments separately with all its trading partners. The total volume is therefore dictated by the country with the lower imports. Multilateral trade enables a country with a deficit in one part of the world to finance it with a surplus earned elsewhere. Total trade is maximised.)

12. Britain's return to protection. While Britain remained wedded to the ideal of free trade long after her competitors had taken refuge in protection the slump brought some of her major industries to the verge of collapse. Under mounting pressure from manufacturers the Government agreed to afford a degree of protection to the home market and in 1932 the *Import Duties Act* was passed. Free trade was now a dead letter.

13. Conclusion. In international economic relationships as in domestic affairs, the Second World War provided a radically new approach. It was appreciated that there would need to be a high degree of co-operation between nations if the pre-war stagnation of world trade was not to be repeated.

The objective was to be a balanced expansion of international trade which would lead to rising world living standards. Instrumental to this ulterior goal would be three subsidiary aims:

(*a*) The gradual reduction and final abolition of protective duties and quotas throughout the world (*see* **19–31** below).

(*b*) International co-operation to improve the means of financing world trade (*see* XII, **31–41**).

(*c*) The promotion of investment by the advanced countries in the developing countries in order that the latter might play a fuller part in an expanding world economy (*see* XII, **42–45**).

While it is true to say that the validity of the general

principle of free trade has now been universally accepted there remain certain reservations.

THE CASE FOR PROTECTION

14. Political and strategic reasons. Government economic policies are by no means based solely upon objective economic considerations. Political or social pressures may be such that a Government finds itself impelled to afford protection to a particular sector of the economy. In the U.S.A. powerful sectional interests have frequently been successful in persuading Government in this way to reduce the intensity of foreign competition.

Again, for strategic reasons a country may feel it necessary to develop domestic sources of supply if it believes that complete dependence upon an overseas source may leave it exposed to unwelcome foreign pressures.

In a more extreme way, when there exists the possibility of military confrontation there will be no inclination to assist the opponent's economy by engaging in trade, *e.g.* until June 1971 there was a complete embargo by the U.S.A. on all trade with China.

In short there may be, at least in the short term, a perfectly valid case for restricting foreign trade based upon factors which override purely economic considerations.

15. Assistance for infant industries. Possibly the only sound economic argument in favour of protection is that which claims that it is necessary to give short-term assistance to new industry in order that it may establish itself.

This argument will be particularly valid where there is initially an investment of a high proportion of capital. At first output will be small and unit costs very high. As output expands and the economies of scale are enjoyed, so unit costs fall and the industry becomes more internationally competitive. At this stage it is then desirable that the protective duty should be removed and that the industry should stand on its own feet. The difficulty is that once interests have become entrenched there is likely to be considerable resistance to the removal of the duty.

Moreover, there is always a considerable possibility that an industry will be encouraged which has no real chance of survival in competitive conditions.

16. Correction of the balance of payments. It may be argued that where there is an adverse balance of payments it is legitimate to restrict the volume of imports and to encourage domestic import-displacing industry. However, pre-war experience suggests that such action invites retaliation from the country against whose exports there is discrimination. The problem then escalates.

The General Agreement on Tariffs and Trade (*see* **24**(*b*) below) exceptionally permits this practice but only after the fullest international consultation.

17. Protection against "dumping." It may occur that a foreign producer is able to practise "discriminating monopoly." He produces on a large scale in order to gain the advantage of low unit costs but restricts supply to his home market in order to secure a high price. He then disposes of the surplus overseas at very low prices, if necessary below total unit cost. The British steel market was exposed to such "unfair competition" from the German steel cartel in the 1920s producing, inevitably, a demand for protection which was finally acceded to in 1932.

18. Protection of vested interests. In old-established industries there may be built up a vast stock of fixed capital which will seem of great value to the owners but may in due course become obsolescent. Similarly, the workers in these industries will acquire specialist skills, in which they too have a vested interest.

If such an industry is now faced with a new foreign competitor whose production costs and selling prices are infinitely lower there will be a demand for protection against "unfair" foreign competition. Such was the appeal of the Lancashire cotton industry when faced with competition from Japan and Hong Kong where wage rates were relatively much lower.

A too simplistic economic answer to such an appeal would be that cheap imports could only be of benefit to the U.K. economy as a whole and that it would be better to divert the factors of production currently devoted to cotton manufacture to some other activity commanding a higher return.

However, factors of production in the form of mills, textile machinery, skilled spinners and weavers are relatively immobile. They cannot suddenly be translated into, for example, a motor assembly plant.

Thus, if the running down of an industry is generally agreed to be desirable it may also be conceded that in the short term a degree of protection is necessary to ease the difficulties of reallocating resources.

THE GENERAL AGREEMENT ON TARIFFS AND TRADE (G.A.T.T.)

19. The goal of global multilateral trade. It has been observed that during the Second World War a good deal of thought was directed towards the creation of a liberal, multilateral system of world trade. Close co-operation was envisaged in the field of international trade relations, payments and investment. Wartime planning produced the most striking results in respect of payments and investment with the setting up of the International Monetary Fund and the International Bank for Reconstruction and Development. Co-operation in respect of trade was somewhat delayed.

After the war, it quickly became apparent that the original objective was overly ambitious and, faced with Communist expansion, attention was concentrated upon promoting European co-operation and reconstruction to meet this threat. In the 1950s and 1960s therefore the most notable achievements in liberalising trade have been regional in nature and have been centred upon Europe (*see* **33** (*b*), (*c*) below).

20. The abortive International Trade Organisation (I.T.O.). The end of excessively ambitious international planning was marked by the failure of the U.S. Congress in 1950 to ratify the treaty setting up an International Trade Organisation. The I.T.O. Charter had been signed by fifty-four countries in March 1948 and covered a very wide range of topics including not only trade but also employment, cartels, economic development and state trading.

The failure of the I.T.O. might have signalled the end of any global attack on tariffs but for the almost accidental birth of G.A.T.T.

to take similar action in respect of the trade of those countries less developed than themselves.

26. Operational procedures.

The signatories of G.A.T.T. meet annually and also at special tariff conferences. Between meetings an Intersessional Committee prepares agendas while working parties report on specific topics. The existence of a permanent secretariat adds continually to the work of G.A.T.T. and enables it to behave more like genuine international organisations.

The work falls into three categories:

(a) The elimination of quota restrictions.
(b) The regulation of disputes.
(c) The reduction of tariffs.

27. Elimination of quota restrictions.

For as long as a chronic imbalance remained in payments between the U.S.A. and the rest of the world the majority of signatories took advantage of the balance of payments exception to the general prohibition of quotas. In 1958, the U.S.A. for the first time moved into deficit and the Western European countries were able both to restore the convertibility of currencies and the following year at the Tokyo session of G.A.T.T to reaffirm their intention to abandon the balance of payments escape clause as soon as possible. Subsequently, all the major trading nations gave up the quantitative restrictions which had been justified on these grounds.

The remaining major problems in this area related to restrictions upon agricultural products in which progress has been disappointingly slow.

Countries which still make use of the balance of payments exception are required to hold periodical consultations with G.A.T.T. as a means of exerting pressure upon them. Discussions are also mandatory when new restrictions are to be imposed.

NOTE: When in 1964 Britain imposed a 15 per cent import surcharge as a measure to correct the balance of payments the rules were violated since although it is permissible to employ quantitative restrictions for this purpose an increased tariff may not be so employed. In consultation with G.A.T.T. considerable pressure was exerted for the early removal of this surcharge.

28. Regulation of disputes. It is in this little publicised area that G.A.T.T has enjoyed some of its most notable successes. Previously trade disputes often went unresolved for many years, souring international relations and normally ending in success for the stronger party.

G.A.T.T. has improved matters by providing a world forum before which grievances can be aired and also a formal complaints procedure. Many disputes have been resolved bilaterally, probably assisted by the knowledge that G.A.T.T. stands in the background, *e.g.* the U.K. Government was persuaded to repeal a restriction upon the manufacture of pure Virginia cigarettes when the U.S.A. protested that this violated the General Agreement.

If the dispute is not settled by the parties concerned an appeal may be made to the collective membership. A report is drafted and recommendations made. If these recommendations are not observed the complainant country may be authorised to suspend certain of its trade obligations to the other country *but* only to a degree which will not escalate the dispute, *e.g.* the 1962 "chicken war." The E.E.C. increased rates of duty on poultry imports which were mainly from the U.S.A. The dispute was unresolved and upon appeal to G.A.T.T. it was calculated that U.S. exports had suffered by $26 million in 1963. The U.S.A. was then authorised to reduce concessions to E.E.C. by an amount which would have a similar effect on the Community's trade. Duties were raised on brandy, trucks and other imports by an amount which affected E.E.C. trade by a sum estimated at $25·4 million.

Although in this case the dispute was not settled the main point is that retaliation was limited and there was no further escalation of the problem.

29. Reduction of tariffs. The major achievement of G.A.T.T. has been a series of six tariff conferences (the last being the "Kennedy Round"), at which reductions have been effected on more than 60,000 rates of duty covering more than half the world's trade.

In each new agreement the mfn principle is applied. Before each conference the participants prepare a list of products on which they are prepared to negotiate. Countries are then paired on the "chief supplier" principle, *i.e.* one country negotiates on those products which are chiefly supplied by a second country. The negotiations result in a large number of bilateral agreements which are then incorporated in a single master agreement to which each country appends a signature. All the signatories then enjoy all the concessions which have been made at that conference. A set of bilateral agreements have been in this way made multilateral in effect.

The advantage of this system lies primarily in the time saved and difficulties avoided were a similar volume of concessions to be negotiated independently by separate trade agreements. Moreover, conferences provide an atmosphere in which countries are disposed to be generous since while negotiating they know that they are about to receive many more benefits from other negotiations taking place concurrently.

30. The Kennedy Round. As duties have been lowered negotiations have become tougher and more protracted, the Kennedy Round lasting from May 1964 to June 1967. At this conference the procedure was somewhat different. Instead of negotiations being based upon specific products it was felt that more rapid progress would be made by linear reductions of all national tariffs with minimal lists of excepted goods. In the case of the U.S.A. the Administration had authority to halve the tariff with only ten excepted products and to abolish all duties which did not exceed 5 per cent. The results although not as spectacular as had been hoped were nevertheless most notable.

The major industrial countries reduced tariffs on imports valued at $26 billion in 1964. Some 70 per cent of the reductions were of the order of 50 per cent or more. In the U.K. cuts on industrial imports averaged 38 per cent. The major benefits to U.K. exports have resulted from the reductions made by the E.E.C., U.S.A. and Japan while the same countries have been the principal beneficiaries of the U.K. cuts.

Although progress at this conference was essentially limited to manufactured goods and to tariff restrictions on trade, it is generally agreed that both the scope and scale of the cuts achieved were infinitely more significant than those resulting from any previous negotiations and that for many manufactured products duties will cease to be a restriction to trade.

31. Appraisal of G.A.T.T. In the first place it must be acknowledged that G.A.T.T. has provided a context for orderly international trade negotiations without historical parallel. In its twenty-three years of existence it has achieved a massive reduction of the obstacles to trade throughout the world.

On the other hand its success has been largely confined to trade in manufactured goods. Relatively little progress has been made in respect of agricultural products. This failure has given rise to some scepticism in the developing countries and the likelihood of continuing pressure through U.N.C.T.A.D. for a revision of G.A.T.T.'s rules in a way more favourable to those countries.

NOTE: United Nations Conference on Trade and Development (U.N.C.T.A.D.), first convened in 1964, is supposed to meet every three years.

32. Organisation for Trade Co-operation (O.T.C.). A weakness of the G.A.T.T. arrangements is that they are provisional and may be dissolved at any time. An attempt to rectify this difficulty was made in 1955 when the signatories negotiated an Organisation for Trade Co-operation, which was to be a permanent world organisation to administer G.A.T.T. Due to the opposition of protectionist interests, primarily in the U.S.A., this agreement has never been ratified.

33. Regional co-operation. Co-existent with G.A.T.T., which is concerned with the liberalisation of trade on a global basis, there exist a number of regional arrangements which have been established for a diversity of political and economic reasons. The most important are:

(a) The Sterling Area (see **34–38** below).

(b) The European Economic Community (see **39–48** below).

(c) The European Free Trade Area (see **49** below).

STERLING AREA

34. Origin. In the second half of the nineteenth century a large part of all international trade payments were made

through London and in sterling.   This practice is explained by
the following reasons:

(a) *Britain observed a full gold standard.*   Sterling was
freely convertible to gold and no restriction was placed
upon the import or export of gold.   The world consequently
had full confidence in sterling as a form of international
money.

(b) *The London money market* was a highly sophisticated
mechanism without parallel elsewhere which permitted the
profitable deployment of short-term funds from all over the
world for the primary purpose of financing international
trade.

(c) *The London capital market* was also highly evolved and
dealt in the securities of the entire world.   It was the
principal international source of long-term investment
capital.

(d) *Britain was the world's chief importer* and very many
overseas countries were enabled to enjoy substantial
sterling earnings.   Rather than hold these earnings in gold
reserves in their own countries it paid to put them to profitable use in the London money and capital markets.

35. The sterling area of the 1930s.   When Britain abandoned
the gold standard in 1931 many countries ceased to hold their
reserves in sterling, because of the uncertainty of the exchange
rate of the pound relative to gold and the dollar.   London
therefore declined as the world's financial centre.   Nevertheless, for the other reasons mentioned above (**34** (b), (c) and (d))
some countries continued to link their currencies to sterling.

36. Characteristics of the modern sterling area.   From 1939
until 1958, when sterling convertibility was restored, the main
characteristics of the area were:

(a) *The centralisation of gold and dollar reserves in London.*
The external earnings of the area are pooled and external
payments made from this pool.

(b) *Free convertibility of all sterling area currencies with
each other.*

(c) *Membership based on the Commonwealth countries
(except Canada), Iraq, Iceland, Ireland and Burma.*

(d) *Exchange controls* which restricted the convertibility of sterling area currencies.

(e) *Tariff and quota restrictions* which discriminated against countries outside the area.

Today the last two features have been dropped and membership has further declined so that it remains essentially a number of Commonwealth countries together with the British possessions.

37. The sterling balances. While each member retains independent control over its trade and payments, it pegs the exchange rate of its currency to sterling and holds its reserves in the form of bank deposits, Treasury bills and other U.K. Government securities in London. These are the sterling balances and are temporary in nature since they will be reduced either by the purchase of U.K. exports or by conversion to foreign currencies for the purpose of making payment outside the area.

In principle they represent short- or long-term lending to the U.K. Government initiated by central banks which acquire sterling holdings from their own nationals in exchange for domestic currency.

Sterling balances may also be held by countries outside the area which acquire them for normal trade and financial purposes and by international organisations such as the I.M.F.

38. Prospects. In the decade following the war the sterling area contributed to the liberalisation of world trade and payments by providing a stable multilateral system for its members. Subsequently, this function was largely superseded by the development of a world system which has permitted the restoration of currency convertibility and which has served directly to promote freer trading relations.

Moreover, Britain's greater participation in European economic affairs and the likelihood of entry into the Common Market almost certainly spell the end of a system which in its time has served a very useful purpose.

EUROPEAN ECONOMIC COMMUNITY (E.E.C.)

39. Organisation for European Economic Co-operation (O.E.E.C.). O.E.E.C. was established in 1948 and comprised sixteen countries. Its initial task was the administration of Marshall Aid (American assistance to Europe) in the Joint European Recovery Programme. It then developed as an organisation for general economic co-operation whose major achievement lay in the progressive removal of quantitative restrictions upon European trade assisted by a system of multilateral payments, the European Payments Union. (When in 1958 ten European countries adopted global convertibility of their currencies on current account, the E.P.U. lost its function and was brought to a close.)

40. Organisation for Economic Co-operation and Development (O.E.C.D.). By the close of the 1950s Europe had made considerable progress in the liberalisation of trade and payments, but simultaneously increasing economic interdependence between Europe and North America had brought the need for fresh forms of co-operation. Therefore, in 1961, O.E.E.C. was replaced by O.E.C.D. (To O.E.E.C.'s membership of Austria, Belgium, Denmark, France, Germany, Greece, Iceland, Ireland, Italy, Luxembourg, the Netherlands, Norway, Portugal, Sweden, Switzerland, Turkey and the U.K. were added Canada, Spain and the U.S.A. and, in 1965, Japan.)

Through a series of committees O.E.C.D. seeks to promote co-operation in a wide variety of economic fields and aims at the development of the whole free world. In this respect it is more outward looking than O.E.E.C. which was concerned only with the development of Europe.

41. European Coal and Steel Community. In the early 1950s strong arguments were being advanced in Europe for much closer economic integration than was possible under the auspices of O.E.E.C. If Europe was to compete with the continental economies of the U.S.A. and the Soviet Union then industrial rationalisation was necessary across frontiers. A single mass European market would enable the economies of scale to be exploited to the full.

The first fruit of this thinking was the establishment in 1952 of the European Coal and Steel Community (E.C.S.C.). All restrictions on trade in coal, steel and iron-ore between Belgium, the Netherlands, Luxembourg, France, Germany and

Italy were abolished while a common tariff on these commodities was adopted against countries outside the group.

42. Treaty establishing the European Economic Community (Treaty of Rome), 1957. In 1955, the members of E.C.S.C. decided to enlarge the scope of their agreement to cover the whole of their economies. Negotiations led to the signing of the Treaty of Rome on 25th March 1957 and its implementation from 1st January 1958. (Simultaneously a separate treaty set up a European Atomic Energy Community, Euratom).

The treaty is a complex document comprising more than 200 Articles. The objectives may be classified in the following way:

(a) *The creation of a full customs union* with free trade in industrial and agricultural products (*see* **43–44** below).

(b) *The creation of a common market in labour, enterprise* (*see* **45** below) *and capital.* The free movement of people, businesses and capital.

(c) *The ultimate integration of national economies into a single European economy* (*see* **46** below).

(d) *Political union* (*see* **47** below).

43. A full customs union. There are two aspects to the creation of a full customs union. Firstly, the abolition of all restrictions upon trade within the group and, secondly, the adoption by the union of a common external tariff and commercial policy.

The treaty envisaged a transitional period of between twelve and fifteen years. In the event progress was more rapid than anticipated and all tariff and quota restrictions (other than in exceptional circumstances) were finally abolished on 1st July 1968.

While the establishment of free trade in industrial products had brought rapid benefits and raised relatively few problems, free trade in agricultural products presented many more difficulties.

44. A common agricultural policy (C.A.P.). The basic problem derives from a technological revolution in European farming methods which is rapidly raising productivity, tending to depress prices and cause vast numbers of farmers to leave the land. Already the Community is fully self-sufficient in pork, sugar, potatoes, vegetables, milk and butter and almost self-sufficient in cheese, poultry, veal, beef, wheat and feed grains. On occasion the output of some commodities outstrips demand. The difficulty has therefore been to establish free trade in these goods and at the same time secure the economic position of the Community's farmers.

The structure of the common agricultural policy is based upon four factors:

(a) *Target price*. This is the base price established by reference to the region of the Community with the least adequate supplies. Subsidies are then paid as necessary to enable farmers to achieve the target price.

(b) *Intervention price*. This is the guaranteed minimum selling price at which the Community will purchase all surpluses. It stands at a given percentage below target price.

(c) *Threshold price*. This provides the basis for calculating the variable import levy. Having allowed for the transportation and marketing costs of imports it is the price necessary to bring the price of these imports into line with the target price. In short, imports from outside the Community are not permitted to compete with any price advantage.

(d) *Variable import levy*. This is constantly recalculated and is equivalent to the difference between the world price of the commodity and the Community's threshold price.

EXAMPLE

	Per bushel of wheat	
	$	$
Target price		2.40
Intervention price		2.20
Threshold price		
Target price	2.40	
Less Marketing/transport costs	0.10	2.30
Variable import levy		
Threshold price	2.30	
Less World price	1.40	0.90

Two important aspects of this policy should be noted. In the first place the Community operates no production controls to eliminate possible surpluses. Secondly, the variable import levy serves to make countries outside the Community the residual suppliers of those products which the Community cannot itself produce in their entirety.

45. A common market in labour, capital and enterprise. Already free movement of individuals in search of work is permitted within the Six and social legislation and labour law are being harmonised so that all workers enjoy the same rights and protection.

Firms also are able to move freely, to expand throughout the union or to participate in mergers. Progress is also being made on the elimination of restrictions which impede the rationalisation of service industries, insurance, banking, law, medicine.

46. The full integration of national economies. Free trade is only the first step in the creation of a wholly effective customs union. Beyond this lies the harmonisation of many aspects of the social and economic life of the uniting countries. It is necessary to develop a common approach to monopolies and mergers, transportation and energy, fiscal and monetary policy, prices and incomes and to social security services to name but a few areas in which differences must be eliminated.

The progress made by E.E.C. in this direction has been quite substantial in those matters specifically covered by the Treaty of Rome but hesitant in matters dependent upon negotiation by the Council of Ministers. The field in which least success has been achieved is that of monetary and fiscal policy since these are subjects which lie at the heart of national sovereignty. Integration here seems to depend upon simultaneous progress towards some form of political union.

47. Political union. Since the Second World War many Europeans have seen political union as the ultimate goal. Early attempts to achieve this objective directly were too ambitious and attention therefore turned to economic union as a first step.

In 1961 the six countries reaffirmed that the ultimate objective of E.E.C. was to achieve a formal political union. However, a gulf has remained between the French concept of a loose confederation of sovereign states and the broadly agreed aim of the remaining five of a supranational federal government. At the present time therefore political integration would seem to be a distant, if desirable, goal.

48. E.E.C. institutions. There are four basic institutions:

(a) *The Commission* represents the Community itself as distinct from the member states. It is a nine-member executive body which administers Community policies and proposes fresh ones to the Council of Ministers.

(b) *Council of Ministers.* The Council comprises six members, one from each country. It makes the final decision on policy proposals made by the Commission and it is therefore through this instrument that national governments are able to influence the evolution of the Community.

(c) *Court of Justice.* The Court is the sole arbiter of the legality of actions taken by the Commission and the Council and its decisions have the force of law throughout the Community.

(d) *European Parliament.* This 142-member body has little real power save for its right to remove the Commission upon a vote of censure.

BRITAIN AND THE EUROPEAN COMMUNITIES

49. European Free Trade Area (E.F.T.A.). In the mid 1950s Britain was unprepared for obligations as far reaching as those implied by the Rome Treaty. Her trade was global rather than focused upon Europe and the Community's common external tariff seemed to threaten old-established relations, particularly those with the Commonwealth. Moreover, the implications of political union seemed unacceptable to a country which had never really visualised itself as an integral part of Europe.

Britain therefore engaged in negotiations to establish a broad free trading area based upon the membership of O.E.E.C. and of which the newly established E.E.C. would be a part. This attempt broke down in 1958, whereupon attention was directed to securing the co-operation of other European countries. In 1960 the Stockholm Convention set up the

European Free Trade Area comprising the U.K., Norway, Sweden, Denmark, Portugal, Switzerland and Austria.

The main provision was that tariff and quantitative restrictions upon trade in industrial products should be progressively removed. This differed from the E.E.C. arrangements in that there was no provision for a common external tariff. Each member was completely free to determine its own trade policies with the rest of the world.

50. U.K. applications to join E.E.C. By the early 1960s opinion in Britain was beginning to shift. The rapid economic expansion in Europe resulting from the creation of E.E.C. could now be observed. Moreover, despite the growing obstacle of the Community's common external tariff this was the segment of the U.K.'s overseas trade which was expanding most rapidly.

Consequently, in 1961 Britain opened negotiations to enter the Community. This was followed in 1962 by the remaining members of E.F.T.A. expressing a willingness to join or become associate members. In 1963 negotiations were abruptly halted when France unilaterally vetoed British entry.

In May 1967, a second application for full membership was lodged. In December of the same year the Council of Ministers failed to reach unanimous agreement on the British application which was nevertheless kept on record and reconsidered over the following two years. Finally, at the end of 1969 it was agreed to open negotiations with the U.K. and other candidate countries as soon as the necessary preparatory work could be completed.

51. The basis of the U.K. application. The reasons for the U.K.'s application and the basic issues for negotiation are to be found in a 1967 White Paper (Cmnd. 3269) and in a statement by the Foreign Secretary on 4th July 1967.

(a) *From the economic point of view* the White Paper spoke of "the long-term potential for Europe, and therefore for Britain, of the creation of a single market of approaching 300 million people with all the scope and incentive which this will provide for British industry, and of the enormous possibilities which an integrated strategy for technology on a truly continental scale, can create."

(b) *From the political point of view* the White Paper pointed out that whatever the economic arguments "the Government's purpose derives above all from our recognition that Europe is now faced with the opportunity of a great move forward in political unity and that we can—and indeed we must—play our full part in it. . . . Together we can ensure that Europe plays in world affairs the part which the Europe of today is not at present playing."

(c) *The fundamental issues for negotiation* were said by the Foreign Secretary to include the inequitable burden upon Britain of E.E.C.'s existing financial arrangements for agriculture; the need for a transitional period; the need to make provision for the interests of the developing countries particularly those dependent on the Commonwealth Sugar Agreement; the need to make provision for New Zealand's dairy products.

These considerations have remained down to the 1971 negotiations the basis of the U.K.'s application for membership.

52. Assessment of the economic consequences of U.K. membership. A White Paper in February 1970 (Cmnd. 4289) sought to make an assessment of the possible economic consequences to the U.K. of joining E.E.C. It frankly admitted the impossibility of arriving at any accurate quantitative conclusions because of the large number of uncertain factors and added that if a basis for judgment was desired there was a further major difficulty. It was necessary to compare the future effects of membership not with the present state of the economy but with the future effects of non-membership.

With these reservations in mind the economic consequences of entry were placed in three categories:

(a) *Effects of adopting the common agricultural policy.*
(b) *Effects upon industry and trade.*
(c) *Effects upon capital movements.*

53. Effects of adopting the common agricultural policy. Clearly the C.A.P. will affect U.K. agricultural production, food consumption and hence imports. The estimated change in the cost of food imports (excluding levies payable on them) ranged from a reduction of £85 million to an increase of £255 million dependent upon the assumption made about the differences between U.K. and E.E.C. prices and the responses to to them by British farmers and consumers. It was further estimated that the maximum likely increase in retail food prices would be of the order of 18–26 per cent, a 4–5 per cent rise in the cost-of-living index.

To this calculation must be added the cost of contributing to the Community budget which at present is mainly concerned with the cost of financing the C.A.P. Here the White Paper was able to make only the broadest possible estimate within the range of £150–£670 million a year offset by U.K. receipts under the C.A.P. of £50–£100 million.

54. Effects upon industry and trade. These may be classified under two headings:

(*a*) *Impact effects* are the immediate effects and arise in the prevailing conditions of demand and supply at the time if entry. They depend upon the reactions of producers, traders and consumers to the tariff changes and are measurable, albeit imperfectly. The estimate made was that the visible trade balance in goods other than food would be adversely affected to the extent of £125–£275 million a year.

(*b*) *Dynamic effects* consist of changes in the underlying conditions of demand and supply "which arise from the opportunities for rationalisation, large-scale investment, and more rapid technological improvements in producing for a quicker and faster growing market and from the pressure for greater efficiency and reduction of unit costs to meet competition within that market."

While it is quite impossible to make any realistic estimate of the dynamic effects it is the general belief that in this area the longer-term balance of advantage lies with the U.K.

55. Effect upon capital movements. The Community's two existing directives on capital movements oblige member states to authorise the free movement of investment funds at the official rate of exchange. The U.K. on the other hand currently imposes exchange control restrictions upon capital movements to E.E.C. as a means of safeguarding the balance of payments.

Although not quantifiable the anticipation is that adherence to the Community's directives would involve substantial cost to the U.K. balance of payments in a typical year. However, to the extent that exchange controls may in any case be relaxed in view of the U.K.'s continuing payments surplus the impact of superimposing E.E.C. obligations would be correspondingly reduced.

56. Total effect upon the U.K. balance of payments. The White Paper concluded that the total cost to the balance of payments could not be calculated simply by adding the extremes of the ranges given in respect of the C.A.P., trade and industry, and capital movements. The resulting figure of £100–£1,100 million not only made no allowance for dynamic effects but was far too wide to provide a basis for decision. The cost at the end of the transitional period was likely to lie well within the two extremes but in what area was a matter for qualitative judgment.

Finally, it may be said that taking the dynamic effects into account it has been the judgment of the Confederation of British Industry that the benefits of membership which are at present unquantifiable should in the long run exceed the balance of payments cost.

PROGRESS TEST 10

1. Explain the theory of comparative costs. **(1–5)**
2. What do you understand by "the terms of trade"? **(5)**
3. What benefit did the U.K. derive from free trade in the nineteenth century? **(8)**
4. Explain the phrase "economic nationalism." **(10)**
5. What effect did the economic nationalism of the 1930s have upon international trade? **(11)**
6. List the reasons which might validly be offered in support of protection. **(14–18)**
7. What was I.T.O.? **(20)**
8. Single out the main features of G.A.T.T. **(22)**
9. What is the mfn principle? **(22(a))**
10. What exceptions are there to the general prohibition of quotas? **(24)**

11. Give an example of G.A.T.T.'s success in reducing the strain of international trade disputes. (**28**)

12. Outline the results of the Kennedy Round. (**30**)

13. Describe the origins of the sterling area. (**34**)

14. What are the principal features of the modern sterling area? (**36**)

15. What are the sterling balances? (**37**)

16. Describe the evolution of O.E.C.D. (**39–40**)

17. What are the main features of the Treaty of Rome? (**42**)

18. Distinguish between a customs union and a free trade area. (**42, 49**)

19. Describe the operation of the C.A.P. (**44**)

20. What are the main institutions of E.E.C.? (**48**)

21. What was the Stockholm Convention? (**49**)

22. Outline the basis of the U.K.'s 1967 application for membership of E.E.C. (**51**)

23. What are the possible effects of adopting the C.A.P. for the U.K.? (**53**)

24. To what degree is it possible to assess the effects of membership upon the U.K. balance of payments? (**56**)

CHAPTER XI

THE U.K. BALANCE OF PAYMENTS

THE BALANCE OF PAYMENTS ACCOUNTS

1. Concept of the balance of payments. The balance of payments accounts of the U.K. include all transactions between U.K. residents and non-residents, transactions being registered when the ownership of goods or assets changes or when services are rendered.

The accounts are set out in sterling values although clearly every transaction involves a foreign currency. Conversions are made simply by applying current rates of exchange.

The term "U.K. residents" includes all individuals residing permanently in the U.K., business undertakings located in the U.K. (but excluding their foreign branches) and U.K. central and local government authorities and agencies.

At the outset, the point should be stressed that international payments must balance. For any deficit resulting from an adverse trading balance there must be a compensatory monetary movement, *i.e.* a running down of national reserves, or alternatively an increase in overseas borrowing.

2. Compilation of the accounts. A Pink Book, *United Kingdom Balance of Payments Accounts*, is published annually in September and *Preliminary Estimates* are made each March.

The presentation of the accounts is currently based upon the definitions which follow and from 1971 falls under five main headings:

(*a*) *Current account.*
(*b*) *Investment and other capital flows.*
(*c*) *Balancing item.*
(*d*) *Total currency flow.*
(*e*) *Official financing.*

3. Current account. The current account comprises two main categories:

197

(a) *Visible trade.* The principal payments and receipts are in respect of imported and exported goods. *The Overseas Trade Statistics of the United Kingdom* provide the basis for the balance of payments figures subject to certain adjustments in respect of valuation and coverage. The most important adjustment is the deduction of freight and insurance from the valuation of imports since these values appear elsewhere under the heading of "Invisible trade."

(b) *Invisible trade.* This includes:

(i) *Government.* All U.K. Government current expenditure and receipts not appropriate to visible or other invisible trade transactions.

(ii) *Transport: shipping.* U.K. payments and receipts in respect of freight, time charter hire, port disbursements and passage money.

(iii) *Transport: civil aviation.* Receipts in respect of all non-resident transactions with British airlines and payments in respect of resident transactions with overseas airlines.

(iv) *Travel.* All personal expenditure by U.K. residents abroad and by non-residents in the U.K.

(v) *Other services.* Among miscellaneous service transactions are included receipts and payments for financial services, royalties, commissions, and education.

(vi) *Interest profits and dividends.* All investment income remitted from and to the U.K. in respect of profits and dividends together with profits remitted or retained for reinvestment. In the public sector are balanced payments and receipts on inter-government loans and on the debit side payments on overseas holdings of U.K. Government, local authority and public corporation securities together with the interest due on official currency liabilities.

(vii) *Private transfers.* Remittance to and from the U.K. of migrants' funds, gifts and legacies.

4. Investment and other capital flows. These fall under the headings:

(a) *Official long-term capital.* Inter-government loans by the U.K. and repaid to the U.K. and to the U.K. and repaid by the U.K. together with subscriptions to certain international organisations, *e.g.* International Development Association.

(b) *Overseas investment in U.K. public sector.* British Government stocks, local authority securities and mortgages, public corporation issues and borrowing by public corporations and local authorities from foreign banks.

(c) *Overseas investment in U.K. private sector.* Direct investments by foreign companies with U.K. branches and portfolio investment in U.K. company shares.

(d) *U.K. private investment overseas.* Both direct and portfolio investment.

(e) *Euro-dollar borrowing in London for investment overseas.*

(f) *Import credit* excluding trade credit between "related" firms but including credit received in connection with import deposits.

(g) *Export credit* excluding trade credit between "related" firms.

(h) *Balances (gross) of sterling area countries.*

(j) *Balances (gross) of non-sterling countries.*

(k) *Foreign currency transactions of U.K. banks.*

(l) *Other short-term flows.*

5. The balancing item. This is the amount necessary to arrive at a balance and represents the net total of errors and omissions throughout the accounts.

The value of the balancing item will be such that total payments will equal total receipts for the balance of payments considered in its entirety. When the item is positive, if we assume the figure for total investments and other capital flows to be correct an unrecorded net export is signified. If we regard the current account as correct an unrecorded net reduction in assets has occurred (*i.e.* U.K. foreign assets have diminished or foreign U.K. assets increased). The opposite conclusions will apply when the balancing item is negative.

In the short term the item is more likely to be the product of unrecorded capital flows but in the longer term is not amenable to reliable analysis.

6. Total currency flow. This is the net currency flow resulting from all external transactions. It includes the current balance, total investment and capital flows and the balancing item.

7. Official financing. This means increases or decreases in the country's reserves or official borrowing drawn or repaid.

They reflect the total currency flow together with the allocation of Special Drawing Rights and the payment of gold subscriptions to the International Monetary Fund.

When the total currency flow is positive, *i.e.* in favour of the U.K., there will be a corresponding increase in the reserves or net repayments of overseas borrowing or a combination of both.

This heading covers the balance of loan transactions with the I.M.F. and other overseas monetary authorities and the drawings on or additions to the official reserves.

8. Relationship of current account and investment and capital flows. It has been observed that the accounts as a whole must balance. If, however, we consider the current account alone it is highly unlikely that in practice a balance will be struck. When payments exceed receipts a current account deficit has arisen and when receipts exceed payments there is a current account surplus.

An immediate conclusion might be that investment and capital flows will be induced by the result achieved in the current account. A deficit may be financed by short- or long-term borrowing which implies a corresponding charge upon the investment and capital-flow sector of the accounts. Similarly, a current account surplus implies a corresponding outward capital flow.

However, it would be erroneous to assume that investment and capital flows are determined solely in this way since many capital transactions occur quite independently and without any reference to the current balance, *e.g.* a Government decision to grant an overseas loan. In simple terms, a decision to invest overseas does not take account of whether the country has earned a sufficient surplus on its current account to finance that investment. It may occur that even with a current deficit there is still a substantial outward movement of investment capital which will add further to the total deficit. This was notably the case in 1964 when a capital account deficit of £370 million was added to a current deficit of £399 million.

When this is the case the total deficit (or surplus) will be matched by a change in the reserves or in short-term borrowing from the I.M.F. and foreign central banks. This change appears under the heading of "Official financing."

TABLE XIX. BALANCE OF PAYMENTS, 1965–70

	1965	1966	1967	1968	1969	1970
Current account						
Visible trade	−237	−73	−552	−643	−141	+3
Invisibles	+160	+128	+255	+337	+578	+628
Current balance	−77	+55	−297	−306	+437	+631
Currency flow and official financing						
Current balance	−77	+55	−297	−306	+437	+631
Investment and other capital flows	−310	−567	−559	−1,010	−15	+499
Balancing item	+34	−35	+185	−94	+321	+157
Total currency flow	−353	−547	−671	−1,410	+743	+1,287
Allocation of Special Drawing Rights (+)	—	—	—	—	—	+171
Gold subscription to I.M.F. (−)	—	−44	—	—	—	−38
Total	−353	−591	−671	−1,410	+743	+1,420
Financed as follows:						
Official borrowing drawn (+)/repaid (−)	+599	+625	+556	+1,296	−699	−1,295
Drawings on (+)/additions to (−) official reserves	−246	−34	+115	+114	−44	−125

(*Source: Preliminary Estimates, 1971.*)

TABLE XX. CURRENT ACCOUNT, 1965–70

	1965	1966	1967	1968	1969	1970
Visible trade						
Exports (f.o.b.)	4,817	5,182	5,122	6,273	7,061	7,885
Imports (f.o.b.)	5,054	5,255	5,674	6,916	7,202	7,882
Visible balance	−237	−73	−552	−643	−141	+3
Invisibles						
Government services and transfers (net)	−447	−470	−463	−466	−463	−480
Other invisibles:						
Private services and transfers (net)	+165	+209	+342	+478	+579	+576
Interest, profits and dividends:						
Private sector	+576	+549	+594	+560	+793	+796
Public sector	−134	−160	−173	−235	−331	−264
Invisible balance	+160	+128	+255	+337	+578	+628
Current balance	−77	+55	−297	−306	+437	+631
Net seasonal influences on current account	—	—	—	—	—	—
Current balance	−77	+55	−297	−306	+437	+631

(*Source: Preliminary Estimates, 1971.*)

9. Summary balance of payments, 1965–70.

Table XIX shows in summary form the major items in the balance of payments accounts. These will be examined in more detail in the following section.

ANALYSIS OF THE ACCOUNTS

10. Current account, 1965–70.

In only very few years since the eighteenth century has the visible trade balance been positive but this has normally been compensated by a surplus on invisible trade to give an overall surplus on current account.

On the invisible account the recurrent deficit in the public sector in respect of services, transfers and interest payments is usually outweighed by the surplus enjoyed in the private sector (*see* Table XX).

11. Trends in visible trade. In the period 1913–45 the volume of British exports declined irregularly and over the whole period 1913–70 increased by only about 33 per cent. (At current values the increase was sixfold.) The visible trade account remained in deficit and its traditional relationship to the invisible account was unchanged.

TABLE XXI. VISIBLE AND INVISIBLE BALANCES, SELECTED PERIODS
1913–70

	1913	1927–29	1937–38	1952–54	1964	1967	1970
Visibles	−134	−373	−388	−242	−537	−552	+3
Invisibles	+340	+480	+355	+384	+138	+255	+628

(*Sources: Abstract of British Historical Statistics* (C.U.P., 1962); *U.K. Balance of Payments* (H.M.S.O.).)

The second trend which we may note is in respect of the U.K.'s share of world export trade in manufactures (which account for about 85 per cent of our visible exports). The decline which had originated in the 1870s but was interrupted in the period 1939–50 continued during the 1950s. In the middle of that decade the U.K.'s share of world markets stood at about 20 per cent. By the late 1960s it had fallen to 11 per cent. The immediate explanation of the decline since 1950 lies in the economic recovery from a standing start of the industrial nations of the world, particularly Germany and Japan, and their subsequent growth rates which greatly exceeded that of the U.K. A lower growth is not of itself particularly significant but taken in conjunction with the U.K.'s recurrent difficulties on current account requires some explanation upon which to base remedial policies.

Certain factors bear upon Britain's competitiveness in international trade and clearly play their part in explaining the post-1955 decline in her share of world markets.

12. Competitive factors in international trade. In the first place it may be noted that during the 1950s and 1960s U.K. prices rose on average twice as fast as those of our major industrial competitors. Until the 1967 devaluation this was clearly a factor which served to diminish the international competitiveness of British goods. The extent to which uncompetitive prices may be viewed as the cause of Britain's declining share of world markets depends upon assumptions made about the elasticity of demand for exports. Early econometric studies suggested that relative prices were comparatively unimportant. Later studies, however, conclude that the elasticity of demand is much greater than was originally believed. At present, the view generally held is that while price is one very important factor there are others.

There then emerges a list of criticisms which have periodically been aimed at British exporters since the nineteenth century:

(a) *Absence of aggressive marketing.*

(b) *Failure to research effectively the requirements of local markets.*

(c) *Unwillingness to vary basic designs to cater for local tastes.*

(d) *Poor after-sales service.*

(e) *Poor quality.*

(f) *Uncompetitive credit terms.*

(g) *Deliveries—long dated, unreliable and late.*

The validity of these criticisms is not amenable to testing by econometric techniques but it is generally agreed that they exert considerable influence.

Finally it must be recognised that the volume of exports depends not only upon the conditions of demand but also upon the conditions of supply. If the economy is being run at a high level of demand then exports are likely to be diverted to home consumption, attracted by the easier market conditions. Manufacturers require more than the assurance of politicians that "exporting is fun."

13. Imports. The visible trade balance depends of course not only upon the receipts from exports but also upon the cost of imports. The first observation therefore is that when aggregate domestic demand is managed at a high level not only are exports diverted to home consumption but an increase in the volume of imports is also encouraged.

Comparison of the rate of increase of imports and exports during the 1960s at first sight seems reassuring.

TABLE XXII. ANNUAL INCREASE IN IMPORTS/EXPORTS, 1961–70

(£ million)

	1961–2	1962–3	1963–4	1964–5	1965–6	1966–7	1967–8	1968–9	1969–70
Imports	53	272	641	46	206	419	1,242	286	680
Exports	102	293	184	311	405	−60	1,151	788	824

(*Source: U.K. Balance of Payments.*)

It will be observed that with the exceptions of the years 1963–64, 1966–67 and 1967–68, the value of exports grew more rapidly than the value of imports. The figures, however, disguise the fact that the volume of imports was growing more rapidly than the volume of exports. This discrepancy between the value and volume growth rate of imports and exports is explained by a continuing movement of the terms of trade in favour of the U.K. A reversal of this trend would have serious consequences for the U.K. balance of payments.

Secondly, it will be noticed that from 1961 to the crisis year of 1964 and again from 1964 to the devaluation year of 1967 the rate of increase of imports far exceeded the rate of increase of exports. Subsequently, imports responded to devaluation in 1968–69 but the trend was re-established in 1969–70 with imports expanding at a far more rapid rate than exports.

It is accepted that since the U.K. is highly dependent upon imported foods and raw materials economic expansion will be related to an increase in such imports. However, since 1950 the growth rate of these items has diminished relative to the growth rate of imported manufactures.

We may therefore conclude that the deterioration in the visible trade account in the period 1961–67 is largely attributed to an acceleration in the growth rate of imports and that the latter is to be explained primarily by an excessive growth of imported manufactures.   Finally, although devaluation produced a small visible account surplus in 1968–70 a comparison of the current growth rates of imports and exports suggests that this cannot be maintained.

14. Invisible trade.   Examination of current account transactions shown in Table XX and the annual average surpluses shown in Table XXII reveals the importance of invisible trade to the balance of payments.   This has long been the position. In the 1930s net earnings on invisible account paid for approximately one-third of U.K. visible imports.   At the outbreak of war invisible receipts stood at 44 per cent of total receipts while payments represented 18 per cent of total payments.

In the immediate post-war years the relative importance of invisibles declined but by the late 1960s had been restored to the position where they produced 38 per cent of total export earnings and accounted for 32 per cent of total payments. Since the invisible account consistently produced a surplus it is clear that it made a major contribution to the current account surpluses of the 1950s and to a reduction of the deficits in the 1960s.

TABLE XXIII. AVERAGE SURPLUSES ON INVISIBLE ACCOUNT, CYCLICAL PERIODS, 1952–70

(£ *million*)

	1952–55	1956–60	1961–64	1965–67	1968–70
Average surplus net	327	230	173	181	514
Average Government account deficit	99	210	378	460	470
Average surplus less Government account	426	440	551	641	984

(*Source: U.K. Balance of Payments.*)

15. Government account.   Reference to Table XXIII shows the significance of Government overseas expenditure to the invisible account and hence to the current account and the total balance of payments position. There was a rapid escalation of the net deficit until the period 1961–64. Thereafter the rate of increase was checked and appears finally to have been contained.

The Government account divides into services and transfers. The first category includes military and diplomatic expenditure. Military-support costs consistently account for well over half the deficit. Transfers include military and economic aid programmes and subscriptions to international organisations.

Whether or not their burden upon the balance of payments is deemed tolerable rests upon the political view of the role which Britain should play in world affairs.

16. Private services and transfers. The accounts show five categories:

(*a*) *Transport: shipping.* The post-war period saw a continuous deterioration in this account with deficits being returned in the 1960s. The trend was reversed in 1967 only to relapse into deficit again in 1970.

TABLE XXIV. TRANSPORT: SHIPPING (NET), 1961–70

(*£ million*)

1961	1962	1963	1964	1965	1966	1967	1968	1969	1970
−36	−21	−26	−43	−4	0	+16	+60	+45	−4

(*Source: U.K. Balance of Payments.*)

The sums involved are by far the largest items in the invisible accounts (in 1970, payments of £1,087 million against receipts of £1,073 million) but Table XXIV shows that the net flows are relatively small.

A number of factors bear upon the U.K.'s weakened position as a maritime power:

(*i*) *Unfair competition* from countries which subsidise their shipping lines for strategic or prestige reasons.

(*ii*) *The rapid increase in world tonnage.* Britain's share shows a relative decline.

(*iii*) *Imports are carried increasingly in foreign ships* and since these tend to be bulk cargoes the freight charges are higher than the export cargoes carried in British ships.

(b) *Transport: civil aviation.* In the past decade both sides of the account have grown quite rapidly but in step, to give a consistent and stable small surplus.

TABLE XXV. TRANSPORT: CIVIL AVIATION (NET), 1961–70

(£ *million*)

1961	1962	1963	1964	1965	1966	1967	1968	1969	1970
+23	+24	+27	+27	+28	+30	+27	+29	+41	+35

(c) *Travel.* This part of the accounts has always shown a fairly substantial deficit and it would seem that Britain has not viewed the tourist industry as a potential major exporter.

However, Table XXVI shows that in 1968 the net surplus expanded quite dramatically.

TABLE XXVI. TRAVEL (NET), 1961–70

(£ *million*)

1961	1962	1963	1964	1965	1966	1967	1968	1969	1970
−24	−27	−53	−71	−97	−78	−38	+11	+35	+45

(d) *Other services.* This category is a major contributor to the net surplus, as shown in Table XXVII, and includes a variety of items such as banking and financial services, royalties, commissions and education.

TABLE XXVII. OTHER SERVICES (NET), 1961–70

(£ *million*)

1961	1962	1963	1964	1965	1966	1967	1968	1969	1970
+247	+254	+246	+267	+270	+306	+395	+474	+535	+582

(e) *Private transfers.* This category normally shows a deficit which has ranged from a low point of £14 million in 1963 to a high point of £96 million in 1968. In 1970 the figure was £72 million.

17. Interest, profits and dividends: private sector. Prior to 1914 Britain was the world's principal overseas investor, the income from her investments making an ever-growing contribution to the total of invisible exports. In the inter-war period the rate of investment slackened and during the

Second World War a substantial portion of her holdings were liquidated to finance imports.

After the war investment abroad was resumed with cumulative benefits for the balance of payments since the net surplus on this item currently makes by far the biggest contribution to the total surplus on the invisible account.

TABLE XXVIII. INTEREST, PROFITS, AND DIVIDENDS: PRIVATE
SECTOR NET SURPLUSES, 1965–70

(£ million)

1965	1966	1967	1968	1969	1970
576	549	549	560	793	796

There is, however, one important new feature in the accounts of the 1960s. During this period the rate of foreign investment in the U.K. has grown substantially with a corresponding rise on the debit side of the account. Until 1968 the rate of growth of debits in fact exceeded that of credits. This clearly has significance for exchange-control restrictions upon outward capital movements which, while they may be justifiable in the short run to correct an adverse balance of payments, in the long run must serve to erode the net surpluses on profits and dividends.

18. Interest, profits and dividends: public sector. Substantial deficits under this heading constitute a major offset to the surpluses in the private sector.

TABLE XXIX. INTEREST, PROFITS AND DIVIDENDS: PUBLIC SECTOR
NET DEFICITS, 1965–70

(£ millions)

1965	1966	1967	1968	1969	1969
−134	−160	−173	−235	−331	−264

Very large debit items arise in respect of overseas holdings of U.K. Government securities, interest paid on official currency liabilities and charges paid on I.M.F. drawings.

19. Investment and other capital flows. The eleven items which make up the segment of the accounts now described as "investment and other capital flows" are shown in Table XXX.

TABLE XXX. INVESTMENT AND OTHER CAPITAL FLOWS, 1965–70

	1965	1966	1967	1968	1969	1970
Investment and other capital flows						
Official long-term capital	−85	−80	−57	+17	−98	−205
Overseas investment in U.K. public sector	−31	+3	+26	+42	+63	−18
Overseas investment in U.K. private sector	+249	+274	+366	+587	+678	+665
U.K. private investment overseas	−368	−303	−456	−727	−652	−735
Euro-dollar borrowing in London for investment overseas	+45	+15	+55	+155	+72	+166
Import credit	+4	−5	+27	+66	+163	+11
Export credit	−69	−183	−185	−345	−323	−303
Balances (gross) of sterling area countries	−10	−33	−81	−150	+256	+389
Balances (gross) of non-sterling countries	−82	−91	−134	−227	−30	+97
Foreign currency transactions of U.K. banks	−73	−162	−47	−124	−108	+313
Other short-term flows	+110	−2	+32	−53	−16	+119
Total investment and other capital flows	−310	−567	−454	−759	−15	+499

(*Source: Preliminary Estimates, 1971.*)

(The first four items used to be known as the "capital account" and together with the current account provided the old "basic balance." The remaining items until 1971 were included in the part of the accounts which used to be headed "monetary movements.")

NOTE: Assets: an increase is signified by $-$, a decrease by $+$.
Liabilities: an increase is signified by $+$, a decrease by $-$.

20. Official long-term capital. During the period 1961–70 the annual rate of official Government overseas lending averaged £80 million and the rate of repayment £32 million. At the same time the annual rate of overseas borrowing averaged £38 million and of repayment £60 million. These figures consolidated signify an average capital outflow of £70 million annually. Other items which include subscriptions to the International Development Association added an average £17½ million to the annual capital outflow.

21. Overseas investment in U.K. public sector. In the period 1965–70 U.K. liabilities in respect of Central Government and local government securities and public corporation issues and borrowing abroad increased at an average rate of £14 million per annum.

22. Inward and outward investment: U.K. private sector. During the decade 1961–70 overseas investment in the U.K. private sector increased at an annual average rate of £391 million counterbalanced by an increase in U.K. overseas investment at the rate of £451 million per annum. This represents an average net increase in U.K. overseas assets (*i.e.* a net capital outflow) of £60 million per annum. However, it has already been observed that exchange-control restrictions upon capital movements which were tightened in the middle sixties served to reduce this net capital outflow.

23. Euro-dollar borrowing. From 1965 to 1970 euro-dollar transactions in London added an average of £85 million per annum to the capital inflow.

24. Import and export credits. In the period 1965–70 the U.K. received import credits at an annual average rate of £45 million and financed export credits at a rate of £235 million.

These credits are the equivalent of inward and outward flows and represent the creation of liabilities and assets respectively.

25. Sterling balances. During the middle sixties there developed a fairly strong tendency for the balance of both sterling-area and non-sterling-area countries to be reduced. The trend was substantially reversed in 1969 and 1970. Overall, the period 1965–70 saw a relatively tiny reduction of total balances by £116 million.

Nevertheless, an examination of the fluctuations revealed in Table XXX draws attention to the pressures which can be exerted upon the exchange rate of sterling as a result of changes in the balances which are not directly related to the U.K. balance of trade.

26. Foreign currency transactions of U.K. banks. Reference to Table XXX reveals a substantial adverse balance from 1965 to 1970 when for the first time in the decade there was a very large surplus.

27. Total investment and other capital flows. From 1962 until 1970 there was a substantial net outward movement of capital, dramatically reduced in 1969 and reversed in 1970 when the net inflow amounted to £499 million. This reflected not only a renewed confidence in sterling associated with a strong British balance of payments but also the high interest rates in London which attracted a large volume of short-term money from overseas.

28. Total currency flow and official financing. When the balances on current account and investment and other capital flow accounts are totalled and adjusted by means of the balancing item a figure for the total currency flow for the year is established. To this figure is added a credit for the annual allocation of Special Drawing Rights begun in 1970 (*see* XII, **41**) and a deduction made when appropriate for gold contributions to the I.M.F.

If the final figure is negative official financing will involve overseas borrowing or drawing upon the reserves. When the figure is positive as it was in 1969 and 1970 official financing implies a repayment of existing short-term loans from foreign central banks and the I.M.F. or an addition to the reserves.

now inevitable that in any expansionary phase, with dome
demand running at a higher level, imports would boom.
the event between 1956 and 1960 total imports rose by 23 p
cent and manufactures upon which restrictions had been mos
stringent by some 56 per cent.

31. Disequilibrium, 1961–64. It has been observed (*see* II,
24) that during the 1950s the major goal of Government
economic policy had been full employment but that in the
1960s attention became increasingly directed to more rapid
growth. Whereas in the preceding period (1956–60) the
annual average growth of Gross Domestic Product was only
2·4 per cent, in the period 1961–64 it increased to 3·6 per cent.
With demand now functioning at a higher level the balance of
payments was subjected to stress and two sterling crises (in
1961 and 1964) resulted.

Due to expansion of imports the visible trade balance
worsened in 1961 to £153 million, recovered marginally in 1962
and 1963 with figures of −£104 million and −£80 million, only
to plummet in 1964 to −£537 million. On the invisible
account moreover the Government deficit was increasing more
rapidly than the private-sector surplus, while one aspect of
the latter was in fact declining. The net surplus on private
services fell from £230 million in 1962 to £177 million in 1963
and £167 million in 1964.

While a net capital inflow relieved the pressure in 1961,
subsequent capital account deficits of £98 million in 1962,
£148 million in 1963 and £370 million in 1964 were clearly not
being financed from the current balance. The cumulative
deficit over the period on current and capital account was
£740 million, largely financed by massive borrowing from the
I.M.F. and a depletion of the reserves by £327 million.

32. Disequilibrium, 1965–67. In this period the balance of
payments and the preservation of the exchange rate of sterling
became a major target of economic policy. Stringent demand
management slowed the growth rate to an average of 1·6 per
cent per annum, initially with some result. The visible trade
deficit shrank to £237 million in 1965 and £73 million in 1966,
only to rocket to £552 million in 1967. The surplus on the
invisible account could not match these figures. In fact the
net yield from invisibles fell in 1966 by £32 million due pri-

EQUILIBRIUM IN THE BALANCE OF PAYMENTS

29. The concept of equilibrium. While international payments must always balance they need not necessarily be in equilibrium. By "long-term equilibrium" is understood a situation in which, at any given rate of exchange, the average current account surplus taken over a period of years is sufficient to finance all net external capital transactions (investment, foreign aid and debt repayment) together with any necessary expansion of official reserves to cover increased liabilities. Further, this equilibrium will be genuine only when it has been achieved without recourse to the management of domestic demand at a level inconsistent with full employment and without dependence upon trade and payment restrictions inconsistent with a country's obligations to G.A.T.T. and the I.M.F.

It should be stressed that disequilibrium will occur not only when a country consistently experiences an adverse balance of payments but also when it recurrently produces large surpluses, *e.g.* this has repeatedly been the case in post-war Germany.

30. Disequilibrium in the U.K. balance of payments: the origin. While the U.K. balance of payments was never very strong during the 1950s it has been argued that the year 1958-59 marked a positive turning-point after which there was a steady deterioration until 1967, significant of a fundamental disequilibrium.

Throughout the 1950s there had been a gradual reduction of the restrictions upon foreign trade and payments which during and immediately after the war had served to limit the volume of imports and restrict the export of capital. In this way the balance of payments had been protected. In 1958 sterling was made freely convertible to gold or dollars for all non-resident holders in respect of current account transactions. In 1958-59 the residual import restrictions which had been designed to conserve foreign exchange were finally removed. Apart from a normal customs tariff which had in any case been lowered as a result of G.A.T.T. the U.K. had now adopted a comparatively liberal system of trade and payments. It was

H

marily to a substantial rise in the Government account deficit and a fall in the net surplus from profits and dividends.

The result was that although the current account deficit was reduced to £77 million in 1965 and converted to a surplus of £55 million in 1966, in 1967 a deficit of £297 million was returned. It is perfectly clear that the current account was not able to support the net outward flow of investment which totalled £462 million.

If a comparison is made with the preceding period in terms of the old "basic balance" (*i.e.* current account plus capital account, the first four lines in Table XXX) the cumulative deficit, ignoring the balancing item, had deteriorated from £740 million to £781 million despite Government remedial policies. The position was further aggravated by a diminution of the sterling balances over the period by £431 million, and by other adverse monetary movements.

Official financing during this time amounted net to £165 million drawn from the I.M.F., £1,095 million borrowed from other monetary authorities, £165 million drawn from the reserves and £520 million transferred to the reserves upon the liquidation of the U.S. dollar portfolio.

33. Deflation or devaluation. From the foregoing discussion it would seem conclusive that a fundamental disequilibrium existed in the U.K. balance of payments from 1959 to 1967. In this situation the balance may be rectified by operating on:

(*a*) *The current account.* Broadly the intention will be to make domestic prices more internationally competitive either by deflation or devaluation. (Detailed consideration will be given to this subject in the following chapter.)

(*b*) *Investment and other capital flows.* Exchange control restrictions upon capital movements may be tightened.

In the event devaluation was forced upon the Government in November 1967 and although this was no voluntary act of policy it was hoped that it would provide in the long run the solution for the hitherto intractable balance of payments problem.

34. Impact of devaluation on the balance of payments. The immediate consequence of devaluation is to raise the price of a given quantity of imports and reduce the receipts from a given quantity of exports. It was not therefore surprising that in 1968 the current balance worsened to £306 million. The "basic balance," however, improved from the 1967 deficit of £418 million to £387 million due primarily to a net inflow of official long-term capital and to an increase in overseas investment in the U.K. public sector.

By 1969 the visible trade balance was responding to devaluation, exports expanding by £788 million and imports by £286 million, to reduce the deficit to £141 million. In 1970 exports continued their sharp upward trend, growing by £824 million while imports disappointingly also rose sharply by £680 million. The result was a highly unusual surplus on visible trade, albeit of only £3 million.

The surplus on invisibles also improved dramatically, having more than doubled from £255 million in 1967 to £628 million in 1970.

The net result was an improvement in the current balance to a surplus of £631 million and in the "basic balance" to a surplus of £338 million in 1970. Short-term capital movements were also especially favourable to the U.K. balance of payments in 1970, adding a further £161 million to the surplus.

The total currency inflow produced in the years of surplus, 1969 and 1970, amounted to £2,163 million. From this position the authorities were enabled to repay £164 million of I.M.F. drawings and £1,830 million of foreign central bank borrowing and also to add £169 million to the reserves.

35. The prospect for long-term equilibrium. Whether stability can be achieved in the long-run balance of payments depends upon a number of highly uncertain factors, some of which are outside the control of the U.K. Government:

(a) *Inflation.* The annual rate of increase of inflation is substantially higher in the U.K. than among her principal industrial competitors. On present trends it seems likely that the price advantage gained by devaluation will be rapidly eroded.

(b) *World markets.* The rate of growth of world markets and their accessibility to U.K. exports, *e.g.* the market potential of the E.E.C. assuming British entry is achieved.

(c) *The cost of E.E.C. membership.* It has already been

indicated that there are no reliable estimates of the cost to the balance of payments of E.E.C. membership.

(d) *Growth of imports.* It has also been pointed out that imports are once more rising more rapidly than exports.

(e) *Terms of trade.* Any adverse movement would have severe consequences for the balance of payments.

(f) *Reform of the international monetary system* which will serve to relieve the U.K. economy of some of the strain of supporting a reserve and trading currency.

PROGRESS TEST 11

1. Why must international payments always balance? **(1)**
2. List the main items in the current account. **(3)**
3. What is the significance of the "balancing item"? **(5)**
4. What does a positive total currency flow indicate? **(7)**
5. How do current account items relate to investment and capital flows? **(8)**
6. Describe the general trend in the visible trade balance in the twentieth century. **(11)**
7. What criticisms have been levelled at British exporters in this century? **(12)**
8. Explain the significance of import trends in the 1960s. **(13)**
9. Explain the importance of invisible trade to the U.K. balance of payments. **(14)**
10. Compare the relative importance of the various items on the invisible account which fall under the heading "private services and transfers." **(16)**
11. What is the significance of restrictions upon outward capital movements for the balance of invisible trade? **(17)**
12. Compare the importance of "official long-term capital" with the other items which appear under the heading "Investment and other capital flows." **(19–28)**
13. Explain the "concept of equilibrium" in the balance of payments. **(29)**
14. What was the source of disequilibrium in the U.K. balance of payments at the end of the 1950s? **(30)**
15. Account for the 1964 sterling crisis. **(31)**
16. What have been the effects of devaluation upon the balance of payments to the present time? **(34)**
17. Upon what factors do the prospects for long-term equilibrium depend? **(35)**

CHAPTER XII

FOREIGN EXCHANGE

THE DETERMINATION OF FOREIGN EXCHANGE RATES

1. The rate of exchange. The rate of exchange may be defined as the domestic money price of foreign currency purchased on the foreign exchange market. The rate varies daily and is derived from the domestic price quoted for bankers' bills of exchange transmitted by cable, the quickest means of international payment. This establishes the "base" rate. Other slower means of international payment, bankers' sight and time bills and trade sight and time bills are carried by airmail and sell at a discount from the base rate to take account of differing liquidity and risk factors.

In this way a pattern of exchange rates is established all of which are geared to the base rate which may be taken as the "key" rate of exchange.

Movements in the rates of exchange depend upon the structure of the foreign exchange market (*see* **2, 3, 4** below).

2. Variable exchange rates. In this situation exchange rates may be completely free to move in response to market forces. Such a foreign exchange system in fact approximates to the classical notion of perfect competition since any given foreign currency is a homogeneous product and the market comprises many buyers and sellers none of whom is able individually to influence the final price.

The demand for foreign currency originates in the debit items in the balance of payments while the supply derives from the credit items. It therefore follows that when demand increases relative to supply the price of foreign currency is forced upward, *i.e.* the exchange rate moves against the home country. The opposite will be the case when supply exceeds demand.

3. Stable exchange rate systems. Exchange rates have in practice rarely been left free to be determined by demand and supply. Stabilisation has been achieved in two ways:

(*a*) *Passive stabilisation.* This system is exemplified by the "gold standard" which functioned throughout the greater part of the nineteenth century and with interruptions to the 1930s. A country observes a full gold standard when its monetary unit is defined in terms of a fixed weight of gold, when the monetary authorities are prepared to buy and sell gold freely at this fixed ratio and when there are no restrictions placed upon the free international movement of gold.

In the situation where a number of countries observe this standard their currencies are linked by a common denominator and must therefore always exchange at this fixed rate.

(*b*) *Active stabilisation.* A genuine international gold standard has not functioned since the 1930s. Subsequently, foreign exchange markets have either been controlled directly or stabilised by official intervention. Intervention requires that the monetary authorities should have at their disposal both supplies of the domestic currency and reserves of gold and convertible foreign currencies. When the flow of domestic currency on to the world's foreign exchange markets is excessive the reserves are used to buy up the surplus in order to support the price (*i.e.* exchange rate) at the fixed level. Similarly, when the domestic currency is in *short* supply on the exchange markets the tendency for its price to rise will be forestalled when the monetary authorities sell domestic currency against gold or foreign currency.

4. Exchange control. In neither of the two preceding systems is any restriction placed upon private transactions in foreign exchange. Where the foreign exchange market is fully controlled all foreign currency earnings must be sold to the control authority at a given exchange rate and all purchases made from the authority at a given rate.

The supply of foreign currency earnings (*i.e.* the credit items in the balance of payments) is largely outside the control of the exchange authority except to the extent that exports or foreign loans can be encouraged. Supply is therefore taken as fixed and the authority turns its attention to restricting demand, usually by a system of licensed imports. Licences are allocated to individuals in a way which restricts the total volume of imports, and hence the demand for foreign exchange, to a level which equates with the supply of foreign currency earnings.

5. Balance of payments disequilibrium and foreign exchange rates. When there exists a fundamental disequilibrium in the balance of payments the effect upon exchange rates varies with the nature of the foreign exchange market.

(a) *Freely fluctuating rates.* When there is a recurrent deficit disequilibrium, there will be a continuing deterioration in the rate of exchange. Conversely, with a surplus disequilibrium the exchange rate will appreciate.

(b) *Stable rates.* Whether the rates of exchange are stabilised actively or passively the results will be the same. With a deficit disequilibrium there will be a continuing diminution in the reserves and/or an accumulation of foreign debt. A surplus disequilibrium will produce additions to the reserves and/or a reduction of foreign debt.

(c) *Exchange control.* The existence of exchange control is itself evidence of a "suppressed" disequilibrium. Were the demand for foreign currency free to rise the result would be an exchange rate lower than the one which currently pertains.

We shall now examine in some detail the adjustment of international payments disequilibrium under different systems of foreign exchange, making special reference to the historical experience of the U.K.

ADJUSTMENT OF PAYMENTS DISEQUILIBRIUM IN A PASSIVE STABLE RATE SYSTEM

6. The classical theory of adjustment. The oldest theory of international payments adjustment was propounded by the eighteenth-century writer David Hulme and refined by the British classical economists of the nineteenth century. It hinges on the concept of "the price-specie flow mechanism."

An inflow of gold resulting from an excess of exports over imports will increase the domestic money supply and raise home prices. Conversely, the outflow of gold from abroad will reduce the foreign money supply and foreign prices. The response will be an expansion of imports and a reduction of exports to the point where international payments are automatically brought into equilibrium.

7. The gold standard. Prior to 1914 and during the second half of the 1920s the pound sterling was defined as 113 grains of gold and the U.S. dollar as $23 \cdot 22$ grains. Since the pound therefore represented $4 \cdot 8665$ times as much gold as the dollar, the so-called "mint parity" of the two currencies was £1 : $4·8665. Any holder of 113 grains of gold could freely acquire £1 or $4·8665 from the U.K. or U.S. monetary authorities respectively or alternatively exchange these sums against 113 grains of gold.

Any tendency for the exchange rate to move away from the mint parity was checked when importers, rather than accept an unfavourable rate, would withdraw and export gold in payment. However, a marginal movement of the exchange rate was possible within the limits set by the "gold points."

(a) *The gold export point* by adding the cost of freight, insurance and handling to the mint parity rate of exchange established the effective rate above which it paid the importer to make payment in gold.

(b) *The gold import point* by similarly subtracting shipment from the mint parity rate of exchange established the lowest rate which the foreign importer would accept rather than make payment in gold.

It therefore follows that on the gold standard any disequilibrium in international payments was compensated by gold movements which left the exchange rate undisturbed within the range of the two gold points.

8. Restoration of equilibrium. A gold standard implies a stringent control over a country's money supply. The 1844 *Bank Charter Act* permitted a small fiduciary issue in Britain but required that every other banknote should have full gold cover (*see* VII, **3**).

Given an unfavourable balance of payments and a movement

of the exchange rate to the gold export point, bullion now flowed out of the country. It followed that the volume of currency had now to be curtailed and the banking system was compelled to follow a policy of deflation. Bank Rate was raised and the Bank of England engaged in open market operations to reduce the cash reserves of the commercial banks which, in turn, were obliged to restrict credit in order to maintain their cash ratio (*see* VII, **36**). In short, there was a contraction of the money supply in terms of both cash and bank deposits.

It was argued that these deflationary policies produced a decline in the domestic price level which encouraged exports and discouraged imports. Equilibrium in the balance of payments was restored automatically, albeit at the expense of a deflation over which there was no control.

Given a favourable balance of payments and an inflow of gold the course of events was reversed.

9. Advantages and disadvantages of the gold standard. Assuming the foregoing explanation to be an accurate account of the sequence of events on an international gold standard, certain advantages and disadvantages are apparent.

(*a*) *Advantages.* Internally it is impossible for inflation to be excessive since the money supply is strictly controlled. The domestic price level must therefore in the long run remain internationally competitive and the balance of payments can be left to adjust itself automatically.

(*b*) *Disadvantages.* Economic expansion may be impeded by a too inflexible and arbitrary restriction of the supply of money and credit. Moreover, the inevitable deflation or inflation which must accompany an outward or inward gold flow may be wholly at odds with internal economic needs, *e.g.* deflation in a situation of high unemployment.

By the 1930s a considerable body of opinion was disposed against a wholly arbitrary system in which gold was the master and a country was robbed of control over its economic fortunes.

10. The validity of the price-specie flow mechanism. Two main criticisms emerge which reduce the validity of the theory as conceived by the classical economists.

(*a*) *Quantity theory of money criticism.* The quantity theory assumes that a change in the money supply will bring about a proportionate change in the price level. However, the effect of a change depends upon the extent to which the volume of spending responds. A decrease in the quantity of money may be compensated by an increase in its velocity of circulation and vice versa. Therefore there can be no direct or certain response from prices to any given change in the money supply.

(*b*) *No allowance for income changes.* In the classical theory of perfect competition and continuing full employment there could be no change in spending which did not simultaneously produce a corresponding change in both prices and incomes. The classical economists saw that deflation (reduced spending) subsequent to an adverse balance of payments reduced the purchasing power (*i.e.* income) of the deficit country since exports were now made at lower prices. However, the view was that the reduction of income was the incidental accompaniment of the reduction in prices, the latter being the key to international payments adjustment. It was not seen that there could be an autonomous change in income unrelated to price change which would itself contribute to adjustment.

11. Income change and the balance of payments.
Modern theory places a great deal of emphasis upon the notion that income changes play a major role in the long-run adjustment of international payments.

Where there exists a recurrent disequilibrium at stable exchange rates and the deficit country is forced to deflate, prices may or may not respond. What is certain is that at lower levels of spending national income will decline, thus inducing a fall in home consumption. The volume of imports will be reduced and goods released from home use for export.

At the same time the income of the surplus country will be inflated with unpredictable consequences for the price level. However, at the higher income level further imports will be attracted and exports diverted to home use.

Nevertheless, it is to be expected that at the same time prices will be falling in the deficit country and rising in the surplus country.

The two sets of circumstances will combine to reduce both deficit and surplus and establish an equilibrium.

12. Variations on the gold standard. In 1914 the gold standard was suspended but fixed rates of exchange maintained. After the war exchange rates between many currencies were permitted to fluctuate and settle at whatever level the market determined. In the resulting chaos many monetary authorities were convinced of the desirability of a return to the gold standard. This course was followed by Austria (1922), Germany (1924), Britain (1925), France (1928).

(a) *The gold bullion standard.* Britain did not readopt a full gold standard as it had functioned before 1914. Rather was it a gold bullion standard. Bank of England paper was convertible but only into gold bars in minimum quantities of 400 ounces, about £1,560. While gold was once more used in settlement of international payments it was no longer circulated internally.

(b) *The gold exchange standard.* This technique enables a country to link its currency to gold without in fact holding gold reserves of its own. Instead, it holds its reserves in the currency of a country observing the gold standard and thus enjoys the advantage of interest receipts on these deposits.

13. Abandonment of the gold standard. For a number of reasons the world was obliged to abandon an international gold standard in the years between 1931 and 1936.

(a) *Failure to observe gold standard obligations.* It has been noted that an automatic consequence of payments disequilibrium will be a degree of inflation in the surplus country and of deflation in the deficit country. During the period of the restored gold standard no country was prepared fully to accept these consequences. In deficit countries such as the U.K. it would have been necessary to permit severe deflation even in the prevailing conditions of industrial depression and rising unemployment. In surplus countries such as the U.S.A. which was receiving huge quantities of gold there was an unwillingness to accept an inflation which might jeopardise exports. The inward flow of gold was therefore stabilised.

(b) *"Hot money."* Before 1914 most capital movements were for the purpose of long-term investment. After the war a huge volume of short-term money shifted from one country to another in search of refuge from depreciation. These movements added instability to the balance of international payments.

(c) *Overvaluation of sterling.* In 1925 the mint parity of sterling was re-established at its 1914 level. In view of the great inflation which had occurred in Britain during the war this rate clearly overvalued the pound. The degree of deflation required to reduce the U.K. price level to a point which made the exchange rate realistic proved impossible of attainment. There followed inevitably a fundamental disequilibrium in the balance of payments which produced a steady drain upon the gold reserves. Following an adverse balance of £100 million, Britain in 1931 was compelled to leave the gold standard. Since sterling was a key reserve and trading currency other countries were obliged to follow suit.

EXCHANGE CONTROL SYSTEMS

14. Origins. Exchange controls were first adopted by many Governments during the First World War as a means of safeguarding those imports vital to the economy. After the war controls were abandoned until the international financial crisis of 1931. Failure of confidence in the ability of one nation after another to honour its short-term international obligations led to massive withdrawals of funds from these countries which were checked only by the reimposition of exchange controls.

In due course confidence in sterling was affected but instead of adopting controls the U.K. reacted first by abandoning the gold standard and allowing the pound to depreciate and then, in 1932, stabilising at a lower parity with the aid of the Exchange Equalisation Account.

By 1935 a clear pattern had emerged in which Germany and the countries of south-east Europe together with Brazil, Argentina and Chile practised stringent exchange controls. The currencies of the rest of the world remained freely convertible.

15. Extension of exchange controls. During the Second World War tight controls were imposed by all countries. After the war while other direct economic controls were dismantled exchange control was retained. By 1958 there were only eleven fully convertible currencies. After 1958 a general easing of international payment difficulties enabled many more countries to revert either to full or partial convertibility. While it is true that exchange controls have not yet been completely eliminated they no longer have the restrictive effect on trade and payments that they had during the post-war years. The exception is in the case of some developing countries where they are used as a major instrument of economic policy.

16. Purposes of an exchange-control system. An exchange-control system will have one or more of the following purposes:

(a) *Correction of a balance of payments disequilibrium.* Since 1945, exchange controls have been, and still are, imposed to correct a disequilibrium which springs from massive capital outflows. For example, half the 1964 U.K. deficit sprang from capital account transactions and controls over these were subsequently tightened.

Current account deficits may be corrected in this way where countries are unwilling to deflate or devalue. However, after 1958, all the world's major trading nations agreed to abandon controls over current account transactions.

(b) *Instrument of economic planning.* We have seen in Part One that in private-enterprise economies Governments seek to implement national economic plans by indirect methods, notably fiscal and monetary policy. Since the achievement of objectives such as full employment or more rapid growth may set up inflationary pressures which induce a balance of payments disequilibrium, exchange controls may be adopted as a short-term planning expedient.

(c) *Source of revenue.* In this case the exchange-control authority arbitrarily sets the price at which it will purchase foreign exchange below that at which it will sell, thus leaving itself a profit margin. Today this objective is mainly restricted to the developing countries.

(d) *Protection.* Like a customs tariff exchange controls may be used to protect domestic industry.

17. Types of system. Exchange-control systems may vary considerably in detail but all will fall into one or other of two categories:

(a) *Single-rate systems.* The exchange-control authority has the sole right to buy and sell foreign currency but does so at one official rate. In this case the price mechanism plays no part in allocating currency between competing importers. The system must therefore be supported by import licences which determine who shall be entitled to foreign currency.

(b) *Multi-rate systems.* There is one official buying rate and one or more selling rates. In this case the price mechanism serves partially to allocate the supply of foreign currency and there need be less reliance on supporting trade controls.

18. Disadvantage of exchange control. The major criticism of any system of exchange control is that by rendering a currency inconvertible it disrupts multilateral settlements which enable a country to offset a deficit in one sector of its trading with a surplus earned elsewhere.

Let us suppose that Peru has traditionally a deficit in its trade with Chile, which has normally been financed by a surplus in its trade with the U.S.A., *i.e.* dollar earnings have been converted to Chilean pesos. If the U.S.A. now adopts exchange control which makes the dollar inconvertible then Peru must balance its payments bilaterally with Chile.

To do so it must reduce its imports (probably by adopting its own exchange controls) to the detriment of Chile and itself. Peru is still left with dollars which can only be utilised in the U.S.A. for the purchase of imports which it might otherwise not wish to take.

In short, the volume of world trade is reduced and the natural pattern distorted. The advantages of international specialisation are lost.

ADJUSTMENT OF PAYMENTS DISEQUILIBRIUM IN VARIABLE EXCHANGE RATE SYSTEMS

19. Variants. Variable exchange rate systems may be of many types ranging from a position in which the rate is determined solely by market forces to the other extreme of an "adjustable peg." The operation of the latter is exemplified by the U.K. Exchange Equalisation Account and has been described earlier under the heading of "active stabilisation" (*see* **3**(*b*)). (The adjustable peg may be considered a variant of either the stable or fluctuating rate systems since it combines both principles.)

Between the two extremes lie a number of *floating rate* systems which display varying degrees of flexibility. However, all the variants share the common principle that the exchange rate moves continuously or occasionally.

20. Adjustment through freely fluctuating exchange rates. When the exchange rate is permitted to move freely and without limit the risk of foreign exchange dealing is intensified. Dealers are unwilling to hold bills of exchange and therefore when exporters supply them in exchange for domestic cash they must be sold immediately to importers who wish to make payment in foreign currency.

An increase in the supply of foreign bills will force down their price (*i.e.* improve the rate of exchange) until there is an increase in demand from importers wishing to settle accounts abroad. If this demand continues to increase the price of bills of exchange will be forced up (*i.e.* the exchange rate deteriorates). In this way imports and exports continuously offset each other at varying exchange ratios. There can consequently be no disequilibrium in the balance of payments and therefore no need for compensatory short-term capital movements. It follows that gold and foreign currency reserves are not required.

21. Adjustment of disequilibrium in an adjustable-peg system. This is the system to which the major trading nations of the world currently adhere. In the short run exchange rates are pegged and adjustment takes place as in a stable rate system. In the long run adjustment is assisted by planned and limited variations in the exchange rate.

In the case of a recurrent deficit disequilibrium a planned devaluation will be effected and in the case of a surplus disequilibrium there will be a planned revaluation.

The problem then arises of selecting the right exchange rate to establish equilibrium. One solution is to allow the market temporary freedom to establish a rate in response to the forces of demand and supply. This was done in the U.K. in 1931 and to a limited degree in Germany in 1971. Equilibrium achieved, the rate is then stabilised. However, this approach is seldom favoured since it unleashes the possibility of large speculative capital movements out of a currency which is depreciating or into a currency which is appreciating. These movements will only serve to exacerbate the disequilibrium.

It is possible nevertheless to make a theoretical approach to the problem through the "Doctrine of Purchasing Power Parity."

22. Doctrine of purchasing power parity. In the 1920s Gustav Cassel argued that the equilibrium rate of exchange between two currencies should reflect the ratio between their respective domestic purchasing powers. For example, if the purchasing power of $1 in the U.S.A. is a half of the purchasing power of £1 in the U.K., the equilibrium rate of exchange is $2 : £1.

Unfortunately, this theoretical approach is beset with difficulties:

(a) *Problem of comparing purchasing power.* It is clearly difficult if not impossible to compare the purchasing power of, say, the pound sterling and the Congolese franc when assortments of goods are purchased in the two countries.

(b) *Inadequate coverage.* The theory in any case only utilises the merchandise price level to determine purchasing power parities, thus excluding the service and capital transactions which also influence the exchange rate.

(c) *Autonomous influences on the rate of exchange.* It is possible that a change in a buyer's tastes or income may act independently upon the exchange rate without any change in comparative price levels.

We may conclude therefore that while this theory is useful in drawing attention to the effect upon the exchanges of differing national rates of inflation or deflation it is of little value in determining an equilibrium rate of exchange.

23. Determining the equilibrium rate in practice. In the absence of any accurate technique reliance has to be placed upon a mixture of economic analysis and guesswork. The test of a genuine new equilibrium rate is whether it reverses those tendencies which have produced a disequilibrium in the first place. In the case of a deficit disequilibrium economic analysis will attempt to establish the degree of devaluation necessary to improve the balance of individual items in the accounts. For example, an assessment of demand and supply elasticities of imports and exports must be made in order to predict the response of these items to a given depreciation in the exchange rate.

24. The effectiveness of devaluation. The effectiveness of devaluation in remedying a fundamental payments disequilibrium depends upon the relative elasticities of demand and supply in respect of foreign exchange. If both are highly elastic then the new more unfavourable exchange rate will induce a greatly increased supply of foreign exchange at the same time as demand is greatly curtailed. The devaluation will have been extremely effective. The opposite will be the case when elasticities are low and a much greater devaluation may be necessary to eliminate even a small deficit.

25. Elasticity of demand for foreign exchange. This depends primarily upon the elasticity of domestic demand for imports. Elasticity will tend to be high where luxury consumer goods and expensive capital equipment constitute a large part of total imports and low when foodstuffs, raw materials and semi-manufactures are the principal element. The ease of substitution of home-produced goods for imports will also affect the degree of elasticity.

When import supply is wholly elastic (*i.e.* when the supply can be varied at constant price) then the elasticity of demand for imports wholly determines the elasticity of demand for foreign exchange.

In this case, when the elasticity of demand for imports is greater than zero, devaluation will produce a reduction in the volume of imports and consequently of the demand for foreign exchange. From the side of demand devaluation has proved effective.

26. Elasticity of supply of foreign exchange. The principal determining factor is the elasticity of foreign demand for domestic exports. When export supply is perfectly elastic, *i.e.* the domestic price remains unchanged after devaluation, then the elasticity of demand for exports wholly determines foreign exchange supply elasticity.

When export demand elasticity has a value of 1 (unit elasticity) a 10 per cent devaluation will produce a 10 per cent increase in the volume of exports and total foreign exchange receipts will therefore remain constant, *i.e.* the supply elasticity of foreign exchange is zero and the effect of devaluation is zero.

When export demand elasticity has a value greater than 1 a 10 per cent devaluation will produce an increase in the volume of exports in excess of 10 per cent and total foreign exchange receipts will be enlarged, *i.e.* the supply elasticity of foreign exchange is greater than zero and devaluation will have been effective.

When export demand elasticity has a value below one then a 10 per cent devaluation will not be matched by an equivalent increase in the volume of imports and total foreign exchange receipts will decline. The deficit has been enlarged.

27. Import and export supply elasticities. In the preceding two paragraphs it was assumed that the supply of imports and exports was wholly elastic, *i.e.* that the "foreign currency" price of imports and the "domestic" price of exports remained unchanged after devaluation. In that case the demand elasticities for imports and exports were the sole determinants of the effectiveness of devaluation. Allowance must now be made for this unrealistic assumption.

In the extreme (and hypothetical) case of perfectly inelastic supply of both imports and exports; by definition there can be no variation in the quantity supplied. A 10 per cent devaluation can have no effect upon the volume of domestic exports but domestic prices will be forced up by 10 per cent as foreign buyers compete to retain their share of the fixed supply. Similarly, foreign exporters, unable to curtail their output, will compete to retain their market in the devaluing country by cutting their prices by 10 per cent. The effect of devaluation is therefore neutral.

On the other hand when the supply elasticity of imports is high then devaluation will have the effect of increasing domestic import prices and it may be expected that imports will contract provided that import demand elasticity is also high.

When the supply elasticity of exports is high then exports will expand at lower foreign exchange prices provided that export demand elasticity is also high.

On the other hand when demand elasticities are low it is preferable that supply elasticities should also be low since the lack of any great response to devaluation in the demand for imports and exports will be compensated by a relatively small fall in foreign exchange export prices and a relatively small rise in domestic import prices.

28. The theoretical case for freely fluctuating rates. The argument in favour of fluctuating exchange rates derives largely from observation of the drawbacks inherent in exchange rates which are too inflexible. When rates are pegged it is expected that a deficit will be adjusted by a deflationary movement of domestic incomes and prices and that, hopefully, output and employment will be undisturbed by lower price and wage levels. In practice oligopolistic industries and powerful trade unions are able to resist the downward pressure on prices and wages, so that the reduced expenditure engendered by deflation manifests itself in declining output and rising unemployment. Since Governments are committed both to growth and full employment they are likely to frustrate deflation by adopting compensatory fiscal and monetary policies. The balance of payments therefore remains in deficit disequilibrium.

Within these limiting circumstances it is unlikely that long-run adjustment can be achieved in a stable rate system without recourse to direct controls on trade and payments. Since these run counter to the world's declared intention to liberalise trade and payments the only alternative is to adopt a system of fluctuating exchange rates. Governments are then free to pursue their own policies for growth and full employment in the knowledge that the external balance of payments is self-regulating.

29. The case against fluctuating rates. Criticism of fluctuating rates is again based upon observation of the difficulties which arose during the early 1920s and again in the 1930s when fixed exchange rates were abandoned. These were periods of great uncertainty which saw violent movements in the exchanges accompanied by massive flows of speculative capital (hot money) and deleterious effects upon trade.

This argument is countered by the suggestion that it confuses cause with effect, that violent exchange rate fluctuations were a product of an instability which sprang from other deep-rooted causes.

A further standard argument against a fluctuating rate system is that it increases the risks of (and therefore deters) international trade. Apart from accepting the normal business risks of their own trade, importers and exporters must also accept the risk of adverse movements in the exchanges.

Against this argument it is claimed that the development of forward exchange markets which may be associated with a fluctuating rate system enables the trader to hedge foreign exchange risks.

Finally, it is claimed that a stable rate system enforces a monetary discipline which makes hyper-inflation impossible. On the other hand, it is argued, a fluctuating rate system leaves a country permanently exposed to this danger.

30. The case for and against an adjustable-peg system. It has already been noted that this is the system, sponsored by the International Monetary Fund, through which the world's major trading nations presently seek to achieve international payments equilibrium.

The intention is to enjoy the combined advantages of stable and fluctuating rate systems while eliminating their disadvantages. Short-term stability is achieved by supporting operations on the exchange markets, in the case of the U.K., through the medium of the Exchange Equalisation Account. If in the long-term a fundamental surplus or deficit disequilibrium develops at the existing exchange rate, then provision is made for an adjustment upward or downward to a new peg.

In practice the weakness of this system has proved twofold. In the first place there is the difficulty of determining the appropriate degree of rate variation (*see* **16–18** above). Secondly, for political and prestige reasons, and in the case of a key currency country such as the U.K. the implications for overseas holders of sterling, a decision to devalue is likely to be postponed in the hope that internal economic measures will rectify the disequilibrium. In the event the decision is likely to be put off until overseas credit is exhausted and the reserves are disappearing. At this point it becomes universally apparent that devaluation is imminent with a resulting capital flight which puts the reserves under further pressure and makes devaluation inevitable. Such proved to be the case in the U.K. devaluation of 1967.

INTERNATIONAL MONETARY FUND (I.M.F.)

31. Objectives. The Articles of Agreement of the International Monetary Fund (I.M.F.) were signed at a 1944 conference in Bretton Woods, New Hampshire, by forty-four nations. The agreement was implemented in March 1947.

The objectives set out in Article I are fivefold:

(a) *International monetary co-operation,* through a permanent institution.

(b) *Balanced expansion of world trade.* This is the key objective since the other purposes are means to this end.

(c) *Exchange stability.* The maintenance of orderly exchange relations and the avoidance of competitive devaluations.

(d) *Multilateral payments.* The elimination of exchange restrictions and the promotion of multilateral payments on current account.

(e) *Short-term credit.* In order to add confidence to trading relations, the provision of short-term credit in the event of a temporary balance of payments disequilibrium experienced by a member.

32. The I.M.F.'s resources and their significance. There are today more than 100 members each of which contributes to the I.M.F. a quota, calculated in U.S. dollars and related to its G.N.P. Of this quota 25 per cent is paid in gold (the gold tranche) and the remainder in its own currency.

The size of the quota is important in that it determines:

(a) *The voting power* of each member's Executive Director.

(b) *The extent of a member's drawing rights.*

33. Drawing rights. Technically the I.M.F. does not grant loans but authorises a member to purchase with its own currency the currency of another member, *i.e.* it has the right to draw foreign currency from the Fund subject to certain conditions. These stipulate that the Fund must not previously have declared the desired currency to be scarce nor the drawer to be ineligible and that drawings should not exceed 25 per cent of a member's quota in any one year or a total of 20 per cent. It follows that as a member exercises its drawing rights so the Fund's holding of that country's currency rises. It can be seen therefore that strictly this is not a loan although the drawing country is expected to redeem the Fund's excess holding of its currency in gold or other acceptable currency normally within three to five years.

It should be stressed therefore that the Fund provides only short-term finance to enable a country to meet a temporary disequilibrium in its payments. The Fund's resources must continue to rotate if they are to carry out their function as an international reserve.

34. Exchange rate policy. Upon joining a member must declare a par value for its currency in terms of the U.S. dollar.

All exchange transactions with other members must then be carried out within 1 per cent of this parity (*see* **44** (*c*) below). Should a member wish to vary this rate it can do so only after consultation with the I.M.F. and then only to correct a fundamental disequilibrium in its payments.

In this way the I.M.F. rules seek to ensure short-term stability of the exchanges which allow for long-term adjustment, *i.e.* this is an adjustable-peg system.

35. Prohibition of exchange control. Article VIII prohibits the application of exchange-control restrictions on current account transactions. On the other hand Article VI permits controls over capital movements.

There are two exceptions to the general prohibition:

(*a*) *Scarce currencies.* If the Fund is unable to supply a particular currency and has declared it to be scarce then controls may be imposed on transactions in that currency. This was the case with the U.S. dollar until 1958 due to a continuing U.S. surplus disequilibrium.

(b) *Existing controls may be retained.* Article XIV permits a country to retain controls over current account payments which existed when it became a member. This was viewed simply as a post-war transitional measure but in the event it was not until 1961 that Western Europe was able to adopt Article VIII. Where advantage is still taken of Article XIV members are obliged to consult annually with I.M.F. in order to justify the continued retention of controls.

36. Appraisal of the I.M.F.'s operations. From the foregoing discussion it can be seen that the I.M.F. has aimed to promote the expansion of world trade by improving the means for international settlement in two ways:

(a) Stabilising the foreign exchange markets.

(b) Providing short-term compensatory finance.

37. Stabilising the foreign exchange markets. The intention at Bretton Woods was to establish a system which combined the advantages of a gold standard with those of a fluctuating rate system. What was desired in the exchanges was short-run stability with long-run flexibility since it was considered inevitable that periodically there would have to be a realignment of exchange rates. A devaluation or revaluation would, however, be carried out in an orderly way and only after international consultation.

In the event the goal of stability has been achieved but at the expense of an almost total inflexibility of the exchanges in the long run. For a variety of reasons Governments have proved unwilling to depart from a rate of exchange once it has been established. The result has been continuing disequilibrium in the payments of a number of countries over protracted periods, *e.g.* the U.K. 1959–67, the U.S.A. 1958–71.

38. Short-term compensatory finance. In this respect the intention was to guarantee the convertibility of currencies by supporting national reserves with the resources of the I.M.F. A country with a deficit disequilibrium would be able to obtain short-term finance while it adopted remedial internal policies which would not include resort to exchange control. However, such an objective would only be achieved in a

world in which there was a substantial degree of equilibrium
overall and no persistent maladjustments such as the dollar
shortage. For this reason throughout the 1950s the world was
compelled to rely upon exchange controls, and only when the
U.S.A. moved into deficit did it become possible to achieve
convertibility. At the same time the Fund's reserves began
to be employed in the way which had been anticipated.

However, the return to convertibility brought another
problem, the massive movement of speculative capital
between the world's financial centres which has had a highly
unstabilising effect upon the balance of international payments. This factor placed the Fund's resources under
strain and led to the "General Arrangements to Borrow."

39. General Arrangements to Borrow (G.A.B.). Since 1962
the I.M.F. resources have had the potential support of up to
£6 billion from the "Group of Ten" (E.E.C., U.S.A., U.K.,
Sweden and Japan).

Additionally, there have been developed "swap arrangements" between central banks whereby each agrees to make
balances available to the others for specified periods of time.
In the late 1960s the U.K. made much use of these facilities.

40. World liquidity problem. Apart from the strain placed
upon national reserves and the resources of the Fund by
speculative capital movements it became increasingly clear in
the 1960s that the rapid expansion of world trade called for
additions to the international money supply. Throughout
the post-war period there has been a steady decline in the
ratio of official world reserves of gold and foreign exchange to
world imports from about 80 per cent in the late 1940s to
about 30 per cent at the end of the 1960s. This decline was
partially offset by the conditional reserves of the I.M.F.
drawing rights, the G.A.B. and the swap arrangements.
However, since the last two devices were purely *ad hoc* measures it was felt there should be a more positive and formal
attempt to raise the level of international reserves. Consequently, in April 1968, the I.M.F. published its plan for
"Special Drawing Rights."

41. Special Drawing Rights (S.D.R.s). The simplest way to
envisage the scheme is to see the S.D.R.s as "international

paper money" which all countries will accept in settlement of debt.

Technically they take the form of an automatic right to receive foreign currency by transferring one's S.D.R.s to another country designated by the Fund. The basic obligation of each member is to provide his own currency upon the Fund's request up to a total of three times his own allocation of S.D.R.s.

There is a very broad requirement for drawing countries to reconstitute their position but the repayment terms are very liberal. In due course this requirement may well be reconsidered.

Individual allocations are related to members' basic quotas and total distributions planned for quinquennial periods. The scheme was activated in 1970 since when there have been two distributions.

REFORM OF THE INTERNATIONAL MONETARY SYSTEM

42. Persistent U.S. disequilibrium. It has previously been noted that in 1958 the U.S. balance of payments moved into a deficit which has subsequently remained unchanged due primarily to overseas military and aid commitments. For the post-war dollar shortage there was consequently substituted a dollar glut which periodically expressed itself in pressure on the dollar exchange rate. In due course this situation led the U.S.A. in 1968 to restrict the convertibility of dollars into gold. Gold from the reserves would now be sold at the official price of $35 only *to central banks*. Parallel to this official gold market there developed a free market with a substantially higher price which gave a truer reflection of the dollar's real international value.

43. Dollar crisis, 1971. In August large sales of surplus dollars by European central banks produced such a heavy drain of U.S. gold reserves that convertibility was now *entirely* suspended. Pressure on dollar exchange rates throughout the world then caused the emergency closure of exchange markets. When dealings were resumed the price of the dollar in terms of all other major currencies had fallen substantially away from the previous parities.

The U.S. monetary authorities were then subjected to considerable pressure from their world trading partners to accept an *official* devaluation against gold in order that markets might be quickly stabilised. Rather than accept a course of action which would depreciate the dollar uniformly against *all* other countries, the U.S. authorities preferred that certain of her major trade competitors, notably Japan and the West European nations, should *revalue* individually and in varying degrees against the dollar. This solution was not acceptable to those countries since they feared that such revaluations might weaken the competitiveness of their export prices and so have adverse effects upon their trade.

In this impasse exchange rates were permitted to float with central banks intervening only to forestall an excessive appreciation of their own currencies. The U.S.A. meanwhile took action to protect her balance of payments by imposing a 10 per cent import surcharge. Over the following four months fears were expressed that possible retaliatory trade and currency restrictions coupled with the existing exchange rate instability were leading to a downturn in trade and conceivably a world depression.

44. Group of Ten meeting, December 1971. After long preliminary negotiations the finance ministers of the Group of Ten met in late December and arrived at a *temporary* solution to which the I.M.F. gave its support. The compromise involved:

(a) *Concessions by the U.S.A.* The U.S.A. agreed to devalue against gold from \$35 per fine ounce to \$38, *i.e.* a devaluation of 8·57 per cent. Since the dollar remains wholly inconvertible the measurement against gold has only numerical significance. Gold provides a useful yardstick. At the same time the import surcharge was abandoned.

(b) *Concessions by the Group of Ten.* The other members of the Group of Ten agreed to revalue against the dollar by varying amounts. At one end of the scale the Japanese yen and the German mark appreciated by 16·9 and 13·5 per cent respectively. At the other extreme, Italy and Sweden appreciated by only 7·5 per cent. Roughly in the middle, the U.K. and France revalued by 8·57 per cent, precisely the same as the increase in the dollar price of gold; *i.e.* while revaluing against the dollar they maintained their existing parities with gold.

(c) *Wider margins*. To give the exchanges greater flexibility and monetary authorities a stronger position in dealing with speculative capital flows, dealing margins were widened to $2\frac{1}{4}$ per cent. The implication for sterling with a new parity of $2·60 is an obligation on the U.K. monetary authorities to support the rate of exchange within the limits of $2·54 and $2·66.

What can be observed in these arrangements is the first realignment of *all* exchange rates since the Bretton Woods agreement of 1944.

45. The Group of Ten communique. The opinion was widely held that the situation had been retrieved only at the eleventh hour and then only temporarily. In their communique, the finance ministers therefore agreed that discussions should be promptly undertaken, particularly within the context of I.M.F., to consider more permanent arrangements for the reform of the international monetary system. It was agreed to direct attention to the appropriate monetary means of stabilising exchange rates and ensuring convertibility: to the proper role of gold, of reserve currencies and of special drawing rights; to the permissible margin of fluctuation on either side of agreed parities and to other means of establishing flexibility; to measures appropriate to dealing with the movement of short-term capital.

It therefore transpired that the weaknesses of the Bretton Woods agreement led ultimately to a world monetary crisis which was temporarily resolved only by long and patient multilateral negotiation which might not easily be repeated. It is clearly a matter of urgency that more permanent solutions should be found.

THE WORLD BANK GROUP

46. Objectives. It has been noted that the ulterior purpose of the I.M.F. is the promotion of international trade as a means to rising world living standards. Similarly, the World Bank Group which is concerned with increasing the flow of investment in the developing countries may be said to have the same objectives. The more rapidly the economies of the developing countries expand the fuller the part they can play in international trade.

47. International Bank for Reconstruction and Development (I.B.R.D.). Basically this is an international investment bank financed by the developed nations and which makes loans to Governments for approved projects for periods up to thirty-five years at the substantial interest rate of $5\frac{1}{2}$ per cent.

A criticism of I.B.R.D. has been that the debt service burden at this rate of interest has grown so rapidly that during the 1960s it was absorbing 10 per cent of the export income of the developing countries, thus jeopardising their economic programmes.

48. International Development Association (I.D.A.). This organisation is also financed by the Governments of the developed countries. It was set up because of the inability of some developing countries either to qualify projects for I.B.R.D. support or to meet the high interest charges. The loan terms are liberal with easily staged repayments and no interest other than a $\frac{3}{4}$ –1 per cent service charge.

49. International Finance Corporation (I.F.C.). Unlike I.B.R.D. and I.D.A., the I.F.C. which was set up in 1956 does not make loans to Governments. Along with private investors it participates in private industrial enterprises.

PROGRESS TEST 12

1. Explain how a rate of exchange is reached. (**1**)
2. What do you understand by a variable exchange rate system? (**2**)
3. Explain how an exchange rate may be actively stabilised. (**3**(*b*))
4. What do you understand by "exchange control"? (**4**)
5. Where exchange rates are stabilised, what will be the effects of a payments disequilibrium? (**5**(*b*))
6. Explain the price-specie flow mechanism. (**6**)
7. What were the main features of the gold standard? (**7**)
8. How was equilibrium supposedly restored on a full gold standard? (**8**)

9.   What were the main disadvantages of the gold standard?
(**9**(*b*))

10.   Criticise the concept of the price-specie flow mechanism.
(**10**)

11.   What is the significance of changes in income to the balance of payments?   (**11**)

12.   Explain one of the variations to the full gold standard.
(**12**)

13.   Why was the gold standard abandoned?   (**13**)

14.   What are the purposes of an exchange-control system?
(**16**)

15.   What are the disadvantages of exchange control?   (**18**)

16.   Define an "adjustable peg."   (**21**)

17.   What are the shortcomings of the theory of purchasing power parity?   (**22**)

18.   Upon what factors does a successful devaluation depend?
(**24–27**)

19.   Compare the main arguments for and against fluctuating exchange rates.   (**28, 29**)

20.   Appraise the case for an adjustable-peg system.   (**30**)

21.   List the objectives of I.M.F.   (**31**)

22.   What are "drawing rights"?   (**33**)

23.   What policy does the I.M.F. pursue in respect of exchange control?   (**35**)

24.   Assess the success of the I.M.F.'s operations.   (**36–38**)

25.   Explain the nature of the world liquidity problem.   (**40**)

26.   What are "Special Drawing Rights"?   (**41**)

27.   List the institutions which fall within the World Bank Group.   (**42–45**)

28.   What are the objectives of the World Bank Group?   (**42**)

GOVERNMENT AND INDUSTRY

CHAPTER XIII

THE RELATIONSHIP BETWEEN GOVERNMENT AND INDUSTRY

PHILOSOPHY OF THE RELATIONSHIP

1. Area of study. In Chapter I an examination was made of the macroeconomic foundation for Government economic policy after 1945. Only then was it recognised that Government should bear the responsibility for the management of the economy at a high level of activity. The instrument was to be the control of aggregate demand (*see* I, **4, 13**). Nevertheless, Government had developed some interest in specific aspects of the country's economic life at an earlier period. Legislation on trade unions and conditions of employment can be traced to the early nineteenth century. By the end of that century there was concern over the effects of monopoly power in certain industries.

During the inter-war depression some rather weak attempts were made to promote industrial rationalisation and to influence the location of industry. After the Second World War Government intervention in these matters became politically more acceptable.

The role of Government in economic affairs may be viewed at two levels. Firstly, the general controls of fiscal and monetary policy. Secondly, controls over specific aspects of economic policy.

Part Four of the **HANDBOOK** is concerned with the second aspect, in particular with the relationship of Government and industry.

2. Laissez-faire attitudes. Nineteenth-century economists and politicians believed that national economic and social benefits would be maximised by the summation of the efforts of each individual consumer and business organisation working unrestrictedly towards their own aims, within the parameter of the "Laws of Supply and Demand" (*see* E. Seddon, *Economics of Public Finance*, M. & E. **HANDBOOK**, 1968, Chapter I).

This concept is economically rationalised in the Theory of Perfect Competition. Resources will be most efficiently allocated and consumer satisfaction maximised in a situation where a large number of firms producing a homogeneous commodity face a horizontal demand curve (the curve is of infinite elasticity). There is no restriction of entry to the industry and factors of production are mobile. No one firm can influence price but they can sell all their output at the prevailing price.

Any deviation from this situation represents a waste of resources.

3. A decline in belief in laissez-faire attitudes. The twentieth century has seen a constant decline in the number of people who believe completely in *laissez-faire* concepts.

The relationships between Government, industry and individuals have developed into a controversial, complex phenomenon. The decline in traditional beliefs has three main causes:

(*a*) *Change in the role of the Government.* It is clear the aims of individual people and organisations are not complementary. They are more likely to conflict. Thus the Government must create an environment in which the individual can pursue his own interest but only at the limited expense of others. This belief was first developed in social legislation, *e.g.* the *Factory Acts* of the 1830s and 1840s, but gradually came into economic thinking, *e.g.* particularly in the pricing policy of nineteenth-century railways, where the consumer was protected from price exploitation.

Today the Government has to seek compromises between the economic interests of various groups within society. They are handicapped because there is no basic set of applied economic truths and goals. Even the previously accepted aim of economic growth is now challenged (*see* E. J. Mishan, *The Cost of Economic Growth*, Staples Press, 1967).

(*b*) *Growth of industrial organisations.* Advances in technology with their huge financial commitment plus the growth of markets based on rising living standards and fast communications has brought the era of giant firms straddling national frontiers. Traditional economic beliefs as expressed in conventional textbooks provide little help in understanding the workings and effects of modern industrial life. The relationship between a company and its markets and the business decisions involved require a rethinking of traditional economic theory.

(c) *Definitions of competition and company aims.* The textbook definitions of competition and company aims are now merely slogans with little connection to reality. G. C. Allen argues that in every buying and selling situation facing the company there are elements of monopoly and fierce competition. The concept of perfect competition, while logically true, is stultifying and cannot explain economic reality. "Experience does not suggest that all the most progressive industries are those which most nearly satisfy the conditions of perfect competition" (G. C. Allen, *Monopoly and Restrictive Practices*, Allen & Unwin, p. 22).

Economic theory of the firm postulates that companies will try to maximise their profits and that use of price will be the major weapon of competition. Empirical research suggests that companies will have various aims and their attitude to profit will centre on achieving a satisfactory level of profit. With certain exceptions, *e.g.* sectors of the retail industry, price changing is not a significant competitive fact. D. C. Hague of the Manchester Business School (*Managerial Economics*, Longman, 1969) suggests that unless costs are rising quickly, prices are sticky and firms will prefer to compete with quality, service, advertisement, promotional gifts or value for money (*e.g.* the sales success of Marks & Spencer is based on value for money which is not the same concept as low prices). Historical studies suggest that businessmen have conservative attitudes towards price cutting and it is an insignificant business practice.

4. Role of Government in industry today. Since 1945 all Western Governments have faced a changing industrial scene without the comforting knowledge and security given by economic truths. A pragmatic approach has developed of treating each problem as it occurs. This method has led to policy contradictions and wild swings of economic fashion. What size of company leads to efficiency? Should mergers be encouraged or banned? Should monopolies at home be allowed in the interest of international competition? Have certain industries such a vital role in the national interest they must not be allowed to die? Is the determination of incomes solely the concern of both sides of industry? The questions are unlimited, the answers ever changing.

Mr. John Davies, representing the Confederation of British Industry, in 1967 suggested the Government had five areas of involvement with industry:

(a) To protect people, *e.g. Trades Description Act* and smoke control legislation.

(b) To provide services, *e.g.* education.

(c) General management of nation's resources, *e.g.* adult retraining schemes.

(d) To provide public utilities, *e.g.* gas and electricity.

(e) Large-scale buyer of private industry products.

Each of these areas contains many points of controversy. Mr. Davies felt the only solution to Government/industry problems was participation, a genuine attempt by both parties to understand the other's difficulties. Too often, he concluded, Government fails to understand the nature and mechanics of industry, thus industrialists become alienated from the Government's desire to improve industrial efficiency.

5. The basic problems of Government intervention. Governments have always created a legal framework in which industry must work and the vast majority of industrialists accept this legislation. It is the financial involvement of Government in industry, *e.g.* textiles, shipbuilding, aircraft, which has proved controversial.

The core of the argument centres on the boundary between the national interest and inefficient subsidising of private industry. National interest can be interpreted from three viewpoints:

(a) *Political, e.g.* defence and diplomatic.

(b) *Economic, e.g.* balance of payments; technology.

(c) *Social, e.g.* unemployment; environment.

It is difficult to envisage other than piecemeal solutions, but Governments must ask themselves:

(a) In what situation will money be given to industry?

(b) What is the ceiling figure of this aid?

(c) How can public accountability be exercised over the money?

6. Conclusion. All Governments wish "To increase the productivity of labour and capital; to raise the rate of new capital formation.   To obtain the maximum return in terms of the production of goods and services" (*Nationalised Industries —A Review of Economic and Financial Objectives, 1967*, Cmnd. 3437).

As A. Schonfield in his book *Modern Capitalism* (O.U.P., 1965) points out, market forces are no longer the flexible economic weapon of the nineteenth century, thus Governments have to devise methods of economic industrial adjustment to achieve the aims outlined above.

METHODS OF GOVERNMENT INTERVENTION PLANNING

7. Control. The Government exercises direct control over the industrial sector by the use of rationing, licensing, quotas and price fixing. Resources are allocated according to a Government-determined need. Controls are acceptable in wartime, as the overriding need to win the war is accepted by the whole nation.

After the Second World War, severe shortages necessitated the use of controls by the Attlee Government. However, by 1948, controls were kept for doctrinaire reasons.   In this situation private industry becomes disillusioned; it has no incentives, rewards are difficult to achieve and industrial inertia sets in.

By 1951, controls were proving useless and the period had proved the peacetime impossibility of influencing industry by direct interference with business decisions.

8. Controls abandoned. After 1951, the new Conservative Government abandoned controls, and the economy leapt forward.   However, the boom was not entirely driven by the freeing of market forces, for a 25 per cent fall in world commodity prices slashed the import bill and the balance of payments surpluses provided the Government with great economic flexibility.

By the end of the 1950s, Great Britain's economic performance was deteriorating and in terms of economic growth we were slipping behind our European neighbours.

France had apparently achieved economic growth by the use of indicative planning and the British Government became interested in economic planning.

9. Indicative planning. Planning might involve a total alteration by the Government of the output decisions of private enterprises. This alteration is to achieve economic and social goals that would be unattainable by private decision-taking. Such planning is called "imperative" and really involves the large-scale use of controls; the system is practised by Communist countries.

Indicative planning implies planning by consent. Government and industry co-operate in deciding how best to utilise resources to achieve agreed goals usually expressed in percentage increases in industrial and national output.

This co-operation should improve Government/industry understanding and give a sense of purpose to the nation by indicating clearly defined, achievable economic goals. Industrial decision-taking is made easier because the Government provides an agreed economic framework (*e.g.* stop-go policies producing wild fluctuations in levels of aggregate demand are avoided).

10. Indicative planning—French style. The system involved three bodies:

(*a*) *Conseil Superieur*, the head of the planning hierarchy, It consisted of representatives of both sides of industry plus some Government representation. Little more than a public relations body, it seldom met.

(*b*) *Commissariat du Plan*, a body of over a hundred economic and industrial technocrats. It was the vital link although it co-ordinated and advised rather than implemented decisions.

(*c*) *Modernisation Committees*. Committees representing various industries and policy sectors, *e.g.* regional planning.

The Modernisation Committee provided the Commissariat with information about output, investment and demand trends. The Commissariat built a picture of economic developments based on the assumptions behind a variety of possible rates of economic growth. The Government and the Conseil then selected a rate of growth on the effective use of resources which would satisfy the country's political, social and economic needs.

The Government created the general economic environment and private industry responded positively because its interests were integrated within the plan. However, in practice the French Government had an iron fist in the velvet glove for they had a tight control over the raising of new capital and firms deviating from the plan's targets found themselves in financial trouble.

France achieved rates of growth of 6–9 per cent per annum in the period 1953–60 when she was committed to indicative planning, but the correlation of planning and growth is too facile (*see* 12 below) and no precise lessons can be learned from the French experience.

11. Indicative planning—British style. This was pioneered by a Conservative Government in the early 1960s, thus marking a significant change in Conservative economic philosophy.

(*a*) *The organisation and aims.* In 1962, the Chancellor of the Exchequer, Mr. Selwyn Lloyd, founded the National Economic Development Council. It has two main parts:

(*i*) *Top Council.* Representatives of both sides of industry and Government. The chairman was the Chancellor and sometimes the Prime Minister.

(*ii*) *The Office.* A body of economic and industrial experts led by a Director-General to carry out the day-to-day research.

N.E.D.C.'s terms of reference were:

(1) To examine the economic performance of the nation.

(2) To find how a sound rate of growth is to be produced.

(3) To find the major obstacles to economic growth in this country.

(*b*) *The planning work of N.E.D.C.* The first major report, *Conditions Favourable to Faster Growth*, published in

1963, assessed the sectoral implications of a 4 per cent per annum rate of growth in the period 1961–65. The plan was based on reports from a cross-section of seventeen industries ranging from coal to electronics. The industrial forecasts of output and investment were promising and the Office felt the likely rise in imports of 4 per cent could be matched by a 5 per cent rise in export earnings.

A subsequent report highlighted the following problem areas:

   (i) *Incomes.* A need for social reasons of more equality.
   (ii) *Education.* Must be given a high-investment priority.
   (iii) *Training.* A complete overhaul of the apprentice-ship system with an extension of adult retraining.
   (iv) *Labour mobility.* A great need for five-yearly manpower-planning exercises.

The above ideas never developed into a coherent economic plan, although N.E.D.C. became a great pressure group for implanting the concept of growth into the nation's subconscious.

The period saw an average economic growth rate of $3 \cdot 4$ per cent, although much of this could be attributed to the use of excess capacity accrued in the previous period of stagnation.

The year 1964 produced two extremely conflicting economic statistics: a growth rate of $5 \cdot 7$ per cent and a balance of payments deficit of nearly £800 million. The new Government under Mr. Wilson decided that the deficit must be removed even at the expense of a thriving rate of growth.

Apart from one hasty effort by George Brown in 1965 to produce a national plan, planning on the national scale passed from the British economic vocabulary, although N.E.D.C. remains and regional economic plans have been prepared (*see* **13** (*c*) below).

12. Problems of planning.

(*a*) Countries have produced economic growth without an economic plan, *e.g.* Germany. The example of France is no real proof of the correlation between economic planning and growth. Do we know what France would have achieved without planning?

(*b*) We have insufficient supportable evidence of what causes growth. Economic development comes from a mix of factors, *e.g.* investment, education, productivity, attitudes. It seems improbable that any country has sufficient knowledge of the relationships of these variables to blend them into a recipe for instant growth.

(c) Indicative planning involves no Government force. It can only produce guidelines, which industry will follow if it trusts the Government. Antagonism rather than trust is the predominant mood between industry and the British Government, although each new administration is granted a short honeymoon.

(d) Economic history suggests that fast growth of the British economy produces a balance of payments crisis as industry absorbs a growing volume of imports to feed its output expansion. A successful plan would need to produce growth led by the exporting industries.

STRUCTURAL CHANGES

13. The need for structural change. The Labour Government of 1964–70 became convinced that general Government economic policies were powerless if there were basic weaknesses and inefficiencies in the key sectors of the economy, particularly in industry. To overcome these weaknesses, industrial structures had to be changed. This was not a new idea. Since 1948 various measures had been taken to increase competition (*see* XV, **7–21**) but the Labour Government felt that "increasing competition" was too vague a concept and they became more interested in precise industrial problems, *e.g.* standardisation in machine tools, market rationalisation in the heavy electrical industry, world competition in the motor industry, economies of scale in shipbuilding, quality of management, levels of advanced technology.

The Government tried to effect these structural changes through:

(a) The structure of Government.

(b) The law.

(c) Specially created bodies.

14. The structure of Government.

(a) *The 1964–70 Labour Government.* The Labour Government came into power in October 1964, convinced that the Treasury had an over-influential conservative effect on

British economic and industrial life. They felt that Treasury thinking was motivated almost entirely by short-term considerations of the balance of payments.

Mr. Wilson founded the Department of Economic Affairs (D.E.A.) with Mr. Brown as its head. Its prime function was to ensure the efficient use of resources. It came to concentrate on the problems of regional development, incomes policy and the effects of industrial structure on industrial efficiency. The D.E.A. lost impetus on the departure of Mr. Brown in 1966. Its role, purpose and power became less and less clear and it was wound up in 1969.

The Wilson administration founded the Ministry of Technology to produce a second Industrial Revolution by encouraging the growth of investment in technology and under the drive of Mr. Wedgwood Benn it enjoyed a degree of success.

(b) *Conservative Government.* The mood for using Government departments to influence industry continued under the 1970 Conservative Government. A Department of Trade and Industry was founded "To assist British Industry and Commerce to improve their economic and technological strength and competitiveness." This Department includes the old Board of Trade and Ministry of Technology; its responsibilities include monopolies and mergers, civil aviation, most of the nationalised industries, relations with private industry and the industrial side of regional development.

15. The use of the law. Many laws affect industry directly or indirectly. They may affect: industrial geography, *e.g. Town and Country Planning Act,* 1947; their organisation, *e.g. Monopolies and Mergers Act,* 1965; their direct business activities, *e.g.* 1968 legislation involving working hours of bus- and lorry-drivers; their relations with labour, *e.g. Redundancy Employment Act,* 1965. Ultimately any Government has the power to limit a firm's activities by law, although controversy will always surround any effort by Government to impose its will on industry by the use of law.

16. Specially created organisations. Since the nineteenth century Governments have created bodies to study and influence industrial problems. In 1962 from the N.E.D.C.

came "Little Neddies"—industrial committees representing all opinions within an industry. They investigated problem areas within their own field under the general headings of Imports-Exports, Structure, Manpower, Forecasting and Miscellaneous. The committees have enjoyed a good deal of success although they have needed a sharing of company information which may have restricted the competitive nature of the industry.

In 1967, the Government created the Industrial Reorganisation Corporation (I.R.C.) (*see* XVI, **26–30**) with the deliberate intention of restructuring sections of industry and trying to improve the general level of management efficiency in key sectors of the economy. The I.R.C. was abolished by the Conservative Government.

17. Conclusion. Modern Governments are committed to influence industry, to maximise the efficiency of industry, although the criteria of efficiency and the weapons of influence are rightly the subject of much debate.

The next chapters investigate how British Governments have affected industry in the realms of competitiveness, size, nationalisation and location.

PROGRESS TEST 13

1. Suggest two ways of viewing the part played by the Government in economic affairs. **(1)**

2. How did the nineteenth-century *laissez-faire* economists think that the nation's social and economic benefits could be maximised? **(2)**

3. What have been the main reasons for the decline of belief in *laissez-faire* attitudes? **(3)**

4. Suggest different interpretations of the term "national interest." **(5)**

5. What is meant by "indicative planning"? **(9)**

6. What is the National Economic Development Council? **(11)**

7. Suggest how sudden economic growth might affect the British balance of payments. **(12(*d*))**

8. Why was the 1964 Labour Government interested in changing industrial structures? **(13)**

9. What are the aims of the Department of Trade and Industry? **(14(*b*))**

10. What is a "Little Neddie"? **(16)**

CHAPTER XIV

MONOPOLIES AND RESTRICTIVE PRACTICES

WHAT IS A MONOPOLIST?

1. Theoretical approach. To clarify the concept of a monopolist, economists have tried to define a perfect monopolist in terms of the completely opposite situation of perfect competition. Thus a perfect monopolist may be defined as a producer facing a totally inelastic demand curve. This in practice is completely unrealistic because it implies that price can be raised without limit.

A producer in this situation would be still competing, for he would be competing for a share of the consumer's income. So a perfect monopolist would have to be the sole producer of all goods and services bought out of the consumer's income. Only a Communist society, with the Government as a producer, would tend to this position.

Clearly a more realistic definition of monopoly is required.

2. A single producer. In a market where the output of a product is controlled by a single firm, that firm is in a monopolistic position. However, branding creates a situation where there is only one producer of the product, *e.g.* only Unilever make "Persil," but the single producer may be in fierce competition with other producers.

3. A lack of substitutes. A firm producing a good for which there is no close substitute is in a monopolistic situation. This is realistic, but a problem remains. A big organisation may own several companies which produce competing brands but unless the policy of the parent firm to its subsidiaries is known, no true assessment can be made of the degree of competition, *e.g.* Distillers own most of the best-selling whisky brands but only insiders know the strength of competition which exists between the brands.

4. Market domination. A firm with a dominant share of the market could be said to be a monopolist, but a definition of market and domination is required. A 100 per cent share is domination, but is 42 per cent? Are boiled sweets in the same market as bars of chocolate and boxes of chocolates?

5. Agreements. A superficially competitive industry could be riddled by agreed restrictive practices (*see* **21–29** below) which remove the competitive element from the market situation.

6. Size. Monopoly should not be exclusively linked to company size, for small firms can have a monopoly through location, *e.g.* a newsagent, or a legal monopoly, *e.g.* patent.

7. Conclusion. Because a precise definition of monopolist is difficult, Governments try to act against a firm or group of firms which use a dominant market position to act against the public interest.

Dominant share can be arbitrarily if not economically defined—the 1948 *Monopolies and Restrictive Practices Act* uses a $33\frac{1}{3}$ per cent share (*see* XV, **8**)—but public interest is capable of infinite definitions and creates a problem for anti-monopoly legislators.

ARGUMENTS AGAINST MONOPOLIES

8. Higher prices. A monopolistic market price may be greater than if the market was competitive because the monopolist is faced with a more inelastic demand. Resources are thus allocated in a way that is not the most efficient, *e.g.* the monopolist can afford to use labour wastefully.

9. Restriction of choice. The buyer is forced if he requires the product to buy from the monopolist. If the consumer is unsatisfied with the good or service, he has no adequate method of expressing dissatisfaction.

10. Lack of innovation. If a company has little competition, there is no incentive to improve its efficiency, its product, its training or any other aspect of business. There is no stimulus to innovate and ultimately this attitude breeds stagnation which kills economic development.

11. Political domination. In a small country, particularly if it is dependent on one crop, a company may come to monopolise the whole economy, *e.g.* the America Sugar Corporation in pre-Castro Cuba. A major part of the nation's resources flow into the company enabling it to dominate the Government and labour force, thus providing a danger to democracy.

ARGUMENTS IN FAVOUR OF MONOPOLY

12. Benefits of economies of scale. If a firm can increase its output by achieving a greater market penetration it should benefit from the economies of large-scale production, *i.e.* output will increase more quickly than costs because of a greater spreading of overheads and cost savings from bulk buying, better financial terms and the use of specialised labour and management. If these benefits are fully realised, cost per unit should fall, giving the opportunity of price reductions.

13. A monopolist as a stable economic force. Any economy is subject to short-term economic fluctuations and smaller businesses may go bankrupt very quickly. This creates both a waste of resources and social hardship. The firm in a monopolistic position is less prone to violent demand fluctuations and gives a greater security to its shareholders and work force. Should a company be the major employer in any area it is more likely to receive Government help in times of temporary stress. While no Government should permanently subsidise a company, no Government can remain indifferent to creating a specific area of very high unemployment.

14. The cost of innovation. Schumpeter, the American economist, thirty years ago pointed out that industry was becoming increasingly technologically and scientifically orientated and that further innovation would involve huge sums of money invested in research and development. In 1970, over £600 million was being spent on research in this country.

The levels of capital required for this investment expenditure are difficult to raise for small companies who have no great access to internal and external sources of capital.

15. Costs of competition. A monopolistic situation may be desirable because competition can create business conditions harmful to the consumer:

(a) *Cut-price wars.* In the short period, consumers gain from price wars but ultimately they lead to reductions in quality of good or service; low profits damage research and drive companies out of business, thus reducing consumer choice.

(b) *Marketing costs.* A fiercely competitive market increases marketing costs as firms fight for their share of the market. Eventually, the marketing costs may be the biggest single cost element, *e.g.* in drugs and cosmetics marketing accounts for 30–45 per cent of total costs.

16. Conclusions. The economic health of a country requires industrial efficiency, rising productivity and the opportunity for new companies to enter any market. Competition theoretically is the key to the solution of these problems, but even in the textbooks some arguments can be found to favour monopoly. An economy gains from both competitive and monopolistic situations. Neither structure is inherently good or bad.

THE PROBLEMS OF APPLYING THE THEORY TO THE REAL WORLD

17. Multi-product firms. Most companies today provide a variety of products for a vast complex of markets. Thus, any one company may be faced with the total textbook range of competitive situations. Satisfactory analysis requires knowledge of each separate market and the companies' policy in that market, *e.g.* how are overheads allocated between the different markets; does each product have a separate pricing policy; is there a cross-subsidisation of products (*e.g.* successful product profits are used to subsidise less successful ones)?

It is even difficult to define a firm in terms of policy decision-taking, *e.g.* what is the relation of J. Crosfield & Sons Ltd., maker of "Persil," to the whole Unilever organisation?   Who actually determines the marketing policy for "Persil"?

18. What is competition?   Economists have a tendency to equate competition solely with prices.   But price is only one form and often an insignificant type of competition.   Many markets are becoming increasingly oligopolistic, *i.e.* a few firms in close competition, *e.g.* petrol, beer, detergents.   In this situation firms are frightened of price competition for if one company significantly cuts its prices the others would follow.   No extra sales would accrue, assuming a static market and revenue and profits would fall.   <u>Falling profits are not in the public interest if they lead to lower investment and poorer quality of good and service.   Firms prefer to compete via the commodity, its use and design and through promotional schemes.</u>

Even where price changes are significant, *e.g.* in the grocery retail trade, there is no evidence to prove that the consumer is a rational economic person.   Reasons for using a particular shop are often more easily explained by Freud than Adam Smith, thus shop layout and background music are more important influences on consumer preference than exciting cut-price offers.

The term "cut price" is not without ambiguity.   All garages may offer 25 per cent off the price of a new tyre.   The economist needs to know:

(*a*) Why in a highly competitive industry is the figure always seemingly 25 per cent?

(*b*) Off what price is the 25 per cent taken?   If it is the manufacturer's recommended price, and nobody charges the price, are we really enjoying a cut-price offer?

19. New competition.   Although a competitive situation is highly desirable, how can it be made to exist?   Even without formal restrictive practices, companies can settle informally for non-aggressive competition.   The petrol industry appears to be highly competitive but the consumer benefits appear to be obscure.

Apathetic competitive attitudes can only be destroyed by newcomers to a market.   Today many markets are closed to small newcomers through the excessive costs of mass production, research and marketing. The ironic situation now exists where new competition in market A is provided by a company which dominates market B, but which finds market B static, thus the company diversifies into market A, *e.g.* Imperial Tobacco entering the potato-crisp market with "Golden Wonder Crisps." This trend will enforce the tendency to oligopolistic situations (*see* **18** above).

20. Innovation. Without new ideas society dies; without innovation industry stagnates., The traditional analysis of innovating influences (*see* **10** and **14** above) appear contradictory and confusing.

Innovation would appear to flourish under three stimulants:

(*a*) *Pressure*

(*i*) The pressure from market forces of either competitor or consumer, *e.g.* colour television sets.

(*ii*) Pressure from within the company. Employees at all levels offering new ideas.

(*b*) *Opportunity*

(*i*) An expanding market with a high income elasticity, e.g. washing-machines.

(*ii*) Is the product capable of change by new ideas, *e.g.* fountain- and ball point-pens.

(*c*) *Capacity*

(*i*) Financial means to foster the innovation.

(*ii*) Management quality to see innovating potential.

The use of this analysis illustrates that innovation is not peculiar to a type of market structure or to the size of a company. It raises doubts about a Government policy based on an optimum market structure or company size (*see* XVI, **35**).

RESTRICTIVE PRACTICES

21. Introduction. Modern thought suggests the size of a company or its share of the market are not the vital criteria in judging a monopolistic situation. The power exercised by the company through its size or market share is the feature to be controlled by monopoly legislation. The power is exercised by the use of restrictive practices which may bring benefit but which restrict the freedom of either the producer, the retailer or the consumer. This section includes a selection of these practices showing how they might affect the public interest.

22. Resale price maintenance. Manufacturers force retailers, through threats of withdrawing supplies, to charge a standard price for a commodity. A retailer is prevented from passing on lower costs via prices that he may achieve from inproving efficiency. This practice is now banned in Great Britain although it is permitted in the sale of books (*see* XV, **20**).

23. Full-line forcing. A manufacturer insists that the retailer takes all his lines and not just those which the retailer feels are good sellers. The freedom of retailer choice is thus abused. The practice was used by the chocolate-manufacturers in the 1950s.

24. Import restrictions. A market dominator in Country A agrees not to export to Country B if a firm in Country B offers a reciprocal agreement. The Swedish and British match industries have operated this system in the past.

25. Exclusive dealings. A group of manufacturers arrange that their products will only be handled by certain outlets, thus a customer of the outlet has his choice of product severely restricted. The petrol and beer industries use this practice although, in these cases, most customers have easy access to a range of outlets.

Competition was more seriously restricted in the dental goods and cast-iron rainwater goods industries, when dealers were forced by the strength of the manufacturers to buy from members of the manufacturers' trade association, membership of which was severely controlled. Thus a basic promise of competition, freedom of entry, was not achieved, as potential newcomers were effectively kept out of the market.

26. Restrictive tendering. In certain industries, *e.g.* civil engineering, the customer orders his product by asking suppliers to bid, by means of tender, for his order. It is easy for the manufacturers to restrict competition by agreeing privately which firm will obtain the contract and the other firms then submit artificially high bids. More sophisticated methods can be devised and it is almost impossible for the individual customer to prove that his choice is being restricted. (*see* Monopolies and Restrictive Practices Commission. *Report on the Supply of Buildings in Greater London*, Chapter 3.)

27. Price fixing. Companies producing closely competing products agree to charge the same price, *e.g.* in the 1950s the Electric Lamp Manufacturers' Association. These type of agreements generally need strengthening because a member of the Association may lower prices to avoid surplus capacity or a newcomer may enter the market with a low-priced good. The first situation is covered by fixing production quotas between firms and the second difficulty could be overcome by producing and selling a product at just above cost, thus driving out newcomers.

28. Restriction in supply of machinery. A company or group of companies is sufficiently powerful to ask their machine-suppliers not to supply to potential competitors, *e.g.* the Swedish Match Corporation also controlled the suppliers of the basic capital equipment for the match industry. They agreed not to supply machinery to their competitors, the British Match Corporation

29. Aggregated rebates. Rebates are given to customers who remain loyal to the producers. This practice may seem innocuous but the period of expected loyalty could extend over a number of years and be exercised by a group of producers.   In this situation new competitors would have to offer almost non-profitable terms to gain a foothold in the market. This system is used by the Shipping Conferences.

PROGRESS TEST 14

1. In theoretical terms how would you define a perfect monopolist? (**1**)

2. Explain how a small company might achieve a monopolistic position. (**6**)

3. Why do Governments view with suspicion companies holding a dominant market position? (**7**)

4. In what way does a lack of innovation create economic difficulties for a country?   (**10**)

5. Are cut-price wars necessarily in the interests of the consumer?   (**15**(*a*))

6. What is meant by a "cross-subsidisation of products"? (**17**)

7. Define an oligopolistic market situation.   (**18**)

8. How does resale price maintenance damage the consumer's interests?   (**22**)

9. Why should a trade association feel that a price-fixing agreement might not achieve its aims?   (**27**)

10. How is competition restricted by an aggregate rebate scheme?   (**29**)

CHAPTER XV

ANTI-MONOPOLY LEGISLATION

POLICY FOR LEGISLATION

1. Introduction. A comparative study of national attitudes to controlling monopoly would show that no two countries adopt the same principles. The criteria of control must allow for certain economic problems which have no clear-cut answer. This chapter discusses some of these problems.

2. General attack on monopolies. There are three areas of attack:

(*a*) *Regulation of structures*. The Government is concerned with the size of companies supplying a market. It will try to prevent any firm or group of firms obtaining more than a given share of the market. This philosophy lies behind American attitudes to monopoly control.

(*b*) *Regulation of behaviour*. A monopolist offends by using restrictive practices (*see* XIV, **21–24**) which adversely affects the consumer and the dynamism of the economy. British legislation has concentrated on this approach (*see* **7–21** below).

(*c*) *Regulation of performance*. This concept believes the monopolist is likely to be less efficient, therefore certain criteria of performance must be checked, *e.g.* price cost relationships, profit levels, innovation record and ability to meet consumer demand. Unfortunately, although the criteria can be listed it is almost impossible to define acceptable standards of measurement, *e.g.* what is a satisfactory level of profit, if profit itself is used as a test of efficiency? If a monopolist obtains a greater rate of return on capital than a similar-sized company in a more competitive market, is it through efficiency or market domination.

The first method of regulation is easier to legislate for, because market shares are easily measurable; however, it could fail to attack companies which are not dominating the market but which limit competition through agreements. Alternatively, it attacks the oligopolistic situation (*see* XIV, **18**). which may be highly competitive, *e.g.* detergents.

To control abuses of power seems the most satisfactory approach, but market circumstances vary so much, this method may become too pragmatic and result in a time-consuming series of investigations (*see* "Monopolies Commission," **8–12** below).

PROBLEM AREAS IN FORMULATING THE LEGISLATION

3. The use of economic criteria.   The textbook approach to monopolies centres on the best use of resources theory (*see* G. L. Thirkettle *Basic Economics* (an M. & E. **HANDBOOK**, 2nd edition, 1971).   A Government must take a wider approach, *e.g.* it has to buy aircraft for defence purposes but cannot order sufficient planes to sustain a highly competitive market, thus only one or two firms can exist.

4. Home and international competition.   Companies and industries are focusing on the world as their market; national boundaries are becoming meaningless.   The development of supranational companies has lead Governments to analyse competition from the view of international markets thus a company may be allowed to dominate the home market if its size and effectiveness allows it to compete with foreign giants.

The legal problem of the future will centre on how Governments can control international monopolies.   Suppose the recently formed Pirelli-Dunlop organisation agreed to share markets with the Goodyear and Firestone companies, what law could deal with this situation.   Already unions are realising they will have to co-operate internationally to bargain with the ever-growing companies and there appears to be a growing need for international anti-monopoly legislation. ?

5. Distinction between economies of scale and market domination.   The legislation must have a system of distinguishing the true reason for a company or companies achieving and using monopoly power.   Most companies claim that big-market shares enable them to reap the economies of scale (*see* XIV, **12**) but seldom is there a quantifying of this claim. The Government should seek answers to such questions as:

(*a*) Are the economies in one plant or through the whole company?

(*b*) Are the economies technical, financial or administrative?

(*c*) What market share is necessary to achieve these economies?

(*d*) How will the economies affect costs and prices?

Gordon Newbould in his book *Management and Merger Activity* (Guthstead, Liverpool, 1970) suggests most firms merge to gain bigger shares of the market, to reduce competition or simply to protect themselves from predatory companies. Rigorous analysis of company claims must be an essential feature of monopoly investigation.

6. Guide lines for companies. In controlling monopolies Governments have to choose between a pragmatic approach, which is non-judicial, and a legalistic approach, which is judicial. The first method treats every monopolistic situation on its merits which seems very equitable. However companies may feel there is no clear Government policy so they are unsure of the types of business behaviour which are acceptable. Companies without a competitive motivation will be tempted to further restrict competition as Government policy is so indecisive.

A legal solution should clarify a company's position although an inflexible attitude to market domination might not be in the public interest, for monopolies in certain circumstances can benefit the public.

The next section illustrates how British Governments have tried to solve this conflict.

BRITISH ANTI-MONOPOLY LEGISLATION

7. Situation before 1948. Before 1948 Governments had few views on industrial structure. Since the late nineteenth century there had been isolated Government intervention in industry, *e.g.* railway law, public utility law, agricultural marketing boards and in the 1930s there were Government-blessed mergers, *e.g.* Lancashire steel, to fight economic depression. A coherent philosophy was totally lacking; indeed monopolistic practices could only be attacked on the grounds of restraint of trade under Common Law. This contrasted directly with the U.S.A. which had severe anti-monopoly legislation from 1890, although many administrations were reluctant to enforce the law.

Prior to the Second World War British industry was sunk in an apathy of market sharing, price fixing and other restrictive practices. This non-competitive outlook was reinforced during the war when the Government obviously had to fix prices and allocate production and resources.

As Germany's war fortunes waned, British civil servants were working on plans for the future of post-war Britain; the Beveridge Plan (*see* I *and* II) was one product of this thinking. The war-time civil service had been invigorated by outside talent and these new minds realised that Britain's future required a dynamic economy, an economy that would have to live with harsh international competition. The old system of permitting industry to avoid competition of any sort would be disastrous. There was the need to encourage low-cost producers by ensuring freedom of market entry and genuine competition. The desire for industrial health was linked to the full-employment aims of the Beveridge Report.

In 1948, the Monopolies and Restrictive Practices Act was passed (*see* **8–14** below). This Act has been attacked for being too weak, but it did represent a fundamental change of Government thinking and many of its weaknesses have been ironed out with experience.

THE 1948 MONOPOLIES AND RESTRICTIVE PRACTICES (INQUIRY AND CONTROL) ACT

8. Constitution of Monopolies Commission. A Commission of ten members (increased in 1953 and 1965) with a small staff was set up to investigate certain types of monopolistic markets. The criteria for investigation were:

(*a*) One-third of final output is in the hands of a single firm or two or more firms being interconnected bodies corporate.

(*b*) Where firms within the industry are acting in such a way as to prevent or restrict competition.

The Commission could only investigate industries referred to it by the then Board of Trade, which received the subsequent report from the Commission. The report would make recommendations but the Commission had no power to enforce its will. Ultimately, responsibility for carrying out the recommendations lay with the Board of Trade, Government and Parliament.

9. The aims. The Commission had two major aims:

(a) To establish if monopolistic practices exist in the industry under review.

(b) If they do exist, are they against the public interest?

"Public interest" was defined as being concerned with efficient production with regard to quality and prices, the most efficient distribution of resources and achievements in the fields of innovation.

The Act makes no comment on the inherent qualities of competition and monopoly, thus the Commission is essentially a pragmatic body analysing each case on its merits.

10. Achievements. Over the last twenty-odd years the Commission has investigated many industries, *e.g.* electric lamps, matches, tyres, building contracts, detergents, film distributors, car accessories, tobacco, glass, coloured films and cellulosic fibres. It has tended to require information under three broad headings:

(a) *Structure: e.g.* What are the conditions of demand in the industry?

(b) *Behaviour: e.g.* Do customers suffer from price discrimination?

(c) *Performance: e.g.* Does the firm restrict output to keep up the price?

11. Principles established. Although legally the Commission has no defined principles, certain strands of thought run through the reports:

(a) The pure economic theory of resource allocation is Utopian and does not provide a helpful criterion to judge an industry.

(b) The most damaging effect of restricting competition is to reduce the incentives to innovate.

(c) Freedom of entry to an industry is the vital stimulant of competition.

(d) Very high profits and return to capital may be signs of lack of competition (unfortunately they may also indicate efficiency).

(e) Competition may well be oligopolistic (see XIV, 8), thus size of company and share of market may be misleading criteria of competitiveness.

12. Criticisms. In its lifetime the Commission has received many criticisms from businessmen who consider its arguments to be too academic and from economists who feel its reports lack the coherent philosophy of the economic textbook. Some criticisms have been made by a consensus of opinion.

(a) The body lacks power. This is true in theory and practice. Very few reported recommendations have been enforced by Governments and the force of bad publicity has been a seven-day wonder. So, Imperial Tobacco own a large proportion of the shares of Gallagher, their main rivals. The majority of cinemas are still owned by Rank and A.B.C. who also control the distribution of films. Courtaulds increased their textile-market share by buying a company inside a year of the Commission suggesting their market domination should not be increased.

(b) When companies voluntarily comply with the report odd circumstances develop. Kodak cut the price of their colour film and drove their biggest rival out of the retail market. The detergent companies produce low-price little-advertised commodities which makes no real impact on the market.

(c) The Commission was too slow. Up to 1965 this was a valid point. Reports were taking from two to four years to produce. Their impact was slight because the Commission could not draw general conclusions about industrial behaviour from their investigation of a particular industry.

(d) References to the Commission came from the Government, rather than an independent body.

Theoretically, the Government was trying to build up a comprehensive casebook of competitive practices throughout

British industry but G. C. Allen suggests that some references came from political pressure within Parliament, *e.g.* constituents complaining to their M.P. about excessive prices. Thus a list of all investigated industries provides no definite pattern of research.

13. Results. The Commission could not be expected to blow a gale of competitive change through British industry. It was essentially an infant body maturing slowly with experience.

However, it did produce excellent case studies showing the workings of sectors of industry, but most importantly it revealed the tip of an iceberg that could wreck British industry. Report after report produced evidence of alarming restrictive practices undermining the competitive effectiveness of our industry. Worried by these results the Government asked the Monopolies Commission to prepare a report on restrictive practices in general.

14. The 1955 Collective Discrimination Report. The Government, realising that an industry by industry report system would stretch into eternity asked the Commission to produce a report on general restrictive practices in industry. It was essential to estimate the prevalence of resale price maintenance, exclusive agencies, discriminating price policies and aggregate rebate schemes.

The Report shocked the Government and public. The practices existed in at least eighty industries; they were basically against the public interest for they frustrated the innovators and created undue rigidity in market situations.

A majority of the Commission recommended a strong policy based on the American concept of using a law to fight monopolistic practices. Impressed, the Government acted with great speed to produce a major piece of British industrial law.

THE 1956 RESTRICTIVE TRADE PRACTICES ACT

15. Main principles. This Act, which is the cornerstone of British anti-monopoly legislation, created two new institutions.

(a) *The Registrar of Restrictive Practices*. This office registers any agreements between two or more companies, which place restrictions on the price of goods supplied, the conditions of sale, the quantity of goods produced and the category of person supplied. In the first two years of the Act's life over 2,000 agreements were registered.

The Registrar codifies the agreements according to their common qualities and if firms wish to maintain the agreements, they are submitted to the Court of Restrictive Practices.

(b) *The Court of Restrictive Practices*. This is a properly constituted court of the British legal system although the judges are given lay advisers. The firms have to prove that the benefits to the public from the agreement are not outweighed by "any detriment to the public or to persons not parties to the agreement."

16. Gateways. The drafters of the Act realised that concepts such as public interest or benefits are vague, so they only permit defence arguments under seven headings or gateways:

(a) The restriction protects the public from danger in the sale, installation or use of the good.

(b) The removal of the restriction would deny the public specific and substantial benefits.

(c) The restriction helps the participants to secure fair terms for the supply of goods for firms who are dominant suppliers.

(d) The restriction protects people against restrictions imposed by persons not parties to the agreement.

(e) The removal of the restriction would seriously affect employment in an area dominated by the parties.

(f) The removal of the restriction would probably cause substantial reduction in the export earnings of the parties to the agreement.

(g) The restriction is necessary for the maintenance of another restrictive agreement which the Court has ruled to be in the public interest.

Words like "specific," and "substantial," seriously mean that defendants have to offer excellent and quantified evidence to prove their case. The gateways have made the benefits of restrictive practices difficult to prove.

17. Economists' reaction to gateways. Economists reacted favourably to the theory if not the application of the gateways.

The first two gateways seem reasonable although gateway (b) is vague. Gateways (c) and (d) are based on the theory of countervailing power, *i.e.* if the seller dominates a market, the power of the buyer should be increased; this principle can be seen in Monopolies Commission Reports on mergers (*see* XVI, **24**). Gateway (e) appears to put the responsibility of full employment on groups of companies rather than the Government and gateway (f) continues the British habit of linking all economic policies to the balance of payments situation. The final gateway ensures the Court does not put itself in a contradictory position.

18. The gateways in practice. As most agreements have been voluntarily abandoned, relatively few cases have come before the Court. The Court's decisions have received mixed reactions from economists. A decision not to legalise an agreement in the yarn-spinning section of the textile industry was acclaimed because the Judge ruled that a protected textile industry was not the answer to Lancashire's employment problem. The Cement Makers' Federation were allowed to have common delivered prices because this reduced business risk and hence the need for large return on capital. Economists argued that common delivery prices meant purchasers near the manufacturer were subsidising more distant buyers thus creating an artificial price system. An even more debateable decision allowed price fixing by the Black Bolt and Nut Association to save their customers the cost of shopping around, an argument which could justify all price fixing. In fact the Court has disallowed the defence in other cases.

One of the most common defences of price fixing has been to ensure product standardisation, although it is difficult to prove price competition would lead to a flood of non-standard products. The need for product standardisation was often reflected in the work of the Industrial Reorganisation Corporation (*see* XVI, **26–30**).

The Restrictive Practices Court like the Monopolies Commission has faced the problem of how far economic theory can be applied to the real economic world and its answers have not always pleased economists.

19. Results of the 1956 Act. The Act has been successful in two ways. Companies now know, through legal advice, what type of competitive behaviour is acceptable and because of this clarity the vast majority of agreements have been voluntarily abandoned. The regular reports issued by the Registrar describe increasing competition within industry.

"Very few major agreements involving price fixing or discriminatory dealing in a substantial part of a trade or industry are now being made and registered and comparatively few cases have now to be referred to the Court.

General experience indicates that a great part of trade and industry is now conducted without recourse to restrictive trading agreements." (*Report of the Registrar of Restrictive Trading Agreements*, March 1970, Cmnd. 4303.)

The reports also reveal a disquieting result of the Act, the growth of the informal agreement. If one managing director shows his price list to a competitor over a social drink, does this constitute a price-fixing agreement? The Registrar seemed convinced that companies could evade the law by these means.

In an attempt to close the loophole of informal agreements further legislation was enacted in 1968.

20. Resale Price Maintenance (R.P.M.). The most common restrictive practice involved the manufacturers forcing all retailers to sell the manufacturers' products at a fixed price, thus removing price competition at the retail level. Concern was most forcible in retailing but R.P.M. was practised throughout industry.

In 1964 R.P.M. was declared illegal and any company wishing to continue with R.P.M. had to appear before the Restrictive Practices Court and prove the removal of R.P.M. would be detrimental to the consumer because:

(a) The number of outlets would be reduced.
(b) The quality and variety of products would be diminished.
(c) After-sales service would be reduced.
(d) The health of the consumer would be affected.
(e) In the long run, price rises would be easier to make.

The manufacturers also had to prove that the benefits outweighed the losses of price competition.

The battle against R.P.M. has been an outstanding success, very few manufacturers tried to defend its use; the most

significant defence has been by the Book Publishers using
gateway (*b*).

21. The 1968 Restrictive Practices Act.   This Act says that
informal agreements must be registered, but their detection is
still almost impossible.

Two new gateways were added to the seven of the 1956 Act
(*see* **16** above).

(*a*) A restriction is permitted if it does not prevent
competition.

(*b*) A temporary exemption for agreements that produce
import substitutes or product standardisation.

22. Extending competition.   The law is a limited force for
ensuring that industry and trade is competitive.   It can ban
practices which appear to restrict competition but it cannot
make producers and traders compete with each other.

There are other stimulants to competition and efficiency
which a Government may use:

(*a*) The removal of tariffs increases the strength of foreign
competitors.   This tactic may be politically unpopular but
world opinion is moving quite quickly towards free trade
attitudes.

(*b*) The Government takes the power to make companies
divest themselves of firms they have bought if the resulting
corporate performance is unsatisfactory.   In the early 1960s
a Monopolies Divestment Bill was unsuccessfully introduced
into the House of Commons but the 1965 Mergers Act does
give Parliament the power to unscramble mergers.   This
concept poses the difficult problem of how to re-create a
company once it has ceased to act as a separate entity; the
selling of the shares is the first and perhaps insurmountable
problem.

(*c*) Companies must reveal more information about their
activities so that the shareholders in particular and the
public in general can better assess the companies' efficiency.
Both political parties and the accountants' professional
bodies are committed to making company reports and
balance sheets more meaningful documents.   The opening
of business activities would ease the task of judging the
competitiveness and performance of industry.

Judging from the history of business, if Governments believe in competition they must find the means of creating a competitive environment, for the natural instinct of companies is to limit the areas of competition.

PROGRESS TEST 15

1. Why should a government try to regulate the behaviour of a monopolist? (**2**(*b*))

2. Is there a need for international anti-monopoly legislation? (**4**)

3. In checking the claim that a company was achieving economies of scale what information would you seek? (**5**)

4. Why in the late 1940s were civil servants determined to improve the competitiveness of British industry? (**7**)

5. How did the 1948 monopolies legislation envisage the "Public interest"? (**8**)

6. From what basic lack of power does the Monopolies Commission suffer? (**12**(*a*))

7. What is the role of the Registrar of Restrictive Practices? (**15**(*a*))

8. In the 1956 Restrictive Practices Act what is a "gateway"? (**16**)

9. Why did some companies voluntarily abandon restrictive practices after the 1956 Act? (**19**)

10. Why is there an interest in making companies produce more informative balance sheets? (**22**(*c*))

CHAPTER XVI

THE PROBLEM OF MERGERS AND THEIR CONTROL

GROWTH OF MERGERS

1. What is a merger? A merger can be defined as the coming together of two or more companies so that the overall policy is determined by a single board of directors. A multitude of words is used to indicate this process, *e.g.* "take-over," "acquisition," "amalgamation," "absorption," "association" and "fusion." Users of the words are trying to distinguish between the method of the merger, *e.g.* were the parties agreeable, were the parties of equal size? In this chapter "merger" will be used for all these situations.

2. The nineteenth century. The economic history of Britain shows that mergers happen in waves as particular economic circumstances seem to indicate the need for big business units.

As R. Evely and I.M.D. Little write in *Concentration in British Industry* (C.U.P., 1960), "In the closing years of the nineteenth century there occurred a series of amalgamations without precedent in British industry," *e.g.* wallpaper manufacturers (1899) and distillers (1877). Most of the mergers involved companies who were competitors facing rapid technological change and a period of declining profits.

3. The 1920s. The second major wave occurred in the 1920s. This period saw the development of the Big Five in banking, the four major railway companies, I.C.I. and the fast growth of Unilever. The biggest proportion of the mergers involved the placing of various processes under one management, *i.e.* vertical integration (*see* **7** below), but again the great stimulant was depressed trade. Companies wished to avoid competition, to rationalise manufacturing processes and to close redundant plant. As stated previously (*see* XV, **7**) the British Government looked with favour on this rationalisation despite its effect on competition.

4. The 1960s. Since the late 1950s a third wave has developed. The Monopolies Commission prepared the *Survey of Mergers Report*, 1958–68 (H.M.S.O., March 1970). The paper studies companies with a Stock Exchange quotation and with assets over £500,000. In the 1958–68 period there was a reduction of 771 in the number of companies (38 per cent). The merger figures were:

Period	1958–60	1961–63	1964–65	1966	1967	1968
Mergers	68	69	59	66	75	100

However, if smaller and unquoted companies are added the figures grow amazingly:

Period	1964	1965	1956	1967	1968	1969
Mergers	939	995	805	661	598	887

REASONS FOR MERGERS

5. Market domination. A company wishes to expand its market share and feels it has not the growth potential within its own resources so it takes over one or more of its competitors. This is called a "horizontal merger."

6. Diversification. The market of a company is reaching saturation point and the company wishes to expand its interests. Rather than build a firm and market up from scratch, the company buys into an existing organisation. An organisation with a whole range of diversified interests is called a "conglomerate."

7. Vertical integration. Companies wishing to have greater control of supplies or outlets buy back or forward in the chain of production. Thus a brewery may own hop-farms and public-houses.

8. Under-utilised assets. All companies do not make full use of their potential resources so they are wasting labour, land or capital. A more enterprising firm realises this waste and takes over the original company to obtain a better rate of return on the assets. These mergers are often cheap for the acquiring company, because the share prices of the inefficient company do not reflect the true value of its potential.

9. Economies of scale. A merger takes place to form a bigger organisation, thus reaping economies of scale (*see* XIV, **12**). These economies do not only arise in production but also in marketing, distributing, personnel, administration and finance. Whether the benefits of economies actually materialise is often a matter of speculation and research (*see* XV, **5**).

10. Product integration. Firms in an industry are all making the same range of goods and wastefully competing against each other with small uneconomic outputs. The firms merge so that each firm or even plant can concentrate on certain items in the range, thus increasing output and perhaps achieving economies of scale.

11. Small company without capital. A small businessman can develop an idea and sell the results at a profit but ultimately his company's development will be handicapped through a lack of capital. The only solution may be merging with a larger organisation. It is worth noting that many mergers are initiated by the company which will lose its identity.

12. Internationalism. Many companies now treat the world as their market and they believe that size is vital to withstand the challenge of foreigners, particularly American companies. Home companies, often with Government blessing, merge to meet this competition.

13. Death of owner. A small firm may be dependent on the talents of one man and if he dies the company can only continue under the management of another company.

14. Monopolies legislation. A side effect of the 1956 *Restrictive Practices Act* (*see* XV, **15–19**) may have been to encourage mergers. It is very difficult for firms to co-operate in such activities as price fixing and market sharing, by the use of agreements. If firms really want to reduce competition, mergers are the most likely way to succeed, for the legal problem of agreements is avoided.

15. Power from size. Companies are managed by men with above-average human desires for power and to prove themselves. A merger may well arise through the desire of management to prove their ability successfully to manage a bigger company.

FEAR OF MERGERS

16. Introduction. Mergers have always aroused controversy at all levels of public debate because, although they may produce economic benefits (*see* **7–13** above) there are certain dangers to a country's industrial structure in unlimited mergers. These dangers are discussed below.

17. Growth of monopoly. Most mergers, particularly among big companies, are bound to place the new organisation in a stronger bargaining position with regard to its supplies and customers. The greater the merger the greater the dangers of monopoly (*see* XIV, **8–11**).

18. Social abuse of power. The dangers of mergers can have tremendous social and political implications, particularly where the merger is in the field of newspapers or radio and television. These implications are also prevalent when the acquiring company is foreign-owned. All Governments are rightly suspicious of large sectors of their industry passing into foreign hands, for decisions affecting the lives of their citizens are being taken overseas.

Such decisions may involve redundancy, for if the economic benefits of the merger materialise plant is often surplus and is closed down. This problem is becoming very serious as firms become more cost-conscious.

19. Are the economic benefits real? The economic benefits of mergers are seldom quantified and they can only be checked after a number of years. Disturbing evidence about efficiency and rates of return is building up. The evidence suggests that huge organisations find the profits of economies of scale whittled away by the costs of size, *e.g.* bureaucracy and lack of communication.

The most serious anti-merger charges are made by Gerald Newbould (*Management and Merger Activity*, Guthstead (Liverpool), 1970). His main points are:

(*a*) Bidding managements did not evaluate an acquisition in the same rational financial fashion they would use for other capital investments.

(*b*) Only in half the mergers investigated did the acquiring company have a plan for the new merged organisation.

(*c*) Size not quality was the biggest factor in determining which company triumphed when there was more than one bidder.

(*d*) The average management's major motives for merging with other companies were the desire for bigger market shares, to reduce competition or to protect themselves from being taken over.

1965

THE 1965 MONOPOLIES AND MERGERS ACT

20. Government reaction to merger growth. Through the 1950s and early 1960s the Government took no action against mergers as such. Only if the merger created a situation *only if* worthy of investigation by the Monopolies Commission was *monop.* there any high-level reaction to mergers. Indeed, in many industries, *e.g.* aircraft and textiles, Governments gave their blessing to mergers which promoted bigger industrial units.

From 1964 the merger boom accelerated and a new facet began to emerge. This was a growing proportion of mergers involving big companies coming together, *e.g.* G.E.C. and English Electric, B.M.C. and Leylands, Boots and Timothy Whites, thus fears of market domination grew rapidly. These fears were deepened when the acquiring company was not British, *e.g.* Chrysler buying Rootes, Nestles buying Crosse & Blackwell.

The fears of the 1960s are best expressed in a speech by Mr. Crosland when he said:

'Mergers raise profound political and social as well as economic issues.' A very large firm has a pervasive influence on people's lives. It provides the means of livelihood for many thousands of workers; its products may enter millions of homes. We can lay down certain principles—they are good if they lead to better management or greater economies of scale, bad if they lead to inertia, a dangerous lack of competition or any abuse of market power. The difficulty comes in applying these general concepts to particular situations" (speech to Manchester Chamber of Commerce, 28th February 1969).

21. Main points of the Monopolies and Mergers Act of 1965. Mr. Crosland's feelings had been embodied in the 1965 Act. The main features were:

(*a*) The Board of Trade will investigate any merger which creates or increases a monopoly in the supply of any good or service in the U.K. The value of the assets to be taken over must exceed £5 million (this covers most mergers of any significance).

(*b*) The Board of Trade will investigate the merger of any independent newspapers whose combined circulation is over 500,000. (This is designed to maintain a variety of opinion within the mass media.)

(*c*) The Board of Trade will investigate any merger involving a foreign company gaining a major shareholding in a British company.

(*d*) The Board of Trade can refer any merger to the Monopolies Commission for further investigation. The latter will report back within six to nine months.

(*e*) Parliament has the power to unscramble a merger which has taken place.

22. The nature of the investigation. The Board of Trade (now the Department of Trade and Industry) seeks information about the companies involved in the merger, the motivation behind the merger, demand factors, market structure, the efficiencies expected to accrue from the merger and any likely effects on the balance of payments. (*See Mergers. A Guide to Board of Trade Practices*, H.M.S.O., 1969.)

23. Results. In the period 1965–69 only 3 per cent of proposed mergers were referred to the Monopolies Commission; of this small number only a third were deemed to be against the public interest and the companies did not merge. It is difficult to decide whether these low figures indicate a laxity of investigation on the part of the Board of Trade or whether growth of business organisation does bring the alleged benefits of size to the economy.

24. Some decisions of the Monopolies Commission.

(a) *Proposed merger of Ross Group & Associated Fisheries.* Disallowed because it would lead to market domination in the Humber ports without strengthening the industry.

(b) *Proposed merger of United Drapery and Burtons.* Disallowed because it would reduce retail competition and give a dominant buying power over the small units of the woollen and worsted industry.

(c) *Proposed merger of B.I.C.C. and Pyrotenax.* Allowed because of cost savings (approximately 4 per cent) and the impact on exports. These points were accepted but the Monopolies Commission felt the public would not have really lost without the merger and B.I.C.C. promised to compile a code of future behaviour. In fact the merger created a near-complete monopoly (95 per cent) of the mineral insulated-cable market.

(d) *Proposed merger of B.M.C. and Pressed Steel.* Allowed because of advantages of integrated production and export potential although the Monopolies Commission felt the first point was exaggerated by the companies.

THE GOVERNMENT IN FAVOUR OF MERGERS

25. Encouragement of mergers. This chapter has concentrated on the control of mergers but it is clear that mergers can be in the public interest, *e.g.* big companies can be more effective in foreign competition, size is often vital for technological development. The Labour Government of 1964–70 were impressed by the arguments in favour of industrial size and despite introducing the 1965 Monopolies and Mergers Act they were sufficiently pragmatic to constitute, late in 1966, the Industrial Reorganisation Corporation (I.R.C.), a body designed to restructure British industry, largely through mergers.

26. The aims of the I.R.C. The aims were:

(a) To promote the restructuring of industry with a view to improving industrial efficiency.

(b) To give the benefits of good management to a greater number of companies.

(c) To achieve the above aims particularly in industries with export expansion potential or the probability of saving imports.

27. Structure. The I.R.C. had a part-time Board of eminent industrialists, unionists and academics. It had a small group of full-time research executives who produced reports for Board consideration, on possible points of restructuring.

28. Method. The I.R.C. was given drawing rights of £150 million. It could use this capital either to lend to companies to finance mergers or to buy a controlling share interest in a company to improve the standards of management and then to sell the shares. The buying and selling of shares would take place at market prices.

29. Results. The I.R.C. influenced many mergers with advice and money, *e.g.* G.E.C. and English Electric; British Leyland; Coats Patons. However, it is difficult to evaluate the work of the I.R.C. because the benefits of mergers take time to materialise and it is impossible to know whether the merger would have happened without I.R.C. guidance.

30. Criticisms. The two major criticisms of the I.R.C. have been:

(a) It was an unnecessary supplement to market forces, particularly the work of merchant banks. If a merger makes economic sense private capital will be found. However, benefits of mergers can be viewed from various interests (*see* **5–15** above) and the market may concentrate on shareholder benefits. It is also debateable whether merchant banks have the experience to evaluate industrial management expertise (according to merchant banker C. Kleinwort, *Sunday Times*, 28th February 1971) and certainly the post-war contribution of institutional shareholders to industrial efficiency has not been good.

(b) The I.R.C. had no clear criteria for restructuring, thus proposals emanated from the small group of executives and were likely to be influenced by their subjective judgements.

It is difficult to counter this criticism. Probably the I.R.C. should have been one of many guiding factors in the search for structural optima.

The Heath administration abolished the I.R.C. for they felt it was an instrument of Government intervention which performed no useful function.

31. The future of mergers. Mergers have become a major problem for the Government and as there are no clear guidelines for policy each new Government has to evolve its own philosophy of industrial structure. As with many economic problems, mergers are fraught with paradoxes, *e.g.* a commitment to competition and market forces will today lead towards more mergers which may lead to a diminution of competition.

Any policy should take into account the following points:

(*a*) Mergers will create large-firm monopolies which escape the 1956 Restrictive Practices Act.

(*b*) The results of mergers can only be judged two to three years after the event. Is it possible to devise retrospective legislation to make a true judgment of mergers?

(*c*) Is a merger for the benefit of the shareholders, the management, the public or the national interest? These interests do not necessarily coincide and may even clash, *e.g.* the creation of a monopoly in the domestic market to gain strength for exports.

(*d*) What are the rights, if any, of the workers involved in a merger?

(*e*) Firms justifying a merger must produce more testable data of cost savings, export performance and expected profits. They should also show how the public is expected to gain from the merger.

In Britain the solution to the problem cuts across political ideologies. Traditionally, Labour Governments have been suspicious of giant business organisations but now their politicians seem to link size to technical growth. Conservatives believe in free enterprise and competition but, unfortunately, free-enterprise industry does not tend to practise competition. Both political parties have found their political philosophies to be unreliable guides to industrial efficiency and this loss of clear principles explains the hesitant piecemeal approach of British Governments to the problem of industrial size and competition.

Some of the biggest units of industrial organisation are the nationalised industries and their problems are investigated in the next chapter.

PROGRESS TEST 16

1. What economic circumstances produced a growth of mergers in the late nineteenth century? (**2**)

2. Explain the meaning of "vertical integration." (**7**)

3. Why might monopolies legislation lead to a growth of mergers? (**14**)

4. In what industries might a merger have dangerous social implications? (**18**)

5. Give two reasons why the benefits of scale might not materialise. (**19**)

6. What size of merger might be investigated by the Department of Trade and Industry? (**21**(*a*))

7. When would a merger be in the public interest? (**25**)

8. What were the aims of the Industrial Reorganisation Corporation? (**26**)

9. To promote mergers why was it necessary to supplement market forces? (**30**(*a*))

10. Why might retrospective legislation be necessary to deal with mergers? (**31**(*b*))

CHAPTER XVII

THE NATIONALISED INDUSTRIES

PRECONCEPTIONS OF THE PROBLEMS OF NATIONALISED INDUSTRIES

1. Introduction.

"The problems of the nationalised industries are complex and changing. With their many operations and outputs the industries are enormously diverse and they are closely involved in the adjustment problems of the entire economy, with important social effects frequently linked to their actions. No single economic criterion for organising and operating the nationalised industries has been found appropriate" (W. G. Shepherd, *Economic Performance Under Public Ownership*, Yale University Press, 1965).

This passage outlines the main features of the British nationalised industries, *i.e.* they are very large business units, they effect the economy, they have a social role and it is difficult to establish criteria to judge the successes and failures of the industries.

This chapter will look at the reasons for nationalising an industry, the methods of running such an industry, the major problems which have arisen in British industries and the likely future of the industries.

The next section must remove some of the myths which have grown round the nationalised industries in this country. Outside academic circles it is difficult to prevent a discussion of the industries being dominated by political attitudes of the most extreme kind. A nationalised industry is a business organisation, thus its problems must be analysed within a business economics framework.

2. Myths.

(*a*) Nationalised industries all lose money. This is patently untrue (*see* Table XXXI). Only British Rail, the National Coal Board and the British Waterways Board have

TABLE XXXI. NATIONALISED INDUSTRIES

Industry	Av. net assets (£m.) 1966-67	Employees 1967 (000's)	Net income as % of assets[2]			
			1957-58	1960-61	1963-64	1966-67
Post Office	1,584	422	7·5	8·5	7·8	8·0
National Coal Board	794	492	3·5	2·3	6·7	3·7
Electricity[1]	4,450	249	5·0[3]	5·0[3]	6·9	5·1
Gas	996	124	4·0	4·0	5·2	4·8
B.O.A.C.	134	19	−1·2	2·7	−6·6	21·7
B.E.A.	102	20	7·6	6·5	8·3	4·8
Airports Authority	54	3	—	—	—	10·3
British Rail	1,931	361	—	—	−4·1	−3·6
London Transport	218	74	—	—	4·5	0·5
Transport Docks Board	95	11	—	—	5·2	5·4
Waterways Board	13	3	—	—	−6·3	−4·9
Transport Holding Co.	175	103	—	—	9·5	8·2

[1] Includes: Electricity Council and Boards of England and Wales
    North of Scotland Hydro-Electric Board
    South of Scotland Electricity Board.

[2] Net income is gross income less depreciation at historic cost and foreseeable obsolescence.

[3] Figure for Electricity Council and Boards in England and Wales.

consistently lost money, although recently in the first two cases profitable years have been known.   Also if one compares railways and coal with their American counterparts which are privately owned the British industries by no means come off worse.   The basic problem of rail and coal throughout most of the world is the growth of car-ownership and alternative fuels; the ownership of the industries, private or *COAL &* public is irrelevant to their fundamental troubles.   The *RAIL .* performance of the British industries is often more favourably evaluated by foreigners than by our own Press.   "There is no consistent evidence that British public corporations have performed their commercial functions less capably than their counterparts in private companies in comparable industries" (Caves, *Britain's Economic Prospects*, Allen & Unwin, 1968, p. 414).

(*b*) Nationalisation is a British phenomenon dating from 1946.   The bulk of the nationalised industries are public utilities, *e.g.* gas, electric, post, railways and public utilities all over the world have been controlled by Governments in one way or another, since the nineteenth century, *e.g.* the *Electric Lighting Act* of 1882, the *Gas Works Clauses Act* of 1871.   The early statutory legislation was primarily concerned with the service provided, prices and financial control, degree of monopoly and labour conditions.   Nationalisation of public utilities is no more than a development of Government interest in monopolistic industries.

However, a nationalised industry may not be a public utility, *e.g.* steel in Britain, alcohol in Sweden, Renault in France.   In these cases other historical and economic forces come into play (*see* **4–7** below).

(*c*) Nationalised industries are monolithic industrial structures run by civil servants.   There are several ways of organising nationalised industries and the role of the civil service in the day-to-day running of the business is negligible (*see* **13–17** below).

REASONS FOR NATIONALISATION

3. Public utilities (gas, electricity, water, rail).   Competition in these industries would be very wasteful of resources because they are capital-intensive industries and competition would involve a duplication of huge expensive equipment.   As was seen in **2** (*b*) above Governments have in the past given the monopoly to a private concern then controlled the activities of the private firm by law. Most countries deem this to be an awkward method of control, thus State-ownership of public utilities is now a world-wide accepted method of business organisation.

4. Economies of scale. Economies of scale can only be truly achieved by large business units, the size of which may create a monopolistic situation. There will usually be laws to prevent the company abusing this position; however, some people argue that it would be easier to let the State run such a company. Whether the change in ownership from private to public would necessarily protect the consumer from the dangers of monopoly is a matter of some doubt.

5. "Commanding heights of the economy." This was an argument much favoured by the late Mr. Aneurin Bevan. He argued that certain industries were the lynchpins of the economy, *e.g.* steel, thus the Government with the responsibility of guiding the economy needed to control these industries and to maintain their efficiency.

It has been suggested the nationalised industries' record was no worse than private industry (*see* **2** above), but there is no real evidence to suggest the Government's ability to run a non-public utility industry is appreciably better than private industry. Only if this argument were true would the "commanding heights" case make sense.

6. Defence industries. Certain industries, *e.g.* aircraft, are very dependent on defence contracts, thus their ability to make money is subject to the great risks of political and diplomatic policies. These industries are also often technological leaders, thus their demise would have serious repercussions for the whole of industry. A further problem involves the armed services who would be forced to buy overseas, a course of action strategically risky and damaging to the balance of payments. So the State should take over these companies and be prepared to run them at a loss in the national interest as defined in the previous sentences.

In practice Governments prefer to encourage the merging of firms in these industries and to create a private monopoly strong enough to compete internationally (*see* XV, **4**).

7. Redistribution of resources. This is a purely political argument held by people who do not believe in the profit motive. They suggest all companies should be nationalised, thus all profits will accrue to the State; a situation leading to an alleged redistribution of income and wealth.

ARGUMENTS AGAINST NATIONALISATION

8. Monopoly. A nationalised industry is usually a monopoly, thus the dangers of monopoly (*see* XVI, **18**) have been deliberately created by the State, the State which may well have anti-monopoly laws. Critics of nationalised industries have emphasised the anti-monopoly argument that a non-competitive market situation results in a misallocation of resources (*see* XIV, **8–11**). The possible flaw in this argument lies in the definition of monopolist (*see* XIV, **1–7**). British Rail is the sole provider of rail services but there is no lack of alternative forms of travel. Only the postal services approximate to a pure monopoly and all other industries will have some markets which are highly competitive, even if the competitors are other nationalised industries.

9. No profit motive. A nationalised industry has no shareholders, thus there is not the incentive to make profits through a search for efficiency. It is true the industries lack shareholders, although Governments have considered the idea of introducing private equity capital. In the 1960s the White Papers of 1961 and 1967 (*see* **21–22** below) have given the nationalised industries greater financial stimulus through setting target rates of return. However, it must be admitted that unless the Government is prepared to sack boards who through inefficiency do not reach the target then the boards may lack the private entrepreneur's incentive.

The foregoing analysis does ignore the complexities of the role of profit in private industry and it evades the question of how many boards of private companies are sacked for poor profit performance.

10. Bureaucracy. The nationalised industries are subject to the evils of bureaucracy, *e.g.* lack of communications, no decision-taking, overmanning and red tape. This criticism may well be true, but is it a criticism of nationalised industries or very large organisations? Any company in public utility work will be huge and may well suffer from bureaucracy. This is essentially a problem of management and not ownership and it revolves round the classic business organisation dilemma of centralised or decentralised control.

11. Democracy. Like the argument in **7** above, this is a political argument. A nationalised industry has evolved out of a transfer of resources from the private to the public sector of the economy; any action which gives the State more power through resource control is a danger to the democratic freedoms of the individual.

12. Summary of 3–11. The arguments for and against nationalised companies or industries have been deliberately given with counter-arguments. This is to show the utter folly of seeing nationalisation as either the cure for all our industrial ills or the demon which produces the ills.

Nationalisation like monopoly is neither good nor bad in itself. Both cases are examples of business organisation which can only be evaluated by business and economic methodology. Thus the nationalisation of public utilities is easy to justify in economic terms but the nationalisation of the whole retail trade would enter the realms of economic fantasy. The real problem is the evaluation of the arguments for nationalising an industry like steel. It is most difficult to uncover the economic facts from the blanket of political emotion and ideology. Although a study of nationalisation cannot ignore the political framework of the control of the industries, the success or failure of nationalisation must be judged by economic and, in certain circumstances, social values. It must be realised that the nationalised industries are only one method of allowing Governments to control the production of goods and services.

METHODS OF ORGANISATION

13. Department of State. The enterprise is organised through a specific Minister and Government department, *e.g.* Carlisle public-houses and the Post Office were until recently run respectively by the Home Office and the Postmaster-General.

14. Semi-independent bodies. These are bodies, set up by Parliament and responsible to a Minister, which are used to regulate non-commercial activities, *e.g.* the Forestry Commission.

15. Local authorities. Most local authorities through their councils and paid official provide a range of non-social services, *e.g.* local buses and markets.

16. Mixed joint-stock companies. The State becomes a shareholder, usually a controlling interest, of a private-enterprise organisation, *e.g.* British Petroleum and Harland-Wolff. The method could well develop if Governments try to bring private capital into existing nationalised industries. The fascinating question in this development will be the exact role of the Government—will it be a dormant or active shareholder?

17. Public board. A board responsible to Parliament, via a Government Minister, is created to run the industry. This has been the normal British practice and in theory it allows the industry to run on commercial principles while remaining accountable to the representatives of the public.

PROBLEMS OF NATIONALISED INDUSTRIES

18. Outline of the problems. The ideal way to run a nationalised industry is to appoint very high-calibre management and leave them to run the industry. Lip service is paid to this ideal but in practice it has scarcely been achieved. The reasons for this deviation are:

(*a*) The industries have been used to further the macro-economic objectives of the Government (*see* II, **1**, **12**), particularly in relation to pricing and investment policy, *e.g.* inflation is fought by cutting back nationalised industry investment programmes.

(*b*) The industries are used to prop up British technology, *e.g.* B.E.A. have been pressured to buy British aircraft.

(c) They have been given social obligations to consumers (maintaining the telegram service) and to employees (maintaining inefficient mines to keep people in work).

(d) Government have interfered with prices not only for economic policy reasons but also to prevent the abuse of monopoly power in relation to the consumer.

(e) Ministers have not always had the political freedom or bravery to buy top management at the going market rate. Especially in their early history the nationalised industries' management were expected to accept low salaries because they believed in the concept of nationalisation. Dr. Beeching on appointment to British Railways received over £20,000, which was a first step towards realistic salaries.

The above points reflect the basic problems of the nationalised industries, *i.e.* their aims, ministerial control, relationships with private industry and financial problems. These specific problems are dealt with in **19–34** below.

THE PROBLEM OF DEFINING AIMS

19. Introduction. The aims of the nationalised industries are the key to the solution of their other problems for without establising aims nothing sensible can be said about pricing and investment policies.

There have been three phases in the evolution of the aims of nationalised industries.

20. Period I: 1948–61. In this period the various statutory obligations were laid down. Broadly, there was a desire to meet the demand for the products and to charge prices which allowed for the industries to break even over a period of time. The vagueness of these aims as a guideline for management policy is revealed in the aims of individual industries, *e.g.* the National Coal Board was expected to provide coal at qualities and prices best calculated to further the public interest. The electricity industry was required to distribute electricity supplies to those who required them and to cheapen supplies as far as was practicable.

No clarification of public interest or efficiency was given, thus the management of the industries were existing in a policy vacuum and results were disappointing.

21. Period II: 1961–67. In 1961 the Government tried to rectify this lack of aims in a White Paper, *The Financial and Economic Obligations of the Nationalised Industries* (Cmnd. 1337). Industries were required to balance their accounts over a five-year period after providing for interest and depreciation at historic cost. Provision also had to be made for reserves to make some contribution towards future investment programmes. Finally, financial targets were to be set for each industry in the light of its capabilities and needs. Most of the targets were expressed as a rate of return on assets, *e.g.*

Industry	*Objectives* %	*Period*
Electricity Boards	12·4	1962/63–1966/67
B.E.A.	6	1963/64–1967/68
Post Office	8	1963/64–1967/68
N.C.B.		To break even after depreciation and interest and £10 million for replacement costs

(These figures are not based on exactly similar definitions of assets.)

The Government also promised the boards greater freedom to fix prices and promised to give a public written explanation for any Departmental intervention over prices. Subsequent Select Committee reports (*see* **26**) reprimanded the Government for ignoring this policy of non-intervention.

22. Period III: 1967–71. The Government published another White Paper, *Nationalised Industries—A Review of Economic and Financial Objectives* (Cmnd. 3437). The Government thought that as investment programmes (*see* **30–32** below) had increased so enormously since 1961, the aims of the industries ought to be seen in the context of the national use of scarce resources. They felt that possibly too much capital was being devoted to the public sector.

The main alteration in 1967 was that investment projects must be subject to Discounted Cash Flow techniques and that the test rate of discount must be sufficient to ensure that resources are efficiently used. It was suggested that investment projects must earn at least an 8 per cent return to keep the industries in line with private investment rates of return.

The Government also required that pricing policy (*see* **34** below) should ensure the customer pays the true cost of the service.

23. Summary of aims.   These two concepts, linked with a rigorous reappraisal of the 1961 target rates of return, should enable the industries to fulfil their role.   The White Paper stated that:

> "Nationalised industries, which command much greater resources than all but the very largest private undertakings should expect to be numbered amongst the most progressive and efficient concerns in the country.   Where there are significant social and wider economic costs and benefits which ought to be taken into account these will be reflected in the industry's policy.   If this means the industry has to act against its commercial interests, the government will accept responsibility by making a special payment to the industry or by an appropriate adjustment to its financial objectives" (p. 14).

It is clear that nationalised industries have become progressively more commercially orientated and their original social obligations are fading into insignificance.   However, the industries are so big that their policies do affect the total economy.   Thus they cannot be precisely compared to a private business undertaking.

THE PROBLEM OF PUBLIC ACCOUNTABILITY

24. Introduction.   Whereas the board of directors of a private company is responsible to its shareholders, the board of a public corporation is ultimately responsible to the electorate.   The problem is to establish channels to make this accountability effective.   The Acts of Parliament establishing the industries deliberately offered no rigid solution in the belief that experience would evolve a satisfactory method of accountability.   Three areas of control have emerged, the Department Minister, Parliamentary Select Committees and Consultative Councils (*see* **25–27** below).

25. The Minister.   The Minister responsible for the industry has been the main weapon of control and back benchers have frequently complained about their inability to influence or

even marginally affect the policies of the nationalised industries. At Question Time, questions seem to investigate the
actions of the Minister rather than the actions of the nationalised boards.

Certain statutory obligations are placed on the Minister. He
appoints board members and fixes their salaries, approves
major policy decisions, *e.g.* investment programmes, and he can
direct the Boards to conduct their activities in the public
interest. These last two points have created most controversy
for they seem to give Ministers almost unfettered power to
affect board decisions on political rather than commercial
grounds, *e.g.* should a Minister refuse a price rise because of a
forthcoming election (*see* the 1961 White Paper and **34** below).
As a general rule the Boards should take day-to-day decisions
and the Minister overall policy decisions, but the border
between these two areas cannot be defined.

The attempt to establish such a distinction is to give the
Boards commercial freedom yet at the same time maintaining
the principle of public accountability.

26. Select Committees. Since 1951, Select Committees in
the Nationalised Industries have been established to increase
Parliament's role in accountability procedure. They have the
power to send for people, paper and records; their aim is to
inform Parliament about the aims, activities and problems of
the industries. From 1956 they have also investigated the
Nationalised Boards' reports and accounts. The Committees
are made up of M.P.s of all parties; their annual reports are
free from political bias and the Committees have won the
confidence of the nationalised industries. They often criticise
Ministerial activities particularly with regard to pricing
decisions and the 1963 Report on the Electricity Industry said
"Because of ministerial interventions accounts laid before
Parliament by Boards do not give a true picture of their
managerial abilities." This extract may summarise the
whole problem of public accountability.

27. Consultative Councils. Each industry has a Consultative Council which is a group of laymen often organised on a
regional basis. Their statutory obligation is to act as general
advisers to their respective Boards but in practice they are
regarded as representing consumer views, *e.g.* in some indus-

tries they have to approve price increases before the increases come into effect. The practical view of the Councils' role is not realistic, for the vast majority of the population are not aware of the existence of these Councils. Thus they exist in limbo, neither representing anybody nor seriously being recognised by the Boards.

The public accountability of the nationalised industries seems to be a myth; responsible Ministers do intervene in the industries' activities but the criterion of intervention appears to be political expediency. Freedom of action or subservience to Ministers may well depend on the political strength of the Boards' chairmen.

COMPETITION

28. Relations with private industry. The nationalised and private industries do not inhabit two separate worlds, their activities are interwoven, e.g. 66 per cent of nationalised industries' output is bought by private industry and the nationalised concerns are huge buyers of plant and equipment from private industry. This relationship poses problems which go to the root of the philosophy of nationalised industries. This section outlines the problems, it cannot solve them.

(a) If the industries are to make commercial rates of return they may well need to raise prices, which affects their industrial customers (*see* **34** below). Does the obligation of nationalised industries to act in the national interest involve them in supplying below-cost services to private industry? Can the industries be both commercial and a weapon of subsidy?

(b) What are the boundaries of the commercial interests of the nationalised industries, *e.g.* has British Rail the right to own hotels and the N.C.B. the need of builders' merchants? If the industries are to be run on a commercial basis should they take commercial decisions? Vertical integration (*see* XVI, **7**) is normal business practice therefore should British Rail, who have the engineering potential, be allowed to build their own rolling stock? Maximisation of asset use is vital to profit achievement—should British Rail turn their empty station forecourts into garages? This problem hinges on whether a nationalised industry with its access to Government money and lack of profit motive, provides fair competition to private industry.

Aspect (b) will be most closely examined by the Conservative Government, which will be under party pressure clearly to define the limits of nationalised industry and to sell off remaining assets.

29. Competition between nationalised industries. Several of the nationalised industries are in direct competition with each other, e.g. gas and electricity, or compete in certain markets, e.g. B.E.A. and British Rail. If competition does stimulate efficiency then the public interest is served by this very active competition; but to what extent does the competition lead to wasteful overheads and excessive investment levels, e.g. gas and electricity showrooms side by side in the main street, the huge advertising campaigns of British Rail and B.E.A? This situation reveals the classic dilemma of judging the merits of competition and monopoly as they affect the consumer.

FINANCIAL PROBLEMS

30. The size of investment. The accompanying table (Table XXXII) shows the enormous levels of investment required by the nationalised industries. This high level, which represents about 20 per cent of investment in this country arises through the nature of the industries not because the industries are nationalised. The sheer volume raises three important issues.

31. The determination of investment levels. The table (Table XXXII) shows the large investment to be of a continuous nature because the industries are capital intensive, thus there is a constant need for replacement capital and new capital to meet demand expansion.

Forecasting demand in the short run is difficult but nationalised industries have to forecast long-run demand patterns because of the time-lags of installing heavy capital equipment, e.g. 150 miles of railway-line electrification can take from five to eight years. The likely inaccuracy of long-term

TABLE XXXII. NATIONALISED INDUSTRIES—BORROWING OUTSTANDING

March 1970

(£ million)

Industry	Gross Gov. advances	Repayments	Net Gov. advances	Borrowing by stock	Temporary borrowing	Foreign borrowing	Total
Post Office	1,921	—	1,921	—	—	—	1,921
Electricity	4,630	950	3,680	701	37	30	4,448
Gas Council	1,927	169	1,128	286	22	32	1,468
British Steel	240	52	188	—	133	—	321
B.O.A.C.	31	14	17	—	—	39	56
B.E.A.	132	30	102	—	14	7	123
British Rail	365	15	350	—	17	—	367
N.C.B.	778	88	690	—	—	—	690
Others	407	—	407	—	18	1	426
Total	£9,801	£1,318	£8,483	£987	£241	£109	£9,820

(Source: Loans from National Loans Fund, 1970–71.)

forecasting reduces the value of modern investment appraisal schemes (*see* **22** above).

The investment decision also involves the choosing of the anticipated modern equipment five years hence, thus a technological unknown is introduced into the decision to invest, *e.g.* in 1969 the electricity industry introduced new generating equipment planned in 1964, it immediately broke down and even by 1971 the technical problems have not been completely solved.

W. G. Shepherd suggests that Treasury influence on investment decisions has led Boards to try to solve single problems rather than view their overall needs, *e.g.* for many years the Post Office ignored the role of telecommunications (Richard E. Caves and associates, *Britain's Economic Prospects*, Allen & Unwin, 1968, p. 14).

The future demand levels on which investment is based are heavily influenced by the industries' own pricing policies (*see* **34** below). Low prices charged now may give demand forecasts which collapse if at a future date a more realistic pricing policy is used by the industry.

32. The problem of raising the capital. The nationalised industries between them raise over £1,000 million per annum, not all of which can be self-financed (*see* Table XXXIII). This quantity of capital-raising produces several problems.

Each of the nationalised industries has a statutory limit to its borrowing powers and each needs Ministry approval to raise and spend this money, but they can borrow working capital without prior consent.

Up to 1956 the nationalised industries (with the exception of the N.C.B.) borrowed on long-dated fixed-interest stock. These levels of interest were low and there was the danger that the industries might be tempted to invest more of this cheap capital than was really necessary, thus wasting part of the nation's capital resources.

The interest rates also bore no relation to industrial risk although the problem of defining risk in a Government-guaranteed industry is difficult.

In 1956 the nationalised industries started to borrow directly from the Treasury and in 1968 from the National Loans Fund which is still the position; this borrowing has been at more commercial rates of interest.

TABLE XXXIII. NATIONALISED INDUSTRIES—FINANCING OF CAPITAL REQUIREMENTS

Industry	Capital requirement 1970–71	Financed by		
		Internal resources	National Loans Fund	Others
Post Office	498	214	284	—
National Coal Board	42	65	—49	26
Electricity (England and Wales)	420	350	80	—10
Gas	335	72	263	—
British Steel	127	224	—21·8	—75·2
B.O.A.C.	97·9	46·3	—2·8	54·4
B.E.A.	46·1	25·2	35·2	—14·3
British Rail	97·6	78·1	15·0	4·5

(Source: Loans from the National Loans Fund, 1970–71, Cmnd. 4333.)

The industries have a desire to raise more of their capital privately, perhaps even overseas, but the Treasury has fought this wish on three grounds:

(a) The risk element is difficult to calculate, allied to which profit performance still has some social criteria limitations, thus the private lender lacks the normal commercial mechanisms for judging an investment opportunity.

(b) The amount of money involved would distort the capital market and perhaps limit the opportunities for private borrowers.

(c) Nationalised industry investment affects the total economy (*see* **33** below), thus it would be wrong for the Treasury to lose control. They also fear the balance of payments consequences of extensive overseas borrowing.

Despite these fears the Treasury have allowed B.O.A.C. and British Steel to borrow from the Government on an equity principle, *i.e.* the interest depends on the profit performance, and the Conservative Government may experiment with the creating of private equity holders to give the nationalised industries a greater commercial incentive.

33. The influence of nationalised industry investment on the economy. All British Governments have used nationalised industries' investment plans as a weapon of counter-cyclical finance (*see* II, **13–23**). Thus the plans have been cut or increased without reference to the needs of the industries; no other businesses have suffered this fate. This policy has so many pitfalls it is amazing that Governments have been so faithful to it. Some of the problems are:

(a) *Timing.* What is the lag after the decision to increase or cut back investment before economic effects can be seen?

(b) *Size of change.* What volume of change is necessary to affect the economy and what effects does this volume have on the industries themselves?

(c) *What is the relation between nationalised and private investment.* Will a cut-back in the former release capital for the latter thus scarcely affecting levels of aggregate demand? (*see* I, **4, 13**).

(d) *Inflexibility of investment programmes.* A nationalised industry invests £x million today for its and the country's needs in five to eight years (*see* **31** above). Do Governments reflect on the long-term repercussions of their short-term policies?

The 1967 White Paper (*see* **22** above) asks the nationalised industries to take a commercial attitude to investment decisions; the evidence suggests it is Governments, not the Boards, which will ignore this advice.

34. Pricing policy. The majority of private companies use the full cost method of price determination, *e.g.* average variable unit cost+a percentage for overheads+a percentage profit margin. In theory, under perfect competition, firms charge a price equal to marginal cost (E. Seddon, *Economics of Public Finance,* Macdonald & Evans, 1968, *see also* IV, **15**). The complexities of the nationalised industries leave them with a policy somewhere between the above positions.

The problem areas are:

(a) In the nationalised industries, because they are capital intensive, variable costs are a low proportion of overheads, thus the concept of "spreading a percentage cost for overheads" is difficult to apply, *e.g.* what proportion of the cost of London to Manchester rail electrification should be borne by a branch line in East Anglia or a commuter in Glasgow?

(b) Until recently the nationalised industries' aims were so vague that the fixing of a percentage profit margin was a meaningless concept.

(c) The use of marginal cost pricing, *e.g.* two-part tariffs on telephones, falls foul of the remaining social obligations of the industries, *e.g.* such a policy in coal pricing would almost immediately close many pits as they would price themselves out of the market; but what effects would it have on regional unemployment? Another problem is the allowance for social costs in marginal costing techniques, *e.g.* on environmental grounds new electrification schemes use underground rather than overhead cables, should the consumer bear this social cost if he rather likes pylons in the countryside?

(d) Should the nationalised industries use a policy of

cross-subsidised prices, *i.e.* charge a very high price in a profitable market to subsidise a non-profit-making service, *e.g.* should Inter-City rail fares be used to subsidise commuter rail fares? Should profitable B.E.A. route prices be used severely to cut internal prices in order to compete against buses and railway routes.

(*e*) The important nationalised industries supply the majority of their outputs to private industry, thus their prices affect the whole structure of industrial costs. Expert as opposed to newspaper opinion has consistently argued that for political reasons nationalised prices have been uneconomically low. "Prices have been kept in general very low in relation to prices elsewhere in the economy largely out of a desire to prevent price increases being passed on in an inflationary manner from these basic industries" (*Growth in the British Economy*, P.E.P., Allen & Unwin, 1960). This Government view is understandable but curiously short-sighted. Under-pricing can lead to a misallocation of resources just as over-pricing can, but more importantly low prices have led to the need of Government help which through its effects on public expenditure (*see* IV, **15–18**) is inflationary.

So often in nationalised industries politics not economics seem to be the prime motivator.

EVALUATING THE SUCCESS OF NATIONALISED INDUSTRIES

35. Guidelines. To judge the results of the nationalised industries it is necessary to establish their aims as envisaged by their political creator. The ideas below indicate the areas into which Government policy has pushed the nationalised Boards:

(*a*) A pricing policy designed to promote the best use of resources and to obtain an acceptable rate of return on capital.

(*b*) To use the industries as the stimulants of innovation and research, which are the fuels of economic growth.

(*c*) To promote economic welfare aims by policies of high wages and low prices.

(*d*) To allow policy for the industries to be dependent on

more general economic policies, *e.g.* obtaining a balance of payments surplus on regional growth.

36. Criteria of success.

The criteria of success must be sought under three main headings:

✗   (*a*) A nationalised undertaking is comparable to a private business organisation and faces problems of output allocation, pricing and investment decisions. The efficient solving of these problems will produce rates of return on capital similar to those in the private sector. To obtain the most efficient resource allocation involves a pricing policy based on the theory of perfect competition, *i.e.* the price of a good or service should approximate to the marginal cost of that good or service.

✗   (*b*) The industries are to assist in the achievement of broad economic targets; they may lead the fight against inflation by standing firm on excessive wage demands; they may keep railway lines open to help a development area.

If this concept is pursued the industries are losing the commercial freedom which is necessary to achieve goal (*a*). Private industry does not live in an economic limbo, its decisions are influenced by Government economic policy, but its policies are seen from the view of self-interest not the national interest. Thus a strike may be suicidal to the firm but not to the Government and the company will try to buy off the strike. If a nationalised industry is used as an economic arm of the Government its profit performance cannot be compared to the private industry.

✗   (*c*) The achievements of social aims may affect Government policy, *e.g.* the use of non-economic pits to keep miners in work. The previous arguments also apply here, a nationalised industry which is not totally pursuing a commercial policy cannot be assessed by commercial criteria.

The nationalised industries are often unjustly criticised because this is not realised. Commercial profits must imply commercial freedom to fix price, to raise capital on the money market and to indulge in vertical integration (*see* XVI, **7**). If this freedom cannot be politically guaranteed, the politician must evolve other standards of judgment, for economic criteria are no longer applicable.

The actual performance of British nationalised industries has confirmed the above analysis. When they have been given top-class management, clear aims and relative commercial freedom their performance in terms of profit and productivity have been satisfactory. This has been particularly so in the 1960s when both political parties have largely substituted economic reality for political doctrine in their dealings with the nationalised industries. Whether the experience from running public-utility industries can be successfully translated to organising an ordinary commercial industry, e.g. steel, is going to arouse great interest and controversy in the 1970s.

37. Conclusions. This chapter has shown the nationalised industries to be a most complex type of business organisation, much affected by political rather than economic considerations. Political decisions have been important, thus the change of government in 1970 from Labour to Conservative may well be significant in the history of the industries.

At first Junior Ministers at the Department of Trade and Industry gave the impression that great sections of the industries would be sold off to private industry. The reasons for and mechanics of this action was never made clear. The senior Departmental Minister in 1972, Mr. John Davies, has pursued a more pragmatic approach.

He has argued that because nationalised industries do not raise their capital on the private market or sell their product in a competitive market politicians have tried to indulge in an excessive scrutiny of the industries which has limited their business initiative. To introduce financial and market disciplines is desirable but difficult. "Some people believe that to achieve this end you find out what parts of the business are or could be profitable and then dispose of them at the best possible price. That is nonsense. The Government by no means intends to clip its own wings by settling for such a crude and ill-thought-out liquidation of national assets" (*Journal of Trade and Industry*, 16th December 1970).

Some of the assets will be sold off, e.g. Thomas Cooks, and the National Coal Board will be the first industry to have its whole operations put under a microscope. It appears that Conservative policy will involve in general terms more stringent rates of return, the selling off of fringe activities and possibly the introduction of private capital, but at the beginning of 1972 it is difficult to envisage a complete new concept of nationalised industries in this country.

PROGRESS TEST 17

1. Do nationalised industries always lose money? (**2**(*a*))
2. Why are public utilities usually nationalised? (**3**)
3. In what way will a lack of profit motive affect a nationalised industry? (**9**)
4. What aspect of nationalised industry policy is used as a weapon of macroeconomic policy? (**18**(*a*))
5. Why are 1961 and 1967 significant dates in the history of the nationalised industries? (**21–22**)
6. What is the problem of "Accountability"? (**24**)
7. Account for the failure of the Consumers' Consultative Councils. (**27**)
8. Suggest two areas of controversy in the relationship of private industry to the nationalised sector. (**28**)
9. What two problems arise in forecasting investment levels for the nationalised industries? (**31**)
10. Why is the Treasury against the raising of private capital for the nationalised industries? (**32**)
11. Outline the difficulties of using marginal costing techniques to determine prices in the nationalised industries. (**34**(*c*))
12. Can the nationalised industries be judged by commercial criteria? (**36**)

CHAPTER XVIII

GOVERNMENT AND INDUSTRIAL LOCATION

NATURE OF PROBLEM

1. Introduction. Throughout history different parts of countries have had varying levels of prosperity as the free play of economic forces has both brought and removed industry, work and income. Governments felt no responsibility for these changes unless a growing depression threatened a political upheaval which might bring the fall of the Government.

In the 1930s, as was seen in the previous chapters, Governments were tentatively pursuing a more interventionist policy towards the economic problems of the day. A major problem in the West was those areas of countries which had unemployment levels well above the national average, *e.g.*. the north-east of England had rates of unemployment in the 30–45 per cent range when the national rate was 10 per cent (compare these rates with the levels of today).

The year 1934 was the first in which the British Government tried to encourage companies to move to areas of high unemployment and these efforts have grown and grown to such an extent that, in 1969, the Government spent £265 million to help areas of high unemployment.

This chapter analyses the methods by which British Governments have tried to solve the problem of the backward regions and it suggests the need for new thinking on what is becoming one of Britain's oldest economic problems. These methods have basically involved the Government in trying to influence the location decisions of private industry and persuading companies to develop new plant in the backward regions.

2. Characteristics of the backward regions. All backward regions appear to have certain common features:

(a) Their unemployment rates will be considerably greater than the national average.

(b) The region relies for its employment on one or two industries whose demand is permanently declining. The resulting unemployment is called "structural unemployment."

(c) The levels of income in the region will be below the national average although the effects of this low-income level will be modified by the transfer of money through Government welfare spending.

(d) Because of (c), the levels of demand in the region will be low, which will adversely affect service industries, particularly the retail trade.

(e) Educational achievements may be lower, as fewer children stay on at school after the statutory leaving age.

(f) The area may be suffering from a net emigration of population. The vast majority of migrants will be young people so the remaining population will have a relatively high proportion of people over forty. This type of age structure creates problems of retraining in new skills and also a problem of a lack of leadership in local affairs.

(g) Several commentators have suggested that firms centred in the backward regions have lower productivity (*National Institute of Economic Research Review*, November 1968) and lower returns on investment (Supplement on the North-West," *Guardian*, 18th November 1969).

(h) The regions have a poor "infrastructure," *i.e.* the quality of housing, schools, hospitals, communications, shopping, social and cultural facilities.

These factors contribute to give most people in the backward regions a quality of social and economic life which would not be acceptable in the rest of the country.

REASONS FOR GOVERNMENT CONCERN WITH THE PROBLEM

3. Waste of resources. Labour is a productive resource which is wasted if it is under-used. Thus to have employable people out of work for long periods of time is as economically nonsensical as having idle plant and equipment. The 1963

National Economic Development Council's report (*see* XIII, 11) argued that "Relatively high unemployment rates also indicate considerable labour reserves.   To draw these reserves into employment would make a substantial contribution to national growth."

4. Contradiction of economic policies.   A Government's economic policy, particularly in its demand management (*see* II, 10(*d*), is trying to influence the economic life of the whole country.   However, the individual parts of the country may have different economic problems, thus to solve these difficulties the Government introduces policies which run counter to the original concepts, *e.g.* a policy of depressing the economy to fight inflation ruins policies designed to rejuvenate industry in the backward regions.   Sir Eric Roll, ex-Permanent Secretary at the now defunct Department of Economic Affairs has written: "A more even distribution of economic prosperity would counteract the inflationary effects of regional concentrations of excess demand, thus facilitating the management of the economy" (*Public Administration*, Spring 1966).

5. Costs of congestion.   If people in the backward areas are forced by economic circumstance to move to more prosperous districts, there will be a growing pressure on the demand for housing and transport in these areas, thus raising living and industrial costs.   A lack of housing and the overcrowding of transport systems both lead to social stresses which can damage the effectiveness of the labour force.

6. The social problem of unemployment.   The backward regions have large numbers of people who have been out of work for long periods of time.   The families of these men, despite welfare aid, undergo great economic and social hardship and the men themselves lose all dignity and belief in themselves and eventually deteriorate into a condition of being unemployable.

Lord Francis Williams in his autobiography describes his first landlord in Bootle, an unemployed engineer.   "He would sit there for hours never saying a word.   You could see a man disintegrating before your eyes" (Francis Williams, *Nothing So Strange*, Cassell, 1970).

7. Summary. Regional backwardness presents severe economic and social problems and provides another example of Governments interfering with market forces to try to prevent the consequences of those forces. In democratic countries the desire to solve the regional problem is strengthened by political fears that extremists might exploit the economic problems for political gain.

Government policy has taken two paths to try to find a solution.

GOVERNMENT REACTION TO THE PROBLEM

8. The movement of workers. Ultimately, if a Government took no action the unemployed would in theory have to starve or move to where there was work. However, the social and economic costs of moving are very heavy, e.g. the cost of a new house, leaving friends and moving children from school, thus labour has tended to be immobile. Occasionally Governments have toyed with subsidising people willing to move out of backward areas, but the social problem and the fear of creating congestion (see **5** above) have prevented the serious use of this policy.

Indeed the Government have through the use of New Towns (see **12** below) tried to move people out of conurbations into less-developed areas. They have hoped to attract industry into the regions by injecting into these areas better housing, younger people and improved amenities.

9. Moving industry into backward areas. The basic Government policy has been to encourage industry, by financial inducement to build new factories in the backward areas. It can be argued that bribing a company to develop where it would not normally have built creates an inefficient use of resources. However, this idea assumes that firms make locational decisions in a rational economic fashion, an assumption not proved by empirical evidence (see **18** below).

Governments are always faced by conflicting priorities and with this problem they prefer to cure unemployment and risk some mislocation of industry. Legislation has centred on persuading companies to move rather than helping labour to be more mobile.

LEGISLATION

10. Introduction. R. Turner in an article "Government Policy on Location" (*Economics*, Summer 1968), suggests that most legislative Acts have common characteristics:

(*a*) They provide for the definition of geographical areas in which benefits are available for industry.

(*b*) They outline criteria for defining the areas.

(*c*) They define the range of industry which will qualify for the benefits.

(*d*) They set out the financial benefits available to industry.

In principle most of the Acts are similar, varying only in detail, *e.g.* re-marking the boundaries of areas or changing the percentage grants. This section mentions the significant legislation but will only discuss changes of principle within the Acts.

11. Pre-1945.

(*a*) *The* 1934 *Special Areas Act.* Four particularly depressed areas, west Cumberland, north-east Coast, South Wales and central Scotland were defined as special areas and industry therein was made eligible for Government assistance. However, the Act had no real effect as the financial assistance was slight and most industries were so depressed they had no incentive to develop anywhere in the country.

(*b*) *The* 1937–40 *Barlow Commission.* This body was asked to study the twin problems of backward areas and congested conurbations. They recommended a central authority to seek three objectives:

   (*i*) Redevelopment of congested urban areas.
   (*ii*) Dispersal of industries from these areas.
   (*iii*) The encouragement of a reasonable balance of industrial development throughout the various regions of Great Britain.

The outbreak of war prevented the implementation of this radical proposal for centralised planning of industrial location.

12. 1945–59.

(a) 1945: *The Distribution of Industry Act*. This Act slightly enlarged the 1934 Special Areas, *e.g.* the inclusion of Wrexham and parts of south Lancashire. It rechristened them "development areas" and gave the Board of Trade powers to build new factories for leasing on trading estates. There was also aid towards the capital cost of moving.

This Act was much influenced by the Barlow Commission and the 1944 White Paper on employment which envisaged attacking unemployment by helping those regions with declining industry.

(b) 1946: *New Towns Act and* 1947: *Town and Country Planning Act*. These two Acts are not strictly to do with the economic problems of development areas but they represent a new strand of thought, the concept that industrial location, location of people and physical planning are all elements in the same problem of improving the quality of life throughout the country.

The 1947 Act introduced Industrial Development Certificates (I.D.C.s). Any company wishing to build plant above a certain size has to have an I.D.C.; they are granted almost automatically within development areas but they may be withheld for development outside the areas. They tend to be negative and their enforcement seems to be very variable so it is nearly impossible to calculate their effect on development areas.

13. 1960–66.

(a) 1960: *Local Employment Act*. Previous legislation was repealed. The areas were replaced by "development districts," localities where a high rate of employment (a high rate was defined as $4\frac{1}{2}$ per cent) exists or is to be expected and is likely to persist. The districts were smaller than the areas, towns or employment areas were often singled out, thus fewer people were in localities receiving aid.

Capital was provided for new buildings and local authorities were given considerable powers and finance to clear unsightly derelict land and to improve local services.

(b) 1963: *Local Employment Act*. This Act extended the available aid to areas within commuting distance of the development districts and also to overspill development of cities within the districts.

The size of capital aid for buildings was increased and for the first time grants were given for the installation of machinery. The Government also promised to give their contracts, where possible, to firms within the development districts.

(c) 1964: *Regional Planning*. When Mr. George Brown helped to found the Department of Economic Affairs in 1964 (*see* XIII, **14**) he assigned a section of the Department to study the problem of "regional imbalance." He created a new philosophy which suggests that the economic discrepancies in the country had to be tackled at a regional and national level, rather than in piecemeal fashion.

Eight regions were created: Scotland, Northern, North-West, Yorkshire and Humberside, East Midlands, West Midlands, Wales and South-West. Each region was given two new bodies:

(i) *Regional Planning Board*. This consisted of senior civil servants from offices within the region. Its function was to co-ordinate government activity in the regions and to draw up a plan to promote regional economic growth.

(ii) *Regional Economic Planning Council*. This body had twenty-five part-time members, men and women of distinction from all walks of life within the region. Each Council had as a chairman, a man with power and influence. The chairman was given, in theory, direct access to Ministers in Whitehall.

The Council's function was to help prepare the regional plan, to advise on its implementation and to study the effect of national policies on the regions. (A third Polytechnic was designated in the North-West after pressure was put on the Department of Education and Science by the North-West Planning Council.)

The Boards and Councils still exist, but their powers have vanished in the mists of obscurity since the demise of the D.E.A. and even by 1966 the Government's thinking had returned to traditional methods.

(d) 1966: *Industrial Development Act*. The development districts of 1960 were widened into development areas (*Board of Trade Journal*, 19th August 1966), namely:

(i) The whole of Scotland except for an area around Edinburgh.

(ii) The whole of the Northern Region plus the Furness peninsula.

(*iii*) A small area in the North-West based on Merseyside.

(*iv*) Most of Wales.

(*v*) An area in the extreme South-West including most of Cornwall and parts of north Devon.

Capital aid was again increased but instead of giving money through tax allowances the aid came in direct grants (*see* **21** below).

14. 1967 onwards.

(*a*) *Special Development Areas..* On 14th November 1967 the President of the Board of Trade, announced the creation of Special Development Areas. These were small parts of development areas (based on labour exchanges) suffering from acute unemployment problems, often because of colliery closures, *e.g.* Workington, Ystalyfera and Sanquhar. In February 1971, more areas were classified as Special; 8·5 per cent of the insured population of Great Britain now live in Special Development Areas (*Trade and Industry*, 24th February 1971).

(*b*) *Regional Employment Premiums.* This was a system springing from the Selective Employment Tax to subsidise labour in the development areas. Manufacturing companies within the areas received £1·50 for each male employed in addition to 38p S.E.T. premium (with corresponding rates for women, girls and boys).

The system is financially wasteful because existing companies in the area may have not created a new job for twenty years yet obtain the subsidy for their work force. The Conservatives are pledged to abolish R.E.P. by 1974.

(*c*) *The* 1970 *Conservative Government.* By the spring of 1971 no comprehensive regional policy had been announced, but the Government late in 1970 replaced investment grants with allowances (*see* **21** below) and suggested that less money would be given direct to industry but more money would be spent on infrastructure (*see* **2** (*g*) above). Whether this idea would be acceptable to the civil service advisers is doubtful because it flies against thirty-five years of continuous policy to help industry directly.

15. Intermediate Areas (Grey Areas). Through the mid-1960s various local authorities complained that their localities were suffering from economic depression but because their unemployment rates were not quite high enough, they did not qualify for aid and consequently could not attract new industry. Such areas included Lancashire, south Yorkshire, Notts/north-east/Derby coalfield, Plymouth.

These areas had certain common economic and social features:

- (*a*) Sluggishly growing and falling employment opportunities.
- (*b*) A slow growth of personal incomes.
- (*c*) A net emigration of population.
- (*d*) An above-average unemployment rate.
- (*e*) Decaying environmental factors.
- (*f*) Poor communications.

The Government set up (under Mr. Hunt a Birmingham industrialist) the Hunt Commission to investigate, and its report was published in April 1969. Its main findings were:

(*a*) Firms moving into intermediate areas or expanding existing firms should receive a 25 per cent grant towards new buildings.

(*b*) Local authorities should have long-term plans for clearing derelict land for which they should obtain 85 per cent grants.

(*c*) The setting up of small business centres to act as management consultants for smaller companies.

(*d*) More assistance for training and education facilities.

(*e*) The removal of development status from Merseyside because its employment possibilities were growing quickly and it pulled industry from north-east Lancashire (a minority report dissented from this finding).

The Government after much hesitation accepted point (*a*) for certain districts within the original intermediate area. It agreed to point (*b*) at a rate of 75 per cent. The money involved in this expenditure had to come from the S.E.T. premium going to the development areas. These decisions were implemented in the *Local Employment Act* of 1970. Point (*e*), politically very awkward, was conveniently forgotten and has not been heard of again.

In February 1971, more areas, ranging from Filey to Tavistock, were given intermediate area status.

16. Results. The following tables are a very brief guide to the money spent in the regions and the general results which ensued from the Government investment.

TABLE XXXIV. TOTAL COST OF SPECIAL REGIONAL ASSISTANCE TO INDUSTRY ABOVE WHAT IS AVAILABLE NATIONALLY

(£ million)

	1963–64	1964–65	1965–66	1966–67	1967–68	1968–69
Local Employment Acts[1]	17	28	30	44	45	50
Free depreciation[2]	—	3	45	25	4	—
Investment grants				—	72	85
Industrial training				1	1	3
S.E.T. Premium[3]					—	25
R.E.P.					34	100
Total	17	31	75	70	156	263

(Source: D.E.A. Progress Report, August 1969.)

[1] Includes building grants and other loans.

[2] Replaced by investment grants.

[3] Abolished in 1969/70 and expenditure transferred to intermediate areas.

NOTE: These figures should be contrasted with the period 1945–63 when the total expenditure was £206 million.

TABLE XXXV. THE MOVEMENT OF MANUFACTURING INDUSTRY TRANSFERS[1] AND BRANCHES[2] 1945–65

Host Regions	1945–51 Moves %		1952–59 Moves %		1960–65 Moves %		1945–65 Moves %	
Peripheral Areas[3]	463	49·6	214	23·8	475	40·3	1,152	38·2
South-East and East Anglia	220	23·6	456	50·6	384	32·5	1,060	35·2
Rest of England	250	26·8	231	25·6	321	27·2	802	26·6
Total	933	100	901	100	1,180	100	3,014	100

(Source: K. D. George, Industrial Organisation; Allen & Unwin, 1971, p. 203.)

[1] Transfer of establishments involving cessation at first locality.

[2] The opening of a second or subsequent establishment.

[3] Peripheral areas correspond closely to those areas where Government aid has been available.

TABLE XXXVI. CHANGES IN REGIONAL DISPARITIES IN UNEMPLOYMENT, NET MIGRATION AND PERSONAL INCOME PER HEAD

Region	Unemployment %			Net migration (000's)		Personal income per head (% of U.K. average)	
	1958	1967	1971 (March)	1956–61	1961–66	1954–55	1964–65
N. Ireland	9·3	7·7	7·0	−93	−38	64	64
Wales	3·8	4·1	4·2	−22	+5	87	84
Scotland	3·7	3·9	5·1	−142	−194	93	88
Northern	2·4	4·0	4·9	−30	−37	93	82
North-West	2·7	2·5	3·2	−60	−13	102	95
South-West	2·2	2·5	3·1	+91	+108	87	91
U.K.	2·1	2·5	2·9	—	—	—	—

(*Source:* G. McCrone, *Regional Policy in Britain*, Allen & Unwin, 1969, Chapter 6.)

It is possible to show that a vast number of jobs have been created in the development areas since 1945. However, these figures must be seen in the context of the number of jobs lost through redundancies and the overall national employment situation.

Table XXXV reveals that despite vast inducements to industry, by 1965 only just over a third of the movements in manufacturing were to development areas. Table XXXVI is the most telling information, for it suggests that in the key areas of employment and income, at best the development areas have stood still, *i.e.* their relative position has not deteriorated, at worst, *e.g.* Scotland and Northern, the situation has worsened rather alarmingly.

The conclusion must be drawn that after thirty-seven years of trying to cure regional backwardness, Governments have not allowed the situation to worsen, but despite large Government expenditure (Table XXXIV), a genuine cure is not in sight.

The next section analyses this curious situation.

REASONS FOR FAILURE OF THE LEGISLATION

17. Introduction. It is perhaps unfair to accuse Governments and their advisers of *naïveté* but the policies pursued seem incredibly simplistic. In district A, a lot of people are unemployed; offer bribes to companies if they go to A; companies go to A and the problem is solved. This section looks at the complexities of the problem, which successive Governments have chosen to ignore.

18. Ignoring market forces. This view is largely held by opponents of Government intervention, who hold that a company changes its location by considering the maximum benefits to be derived from siting the plant in proximity to raw materials, fuels, markets, labour supply and transport, or some combination of these elements. However, judging from recent research at the University of East Anglia, companies locate new plant for a myriad reasons, not all of them economically logical (P. M. Townroe, "How Managers

Pick Plants," *Management Today*, October 1970). Thus Government incentives do not necessarily go against normal location decisions but are merely another factor in location decision-taking.

Assuming firms do act according to the economic textbook, their decision will rest on economic costs but their choice of site may well incur social costs, *e.g.* costs of congestion (*see* **5** above) or the costs of creating pockets of permanent unemployment (*see* **6** above). Governments cannot ignore these social costs, thus they may pursue a policy which creates a higher economic cost but which reduces social costs.

It is worth noting that structural unemployment is caused by the free play of market forces.

19. The use of blanket solutions. Governments have treated all development areas as identical units, having identical causes of backwardness. This is a distortion of the truth, *e.g.* Scotland is troubled by a dramatic decline in population (*see* Table XXXVI), Wales suffers partly from the collapse of hill farming; neither of these difficulties are inherent in the Merseyside economic troubles.

A clear identification of the underlying causes of each area's unemployment is required, then Governments should devise a whole armoury of aid, which the areas could choose from to suit their own circumstances.

20. Growth points or growth areas. Conservative Governments have advocated the concentration of aid in small areas, perhaps one town, rather than spreading financial incentives over a bigger geographical unit. This argument is based on achieving external economies of scale (*see* XIV, **12**), for if companies are spread haphazardly over a wide area it will be difficult to provide the required education, communication and housing facilities, *i.e.* growth points cut down the cost of infrastructure renewal. Surrounding areas of the growth point benefit as economic stimulants spread from the growth centre like ripples in a pond. This concept also avoids the cost of giving aid to areas beyond all economic recovery. Critics deny the ripple argument and say the method will still lead to a vast under-utilisation of resources.

Vacillation on the size of aid-receiving areas has undermined industrial confidence, for they may plan to go to Area A but as their plans ripen into fruition, a new Government cuts off aid from A, thus altering all the company's calculations.

21. Capital grants or capital allowances. The method of granting aid has also led to sudden changes in policy. Capital allowances are linked to the company taxation system and thus the more efficient company making a larger profit is likely to obtain more aid. Grants are direct payments to companies moving to development areas and thus there is a direct connection between moving and receipt of aid.

The Conservatives on taking office in 1970 almost immediately switched from the grant to the allowance system, thus reducing the liquidity of low-profit companies. (This was the last nail in the Rolls Royce coffin.) These sudden switches of policy are not helpful to companies (*see* **20** above).

22. Over-use of capital incentives. Apart from the Regional Employment Premium (*see* **13** (*b*)) all the major weapons of aid have been subsidies to capital. The *National Institute Economic Review* (November 1968) suggested that the development areas were becoming full of capital-intensive industries which seems strange when unemployment is the significant difficulty. More labour subsidies might be a better policy (*see* **31** and **32** below) unless it leads to an inefficient use of manpower.

23. Lack of analysis of the unemployed. Blanket solutions have already been condemned (*see* **19** above). This approach is most noticeable and dangerous in the analysis of who are the people out of work and what types of job will the new company offer. Parts of the Northern area have received female-intensive companies when the unemployment crisis centres on older miners; Liverpool is short of work for the semi-skilled but its factories ceaselessly search and compete for almost non-existent skilled men. This problem springs from discussing the unemployed and new jobs in round abstract figures, rather than in terms of people and skills. The infant science of manpower-planning is surprisingly absent from regional economic discussion.

24. The mobility of labour. The assumption of an immobile labour force has invariably led Governments to concentrate on the movement of industry (*see* **9** above), but how valid is the assumption? If housing costs are a stronger disincentive to mobility than social costs then a different Government attitude to housing subsidies and rented accommodation might ease the cost of movement.

At the moment subsidies are on the house, thus if a person moves to an area and is not on the housing list his chances of a council house are remote. If the subsidy went to people in genuine need a person changing areas would still have a chance of obtaining a housing subsidy.

Advocates of a greater use of labour mobility do not see it as a complete answer but as an aid to the problems of the development areas, although the congestion problem (*see* **5** above) might grow if labour really becomes more mobile.

25. Lack of national economic growth. The disappointing growth of the British economy has been the fundamental reason for the lack of work in the regions. If a company cannot sell its products it is not going to create new work anywhere. In two years out of five, on average, since 1945, Government policy has tried to reduce the level of aggregate demand (*see* **I**, **4** and **13**) and there is no economic reason why a particular region, already handicapped, can raise the pressure of demand against the national trend.

It may take two years to persuade a company to move to Merseyside and create 200 jobs. Within twenty-four hours of the opening of the plant, two firms announce redundancies involving 800 men. This is the nub of the problem of lack of national growth.

Some people have argued that a lack of growth in certain regions have caused the lack of national growth, but this is putting the cart before the horse. In the mid-1950s when the economy was expanding, the prospects in the regions brightened. The development areas, perhaps dependent on a declining industry, have not the strength to be the engine-room of economic growth.

The erratic nature of post-war economic policies have led to very low-investment levels in industry in general and in the development areas in particular; Government financial aid has been inadequate to fill the investment gap. The nonsense of reducing the demand for a company's products, through taxes or credit squeezes, and then trying to bribe it to increase its plant is now clearly exposed.

26. Psychological defeatism. The non-success of economic policies is now often explained in psychological terms and development-area policy is no exception. Many of the areas have suffered economic depression for twenty-five years and the people in the area have become defeatist and dejected. They are dependent on aid and the urge to fight, the desire to create new businesses, have gone. The final proof of this mental attitude would be difficult but odd statistics are disturbing, *e.g.* companies with headquarters in the North-West have lower rates of return than their southern counterparts and the educational qualifications of top management are lower (*Guardian*, 18th November 1969).

We know that a long period of unemployment can seriously undermine an individual (*see* **6** above), perhaps a whole area can mentally and physically rot, *e.g.* the west coast of Ireland.

POSSIBLE SOLUTIONS

27. Introduction. These solutions are not offered with great hope of adoption but from the desire to try a different policy. Governments have really become stuck since 1945 and radical new thinking is needed.

These ideas will be redundant if the economy does not grow at a quicker rate (*see* **25** above), for without that stimulant the development areas are doomed to living off Government welfare schemes.

28. The need for more research. There are three areas where the Government's economic knowledge seems slight:

(*a*) The relationship between rates of growth in the total economy and the rates in the regions and how these two rates influence each other.

(*b*) A cost-benefit analysis of the aid given to development areas. It is known that the creation of one job can cost between £900 and £1,500, but does this represent a gain or loss in real resources to the economy?

(c) How do firms decide where to locate their new plant? Without this knowledge, Governments are merely guessing at the best policy.

29. Types of aid.   There has been little change in the type of aid given; only the details have varied.   Would it be possible to give companies a lump sum per x jobs created, thus cutting down the paper work of capital grants and allowances and more directly linking the sums of money with the purpose of giving the aid?

If there are doubts about the best method of inducing companies to move, why not offer them a selection of incentives allowing them to choose the most suitable for their needs?

30. Industry not firms.   Development areas announce with pride that one company has opened one plant in the area, but this is false optimism because in times of economic stress companies invariably retrench at their traditional headquarters and close the one-off plants.

The areas need to tempt whole sections of industry so that there is an underlying strength and companies can reap economies of scale, *e.g.* Merseyside has built up a motor-car industry, not just a few assemblers of cars.

31. Differential social security schemes.   Two ideas are possible, if administratively difficult:

(a) Firms moving to development areas would pay lower National Insurance contributions, thus obtaining a labour subsidy.

(b) Unemployment benefits would be raised in development areas to raise the levels of demand through the multiplier effect of the extra spending (*see* I, **17**).

32. Pay-roll tax.   All companies would pay a tax on their labour but the rates would be very low in the development areas.   This would be a labour subsidy and it is also argued it would be a regional anti-congestion tax.

33. Attracting head offices to regions.   Many companies have head offices in the South-East largely as a matter of prestige.   If they could be persuaded to move to the regions, the latter would benefit in two ways:

(a) Head offices usually contain a large proportion of people in the higher income brackets, whose spending power would have an effect on regional demand.

(b) These people would not tolerate the low regional levels of infrastructure (see 5 above) and they would form pressure groups to improve the amenities.

34. Regional government.   Head offices may be in London because they are close to the seats of power and decision. The regions have little influence on the policies which affect them, thus a restructuring of Government decision-taking would raise the morale of the regions and give them greater impetus and perhaps lead to a wider dispersion of industry.

This idea involves matters of constitution and government which are not within the scope of this section.   However, more and more today we are realising the solution to economic problems may involve a multiplicity of other disciplines, and regional backwardness certainly has no simplistic economic solution.

PROGRESS TEST 18

1.   What is meant by "structural unemployment"?   (2)

2.   Explain the term "infrastructure."   (2)

3.   How could congestion create economic costs?   (5)

4.   Describe two deterrents to the mobility of labour.   (8)

5.   What is an Industrial Development Certificate?   (12)

6.   Name the functions of a Regional Planning Council.   (13)

7.   What are the major characteristics of an Intermediate Area?   (15)

8.   Which circumstances influence an entrepreneur in decisions to locate his plant?   (18)

9.   Explain why some economists prefer growth points to growth areas.   (20)

10.   Which factor of production has been most subsidised by the various aid schemes for backward areas?   (22)

11.   What has been the major cause of the lack of employment opportunities in the development regions?   (25)

12.   How might a pay-roll tax help to bring work to a development area?   (32)

BIBLIOGRAPHY

PART ONE: THE MACROECONOMIC APPROACH

Beveridge, W. H. *Full Employment in a Free Society*. Allen & Unwin.

Brittain, Sir Herbert. *The British Budgetary System*. Allen & Unwin, 1959.

Brittan, S. *Steering the Economy*. Penguin Books, 1971.

Brooman, F. S. *Macroeconomics*. Allen & Unwin, 1967.

Caves, Richard E. *Britain's Economic Prospects*. Allen & Unwin, 1968

Chubb, Basil. *The Control of Public Expenditure*. Oxford University Press, 1952.

Dicks-Mireaux, L. A. *The Inter-relationship between Cost and Price Changes 1946–1959*. Oxford Economic Papers, October, 1961.

Dow, J. C. R. *The Management of the British Economy 1945–1960*. Cambridge University Press, 1964.

Galbraith, J. K. *Economic Development*. Oxford University Press.

Hansen, A. H. *A Guide to Keynes*. McGraw–Hill.

Lewis, W. Arthur *Theory of Economic Growth*. Allen & Unwin.

Lipsey, R. G. "The Relation between Unemployment and the Rate of Change of Money Wage Rates in the United Kingdom 1862–1957." *Economica*, February 1960.

Nevin, E. *The Problem of the National Debt*. University of Wales Press.

Phillips, A. W. "The Relation between Unemployment and the Rate of Change of Money Wage Rates in the United Kingdom 1861–1957." *Economica*, November 1958

Prest, A. R. *Public Finance in Theory and Practive*. Weidenfeld & Nicolson, 1967.

Seddon, E. *Economics of Public Finance*. Macdonald & Evans, 1969.

Official publications

Appropriation Accounts. Annual. H.M.S.O.

The British System of Taxation. Central Office of Information, Reference Pamphlet No. 10. H.M.S.O., 1965

Estimates. Annual. H.M.S.O.

Economic Trends. H.M.S.O.

Finance Accounts of the U.K. Annual. H.M.S.O.

Finance Act. Annual. H.M.S.O.

Finance Statement. Annual. H.M.S.O.

Loans from the National Loans Fund. Annual White Paper. H.M.S.O.

National Income and Expenditure. Annual Blue Book. H.M.S.O.

National Income Statistics: Sources and Methods. H.M.S.O.

Preliminary Estimates of National Income and Expenditure Annual White Paper. H.M.S.O.

Prices and Incomes Act, 1966. H.M.S.O.

Public Expenditure 1968–9 to 1973–4. Cmnd. 4234. H.M.S.O., 1970.

Value-added Tax. 1971 Green Paper. Cmnd. 4621. H.M.S.O.

PART TWO: THE MONETARY SYSTEM

Dacey, W. Manning. *The British Banking Mechanism.* Hutchinson, 1962.

Day, A. C. L. *An Outline of Monetary Economics.* Clarendon Press, 1957.

Friedman, M. *The Counter-Revolution in Monetary Theory.* Occasional Paper 33, Institute of Economic Affairs, 1970

Gibson, N. J. *Financial Intermediaries and Monetary Policy.* Hobart Paper 39, Institute of Economic Affairs, 1967

Hanson, J. L. *Monetary Theory and Practice.* Macdonald & Evans, 1965.

Hobson, Sir Oscar *How the City Works.* Dickens Press, 1962.

Macrae, N. *London Capital Market.* Staples Press, 1957.

Morgan, E. Victor. *Monetary Policy for Stable Growth.* Hobart Paper 27, Institute of Economic Affairs, 1966.

Paish, F. W. *Business Finance.* Pitman, 1965.

Sayers, R. S. *Modern Banking.* Oxford University Press, 1967.

Banking publications

Bank of England Annual Report.

Bank of England Quarterly Bulletin.

The Banker.

The Bankers' Magazine.

Journal of the Institute of Bankers.

The reviews of the London clearing banks.

Official publications

 The British Banking System. Central Office of Information
  Pamphlet No. 65. H.M.S.O.
 British Financial Institutions. Central Office of Information
  Pamphlet No. 24. H.M.S.O.
 Report of the Committee on the Working of the Monetary System
  (Radcliffe Report). Cmnd. 827. H.M.S.O., 1959.

PART THREE: INTERNATIONAL TRADE AND PAYMENTS

Friedman, M. "The Case for Flexible Exchange Rates." *Essays
 in Positive Economics*, pp. 157–187. University of Chicago
 Press, 1953.
Haberler, G. von. *The Theory of International Trade.* Macmillan,
 1937.
Kindleberger, C. P. *International Economics.* Irwin, 1963.
Machlup, F. *Plans for Reform of the International Monetary
 System.* Special Papers in International Economics No. 3.
 Princeton University Press, 1962.
Scammell, W. M. *International Monetary Policy.* Macmillan,
 1964.
Triffin, R. *Gold and the Dollar Crisis.* Yale University Press,
 1961.
Worswick, G. D. N., and Ady, P. H. *The British Economy in the
 1950s.* Oxford University Press, 1962.

Official publications

 The Activities of GATT. Annual. Geneva.
 Britain and the European Communities: An Economic Assessment.
  1970 White Paper. Cmnd. 4289. H.M.S.O.
 Britain's Financial Services for Overseas. Reference Paper
  R.4881/65. C.O.I.
 Britain's Overseas Investment. Reference Paper R.5732/66.
  C.O.I.
 European Free Trade Association. Annual Report. Geneva.
 I.M.F. Annual Report. Washington.
 *Preliminary Estimates of National Income and Balance of
  Payments.* Annual White Paper. H.M.S.O.
 U.K. Balance of Payments. Annual Orange Book. H.M.S.O.

PART FOUR: GOVERNMENT AND INDUSTRY

Allen, G. C. *Monopoly and Restrictive Practices.* Allen & Unwin.
Cameron, G. C., and Clark, B.D. *Industrial Movement and the
 Regional Problem.* Oliver & Boyd.

Caves, Richard E. *Britain's Economic Prospects*. Allen & Unwin.

Evely, R., and Little, I. M. D. *Concentration in British Industry*. Cambridge University Press.

Hague, D. C. *Managerial Economics*. Longmans.

Henderson, P. *Economic Growth in Britain*. Weidenfeld & Nicolson.

McCrone, G. *Regional Policy in Britain*. Allen & Unwin.

Newbould, G. *Management and Mergers Activity*. Guthstead (Liverpool).

Schonfield, A. *Modern Capitalism*. Oxford University Press.

Shepherd, W. G. *Economic Performance under Public Ownership*. Yale University Press.

Sutherland, A. *Monopolies Commission in Action*. Cambridge University Press.

Thornhill, W. *Nationalised Industries*. Nelson.

Official publications.

Financial and Economic Obligations of Nationalised Industries. Cmnd. 1337, 1961. H.M.S.O.

Mergers: A Guide to Board of Trade Practices. H.M.S.O. 1969.

Monopolies and Restrictive Practices Commission Reports H.M.S.O.

Nationalised Industries: A Review of Economic and Financial Objectives. Cmnd, 3437, 1967. H.M.S.O.

Registrar of Restrictive Trading Agreements Reports. H.M.S.O.

Survey of Mergers Report 1958–1968. H.M.S.O. 1970.

EXAMINATION TECHNIQUE

SUCCESS in examination depends not only upon a knowledge of facts but also upon the ability to marshal evidence systematically in a succinct answer to a specific question. In developing an examination technique the candidate will benefit from the following advice:

1. Read the whole paper carefully and unhurriedly and make a selection of those questions you intend to answer. You should be confident that you understand quite clearly the meaning of the questions selected. Avoid those questions where it seems that you will simply duplicate what you will write elsewhere.

2. Having understood a question let it remain uppermost in your mind so that your answer is wholly relevant. Too many failures result from candidates answering questions which do not appear in the paper.

3. Apportion your time so that you are certain of answering the required number of questions. Failure to complete the paper automatically lowers your maximum possible marks.

4. Many problems in Applied Economics have a highly controversial content with no clear-cut solutions. You should therefore avoid dogmatic answers. It is preferable to present the arguments of opposing schools of thought and to arrive at a balanced conclusion. You must certainly avoid the superficial and politically emotive approach of popular journalism.

5. Plan your answers systematically so that there is a logical progression of ideas leading to a natural conclusion. Avoid arguments based upon a series of disconnected points which do nothing to support your conclusion.

6. Finally, it is important to give attention to the composition of your script. A slipshod presentation immediately creates an unfavourable impression.

EXAMINATION QUESTIONS

PART ONE: THE MACROECONOMIC APPROACH

THIS selection of examination questions is related to the four parts of the text. However, it should be understood that in some cases it will be necessary to refer to material covered elsewhere in the book.

1. Explain how the level of income and employment are determined in a private enterprise economy. (*G.C.E.(A)*, *J.M.B.*)

2. Consider the relative merits of direct and indirect taxation. What are the advantages and disadvantages of increasing the proportion of revenue derived from indirect taxation in the United Kingdom? (*G.C.E.(A)*, *J.M.B.*)

3. Is it possible to reconcile the views that (*a*) savings are necessary for growth and (*b*) savings create unemployment? (*G.C.E.(A)*, *J.M.B.*)

4. To what extent, if any, is the National Debt a burden? (*G.C.E.(A)*, *J.M.B.*)

5. How may redistribution of income offset the level of total demand? (*B.Sc. (Econ.)*, *Part I*, *London Internal*)

6. Explain the multiplier concept and discuss its implications for economic policy. (*B.Sc. (Econ.)*, *Part I*, *London External*)

7. Control over the money supply is increasingly advocated as a means of preventing inflation. Examine briefly the theoretical rationale of this argument. (*B.Sc.(Econ.)*, *Part I*, *London External*)

8. "Higher taxes will never solve our problems." (Mr. Edward Heath, March 22nd 1969.) Explain how the pressure of demand on the country's productive capacity is reduced:

(*a*) by higher taxes;
(*b*) by higher saving. (*B.Sc.(Econ.)*, *Part I*, *London Internal*)

9. Discuss the policy implications of the Phillips Curve which relates changes in money wages and prices to the percentage of unemployment. (*B.Sc.(Econ.)*, *Part I*, *London Internal*)

10. How do you distinguish between macroeconomic and microeconomic theories? (*B.Sc.(Econ.)*, *Part I*, *London Internal*)

11. Why has the British economy experienced a relatively low level of unemployment since the war? (*B.Sc.(Econ.), Part I, London Internal*)

12. Discuss critically recent developments in the forecasting and control of public expenditure in the U.K. (*B.Sc.(Econ.), Part II, Public Finance, London Internal and External*)

13. "Post-war stabilisation policy has replaced ten-yearly major depressions with much more frequent minor recessions." Discuss. (*B.Sc.(Econ.), Part II, Public Finance, London Internal and External*)

14. Discuss the influence of short-term stabilisation policies on long-term growth. (*B.Sc.(Econ.), Part II, Public Finance, London Internal and External*)

15. Discuss the influence of the progressivity of the income tax on the aggregate supply of labour. (*B.Sc.(Econ.), Part II, Public Finance, London Internal and External*)

16. What measures would you recommend to improve the built-in stability of the U.K. economy? (*B.Sc.(Econ.), Part II, Public Finance, London Internal and External*)

17. How would you explain the comparatively slow rate of growth in the British economy in recent years? In what ways do you consider that public finance may best be directed to achieving an improvement? (*H.N.D. Business Studies, Liverpool Polytechnic*).

18. Explain why measures to sustain the level of effective demand are not appropriate in dealing with all forms of unemployment. What alternative measures have been developed and with what results? (*H.N.D. Business Studies, Liverpool Polytechnic*)

19. Explain the belief that it is not necessarily sound public finance to insist upon balancing the national budget. (*H.N.D. Business Studies, Liverpool Polytechnic*)

20. Detail the structure of the National Debt. Examine the significance of its burden and the possibilities of reducing this burden. (*H.N.D. Business Studies, Liverpool Polytechnic*)

21. What difficulties hinder a prices and incomes policy in conditions of full employment and free collective bargaining? (*H.N.C. Business Studies, Liverpool Polytechnic*)

22. "The acceptance by governments of responsibility for the level of employment cannot be understood without reference to the changes in economic theory associated with Keynes." What in economic thought do you associate with Keynes? (*H.N.C. Business Studies, Liverpool Polytechnic*)

23. Present government economic policy faces a conflict of interest between short-term "stop-go" and long-term planning for growth. Explain, with examples, why this is so. (*H.N.C. Business Studies, Liverpool Polytechnic*)

24. Outline the main characteristics of the "national debt." How far is such a debt a burden on a country's economy? (*I.O.B.*)

25. Outline the general principles a government should adopt when levying taxation. (*I.O.B.*)

26. Contrast the place of the budget in the modern economy with its position before 1939, illustrating your answer by reference to any particular country. (*I.O.B.*)

27. Discuss the relationship between rising wages and rising costs. (*I.M.T.A.*)

28. "Since the second world war the centre of interest in economics has shifted from the study of equilibrium to the study of growth." How do you explain the change? (*Economics, Final Part I, I.M.T.A.*)

29. To what extent can the Government use the level of public expenditure as an instrument of economic stabilisation? (*Public Finance, Final Part I, I.M.T.A.*)

30. Is the short-run control over the supply of money a necessary condition for ensuring price stability? (*Public Finance, Final Part I, I.M.T.A.*)

31. "Savings and investment are always equal."
    "In equilibrium savings equal investment."
    Reconcile these two statements. (*Public Finance, Final Part I, I.M.T.A.*)

32. What are the causes of unemployment? Illustrate your answer with examples. (*I.C.W.A.*)

33. Why has the United Kingdom experienced inflation since 1945? (*I.C.W.A.*)

34. "Savings and investment are done by different people at different times for different reasons." Explain this statement. (*I.C.W.A.*)

35. In what ways may the budget be used as an instrument of economic policy? (*I.C.W.A.*)

36. What do you understand by the "multiplier"? Explain its usefulness to a government seeking to control an economy. (*I.O.T.*)

37. Is it true to say that the trade cycle belongs nowadays to Economic History? (*I.O.T.*)

38. What do you understand by a full employment policy? How likely is it to cause inflation? (*I.O.T.*)

39. What do you understand by inflation? Why do governments seek to control it? (*I.O.T.*)

PART TWO: THE MONETARY SYSTEM

40. What factors determine the supply of money in the United Kingdom? (*G.C.E.(A), J.M.B.*)

41. What part do the discount houses play in the system of monetary control operated by the Bank of England? (*G.C.E.(A)*, *J.M.B.*)

42. What are the main instruments of monetary policy? Assess their efficacy as economic stabilisers. (*G.C.E.(A)*, *J.M.B.*)

43. Outline the chief problems involved in the value of money in time. (*G.C.E.(A)*, *J.M.B.*)

44. Explain how the London discount market acts as a buffer between the monetary authorities on the one hand and the clearing banks on the other. (*B.Sc.(Econ.)*, *Part I, London External*)

45. "Bankers cannot create anything; they merely exchange one kind of asset for another." Discuss. (*B.Sc.(Econ.)*, *Part I, London External*)

46. Discuss fully the meaning attached to the concept of liquidity in the Radcliffe Report. (*B.Sc.(Econ.)*, *Part I, London External*)

47. Outline the ways in which an efficient capital market can assist the finance of industry. (*B.Sc.(Econ.)*, *Part I, London External*)

48. "Recent theoretical attempts to arrive at a definition of money suggest that the problem can be usefully pursued only as an empirical question." Discuss. (*B.Sc.(Econ.)*, *Part II, Principles of Monetary Economics, London Internal*)

49. The experience of the 1960s seems to suggest that rising interest rates are associated with an expansion rather than a contraction of the money supply. How can this experience be explained? (*B.Sc.(Econ.)*, *Part II, Principles of Monetary Economics, London Internal*)

50. Non-bank financial intermediaries have grown in size and number in the past two decades. What effects may this have had on the supply of money, rates of interest and the effectiveness of monetary policy? (*B.Sc.(Econ.)*, *Part II, Principles of Monetary Economics, London Internal*)

51. "The quantity of money in the United Kingdom since 1945 has been entirely demand determined." Consider whether this statement is true and, if so, why. (*B.Sc.(Econ.)*, *Part II, Principles of Monetary Economics, London External*)

52. "The authorities can choose interest rates or the supply of money but cannot choose both independently of each other" (Sayers). On what basis should the authorities make their choice? (*B.Sc.(Econ.)*, *Part II, Principles of Monetary Economics, London External*)

53. "A firm control of the money supply is both necessary and sufficient to control inflation." Discuss. (*B.Sc.(Econ.)*, *Part II, Principles of Monetary Economics, London External*)

54. To what extent is it true to say that money is the creation

of the banking system? (*H.N.D. Business Studies, Liverpool Polytechnic*)

55. Describe the structure and operation of the London discount market. Do you believe that it performs a useful function? (*H.N.D. Business Studies, Liverpool Polytechnic*)

56. The methods by which the Bank of England traditionally exercised the ultimate control over the supply of money are no longer effective. Explain and evaluate this statement. (*H.N.D. Business Studies, Liverpool Polytechnic*)

57. "The commercial banker's basic problem is to achieve a proper balance between liquidity and profitability." Explain. (*H.N.C. Business Studies, Liverpool Polytechnic*)

58. How can the authorities control the amount of money and why should they wish to do so? (*H.N.C. Business Studies, Liverpool Polytechnic*)

59. Why is it that whilst opinion seems to be that Bank-rate changes are an outmoded instrument of economic policy, the authorities continue to attribute to them an important role? (*H.N.C. Business Studies, Liverpool Polytechnic*)

60. Describe the structure and operations of the London money market. (*I.O.B.*)

61. Discuss the special characteristics that distinguish money from other economic goods. (*I.O.B.*)

62. Examine the various factors which in present-day Britain set a limit to an increase in the money supply. (*I.O.B.*)

63. Describe the demand for, and the supply of, funds in the London money market. (*I.O.B.*)

64. Examine the present-day effectiveness of Bank rate as a deflationary control. (*I.O.B.*)

65. To what extent is the ability of money to fulfil its functions affected by changes in its value? (*I.O.B.*)

66. "It is impossible in practice to achieve together all the objectives of monetary policy." Discuss this statement. (*I.O.B.*)

67. Describe the components of the supply of money in Britain and examine carefully the consequences of a reduction in the supply. (*S.B.I.*)

68. "The effectiveness of Bank Rate as an instrument of economic policy depends more on the fact that it changes than on its particular level." Discuss. (*S.B.I.*)

69. Set out the sources of borrowing by the central government in Britain and show the importance of the Savings Banks in this borrowing. (*S.B.I.*)

70. Explain the function of the Bank of England as "lender of last resort." What role does the discount market play in the fulfilment of this function? (*S.B.I.*)

71. Consider the consequences on the supply of money of my

withdrawing a deposit from a savings bank and depositing it instead with a commercial bank. (*S.B.I.*)

72. Discuss briefly the asset structure of joint-stock banks. How is it influenced by changes in interest rates? (*Public Finance, Final, Part I, I.M.T.A.*)

73. "The Discount Market makes a living by borrowing short and lending long." Discuss. (*Public Finance, Final Part I, I.M.T.A.*)

74. Assess the view that the management of the national debt is an integral part of monetary policy. (*Public Finance, Final Part I, I.M.T.A.*)

75. Outline the economic services provided by a Joint Stock Bank. (*I.C.W.A.*)

76. Define Bank rate and describe the possible economic effects of a rise in Bank rate. (*I.C.W.A.*)

77. Distinguish between the characteristics of the Bank of England and those of the Joint-Stock Banks. (*I.C.W.A.*)

78. What do you understand by the supply of, and the demand for, money? (*I.C.W.A.*)

79. Distinguish between (*a*) finance houses and (*b*) building societies, making clear the economic role of each. (*I.C.W.A.*)

80. If Banks are merely financial intermediaries, how can they create credit? (*I.O.T.*)

81. Why is Bank rate raised or lowered? (*I.O.T.*)

82. Bankers claim that they can only lend what is lent to them. How then is it possible for them to "create credit"? (*I.O.T.*)

83. Contrast the functions of a central bank and a commercial bank. (*I.O.T.*)

PART THREE: INTERNATIONAL TRADE AND PAYMENTS

84. Explain what is meant by the *terms of trade* and the *balance of trade*. What relationship exists between these two concepts? (*G.C.E.(A), J.M.B.*)

85. Explain what is meant by "devaluation." How is a devaluation likely to affect the balance of payments of an economy? (*G.C.E.(A), J.M.B.*)

86. State precisely what you understand by the "fundamental disequilibrium" in the British balance of payments. (*G.C.E.(A), J.M.B.*)

87. Assess the relative merits of devaluation and tariff imposition as instruments for correcting an adverse current balance. (*G.C.E.(A), J.M.B.*)

88.   Consider the relative merits of devaluation and deflation as correctives of a Balance of Payments deficit.   (*B.Sc.(Econ.), Part I, London External*)

89.   Why is it mutually profitable for two or more countries to engage in international trade?   Can the existence of unemployment modify your conclusions?   (*B.Sc.(Econ.), Part I, London External*)

90.   Argue the case for and against flexible exchange rates. (*B.Sc.(Econ.), Part I, London External*)

91.   Consider the view that restrictions on British investment can secure short-run improvement in the balance of payments only at the expense of a long-run worsening.   (*B.Sc.(Econ.), Part I, London External*)

92.   Under what conditions would you expect a fixed exchange rate system to permit major trading countries to maximise their own welfare?   (*B.Sc.(Econ.), Part II, Principles of Monetary Economics, London Internal*)

93.   "The problems surrounding the supply of international means of payment arise because the countries which are the world's bankers are also its chief traders; these problems will be solved only when these roles are separated."   Discuss.   (*B.Sc. (Econ.), Part II, Principles of Monetary Economics, London Internal*)

94.   Discuss the merits of the "crawling peg" scheme for exchange-rate adjustments.   (*B.Sc.(Econ.), Part II, Principles of Monetary Economics, London External*)

95.   "Under a regime of fixed exchange rates a government cannot maintain both internal and external balance."   Comment. (*B.Sc.(Econ.), Part II, Principles of Monetary Economics, London External*)

96.   "The general adoption of flexible exchange rates would increase, not lessen, both the need for the authorities to intervene in the foreign exchange market and the need for international co-operation."   Discuss.   (*B.Sc.(Econ.), Part II, Principles of Monetary Economics, London External*)

97.   Explain the concepts of over-valuation and under-valuation when applied to a currency.   What are the possible remedies in each case?   (*H.N.D. Business Studies, Liverpool Polytechnic*)

98.   Explain the composition of the balance of payments and assess the relative importance of each of its components.   Consider some of the measures which might be applied to the improvement of this balance.   (*H.N.D. Business Studies, Liverpool Polytechnic*)

99.   Examine the advantages and disadvantages to the British balance of payments of sterling's function as a world reserve and

trading currency. Could this function be abandoned? (*H.N.D. Business Studies, Liverpool Polytechnic*)

100. Despite the advantages of international trade based upon the principle of comparative costs, countries do in fact impose restrictions on trade. Why is this? (*H.N.C. Business Studies, Liverpool Polytechnic*)

101. Argue the merits of devaluation rather than deflation as an answer to balance of payments problems. (*H.N.C. Business Studies, Liverpool Polytechnic*)

102. For what reasons do some economists advocate a rise in the price of gold? What objections are raised to such a proposal? (*H.N.C. Business Studies, Liverpool Polytechnic*)

103. Show how the total of the debits and credits on a country's balance of payments account must always equal one another. (*I.O.B.*)

104. "Deflation and devaluation are not alternatives. Some deflation is necessary if devaluation is to succeed." Comment on this statement. (*I.O.B.*)

105. "For international monetary equilibrium a properly functioning adjustment process is as important as sufficient liquidity." Discuss this statement. (*I.O.B.*)

106. Define the term "international liquidity" and comment on the main elements of such liquidity today. (*I.O.B.*)

107. How can a country have a surplus in its balance of trade but a deficit in its balance of payments? Why must a country take steps to reduce a persistent payments deficit? (*S.B.I.*)

108. Why has the present international monetary system been described as the New Gold Standard? Indicate the chief defects of the present system and how they might be resolved. (*S.B.I.*)

109. Give an account of the objectives and principles of operation of the International Monetary Fund. (*S.B.I.*)

110. What are the "sterling balances"? In what way do they create a problem for Britain? Suggest possible solutions. (*S.B.I.*)

111. Outline the functions of the International Monetary Fund. Will the issue of Special Drawing Rights enable the Fund to play a more effective role in the international monetary system? (*S.B.I.*)

112. "Whatever policy is used, a Balance of Payments deficit can only be corrected through a reduction in the standard of living of the economy as a whole." Discuss. (*Public Finance, Final Part I, I.M.T.A.*)

113. Will export subsidies increase the competitiveness of British exports in the long run? (*Public Finance, Final Part I, I.M.T.A.*)

114. Why may it pay a country to import goods which it can produce itself? (*I.C.W.A.*)

115. How may the Government finance a deficit on the balance of payments in the short run? (*I.C.W.A.*)

116. Discuss the advantages and disadvantages of imposing restrictions on international trading relations. (*I.O.T.*)

117. Why does the economist suggest that international trade is gainful? (*I.O.T.*)

118. "Overseas investment merely creates overseas competitors and should be discouraged." Discuss. (*I.O.T.*)

PART FOUR: GOVERNMENT AND INDUSTRY

119. Why are monopolistic practices in general thought to be against the public interest? How has the Government attempted to deal with them? (*G.C.E.(A)*, *J.M.B.*)

120. "In the industrial structure of the U.K., all competition is monopolistic, all monopoly is to some extent competitive." Discuss this statement. (*G.C.E.(A)*, *J.M.B.*)

121. What factors encourage (*a*) horizontal integration and (*b*) vertical integration in an industry? (*G.C.E.(A)*, *J.M.B.*)

122. Is increasing concentration in industrial markets inevitable? (*G.C.E.(A)*, *J.M.B.*)

123. How and why has the Government intervened in the location of industry since 1945? (*G.C.E.(A)*, *J.M.B.*)

124. Examine the view that public sector industry should be run like ordinary commercial enterprises. (*G.C.E.(A)*, *J.M.B.*)

125. What criteria of efficiency can and should be applied to nationalised industries? (*G.C.E.(A)*, *J.M.B.*)

126. What are the advantages and disadvantages of setting price equal to marginal cost in public enterprises? (*G.C.E.(A)*, *J.M.B.*)

127. In what ways does the functioning of a "planned" economy differ from that of a "free" economy? (*G.C.E.(A)*, *J.M.B.*)

128. "To check and reverse the drift of population to the South-East and Midlands would be to impose an unwarrantable cost upon the national economy." Discuss. (*B.Sc.(Econ.)*, *Part II*, *London*)

129. Should the financial targets for nationalised industries be based on the rate of return on capital earned by private industry? (*B.Sc.(Econ.)*, *Part II*, *London*)

130. Would a policy to outlaw monopolies necessarily be in the public interest? (*H.N.D. Business Studies*, *Liverpool Polytechnic*)

131. Governments have tried to cure regional economic imbalance for over thirty years, yet the problem remains. Discuss

possible reasons for this lack of success. (*H.N.D. Business Studies, Liverpool Polytechnic*)

132. What difficulties arise in applying commercial criteria as a measure of efficiency to nationalised industries? (*H.N.D. Business Studies, Liverpool Polytechnic*)

133. Discuss the assertion that a ruthless breaking up of monopolies might create more inefficiency than it would eliminate. (*H.N.C. Business Studies, Liverpool Polytechnic*)

134. "No policy for dealing with the regional problem ought to interfere with the fundamentals of economic efficiency" (Professor Wilson). In what ways might Government policy have offended this precept? (*H.N.C. Business Studies, Liverpool Polytechnic*)

135. What main factors influence an entrepreneur in his choice of locality for a new factory? (*I.O.B.*)

136. Monopoly is usually regarded as undesirable. Outline the case that can be made against this view. (*I.O.B.*)

137. To what extent do you agree that nationalised industries should finance their capital investment out of profits? (*I.O.B.*)

138. How may companies with "Monopoly Powers" attempt to strengthen their market position? (*I.C.W.A.*)

139. Some authorities take the view that the security of monopoly provides conditions in which the most rapid technical progress will take place in industry. Others hold that the pressure of competitive conditions is more favourable to this process. Discuss. (*C.I.S.*)

140. "The taking over of one company by another is always in the interest of the shareholders but rarely in the interest of the country as a whole." Discuss this statement. (*C.I.S.*)

141. "The main disadvantage of monopoly is not that it causes high prices but that it is inefficient." Discuss. (*C.I.S.*)

142. Does economic theory indicate any rules which should govern the policies pursued by nationalised industries? (*C.I.S.*)

143. "Planning without specific targets is a useless operation for raising economic growth." Do you agree? (*C.I.S.*)

144. "The economic activities of the state have increased and are increasing." How far economically is such increase (*a*) desirable, (*b*) undesirable? (*C.I.S.*)

INDEX